WHO IS MARKIE?

Martha Custis Williams "Markie"
Portrait by William G. Williams
Courtesy of National Park Service, Arlington House,
The Robert E. Lee Memorial

Who Is Markie?

THE LIFE OF
MARTHA CUSTIS WILLIAMS CARTER
COUSIN AND CONFIDANTE
OF ROBERT E. LEE

Frances Scott
and
Anne Cipriani Webb

HERITAGE BOOKS
2007

HERITAGE BOOKS

AN IMPRINT OF HERITAGE BOOKS, INC.

Books, CDs, and more—Worldwide

For our listing of thousands of titles see our website
at
www.HeritageBooks.com

Published 2007 by
HERITAGE BOOKS, INC.
Publishing Division
65 East Main Street
Westminster, Maryland 21157-5026

International Standard Book Number: 978-0-7884-3745-8

CONTENTS

LIST OF ILLUSTRATIONS
Unless otherwise noted, all images courtesy of Tudor Place Historic
House and Garden

vii

PREFACE AND ACKNOWLEDGEMENTS

This biography began with the typing at Tudor Place of the diaries of Martha Custis Williams Carter (Markie) to provide easier research access to their rich trove of history. Frances Scott, who did the bulk of the transcription, and Anne Webb, the former Tudor Place archivist, soon determined that the diaries were the core of a story that would be of wide interest and had never been told.

Much to our surprise at times, our research took us far afield from the two houses most identified with Markie, Tudor Place and Arlington House. We have many people to thank for helping us along the way.

First, we must thank Leslie Buhler, the executive director, Wendy Kail, the archivist, and many other members of the staff at Tudor Place, where we did the most extensive research. At Arlington House, the Robert E. Lee Memorial, Colleen Curry, the former curator, gave us unlimited access to Markie's diaries there and to objects associated with her. The present curator, Mary Troy, has also been most helpful. Karen Kinzey, the former historian at Arlington House, not only helped us with our research but also reviewed the manuscript and gave helpful suggestions.

At the Pierpont Morgan library in New York, Inge Dupont and other members of the staff could not have been more gracious as we perused Markie's Baltimore diary. Staff at the Eleanor Brockenbrough Library of the Museum of the Confederacy in Richmond, Virginia were also most helpful. We are also indebted to archivists at Washington and Lee University in Lexington, Virginia; the Library of Virginia and the Virginia Historical Society, both in Richmond, Virginia.

Laura Vetter, archivist at Episcopal High School in Alexandria, Virginia, graciously provided us access to Orton Williams' school records and a splendid image of him as a young man. Judy Carter, a descendant of Admiral Carter's brother, was a great help in matters related to Markie's husband. We also had wonderful experiences at the District of Columbia Archives and the Office of the Recorder of Deeds in Washington, DC.

Many thanks go to Osborne Mackie, former director of Tudor Place, for arranging access to the Upshur-Brown family papers, and to the family that agreed to let us quote from their collection of Markie's papers.

A group of former and present Tudor Place volunteers helped us in many ways along the journey as well: Irene Navarro, Jean Oseth, Anne Rollins, Joan Sweeney, and Martha Wilson. Last but not least, our undying gratitude to Willard Webb and Leni Preston, who provided continuing and what seemed at times, endless, moral support, and who also reviewed the completed manuscript, much to its improvement.

Frances Scott
Anne Webb
Arlington, Virginia
July 2007

INTRODUCTION

WHO IS MARKIE?

Over 70 years ago, the Huntington Library published a slim volume of the letters of Robert E. Lee, *To Markie*. Who was Markie? The short answer is that she was Martha Custis Williams, a cousin of Lee's wife, Mary Custis Lee. But she is worth knowing in her own right. Hers was a life that spanned three quarters of the 19th century, filled with life's joys and sorrows, and connected with prominent people and historic events that we know well from our history books. She left us a considerable record of her response to these people and events in her correspondence and diaries, for she was aware of their importance, and they were interesting to her. Thus she opens a new window through which we can view an important period in American history, as well as learn about the life of an articulate and accomplished woman and her response to the conditions imposed on a woman, single for most of her life, in the 19th century.

First, a brief background. Markie was the eldest child of America Pinckney Peter and William G. Williams. Her mother was the great-granddaughter of Martha Washington and her father a rising star in the U.S. Army's elite Corps of Topographical Engineers. She spent much of her childhood and early adult life at Tudor Place, the elegant Georgetown home of her maternal grandparents. She also lived for extended periods at Arlington House, the home of her grandmother's brother, George Washington Parke Custis, who was Robert E. Lee's father-in-law and George Washington's adopted grandson.

At the early age of 15, Markie lost her mother and began a lifelong responsibility for her four younger siblings. Just four years later, her father was killed at the Battle of Monterrey in the Mexican War. At this point, her youngest brother, Orton, was only seven.

This early burden of responsibility, coupled with a serious and religious disposition and devotion to duty, shaped the rest of Markie's life. She was always the one to take charge when someone was ill, or when there were children to be nurtured. When the Lees were posted away from Washington, she was at the side of the widowed George Washington Parke Custis as his health deteriorated; when her sister Kate died leaving young children, she raised them while her brother-in-law pursued his naval career; when her brother Laurence was dismissed from the Union Army during the Civil War, she spent many years fighting for his reinstatement.

At the same time, she was remarkably independent and strong-minded in pursuing her own many and varied interests. She traveled extensively, pursued art studies in New York and Philadelphia, and wrote articles for publication, all while being the one available to the family in times of trouble. Through her family connections, she knew many of the prominent figures of her time, and with her gift for friendship, she became the confidante of some of them, including Robert E. Lee, George Washington Parke Custis, Elizabeth Patterson Bonaparte, and Eleanor Custis Lewis.

When she was 50, Markie married Samuel Powhatan Carter, the only person ever to hold flag rank in both the U.S. Army and Navy. They settled in Washington, D.C., where for the first time Markie had a home of her own.

No one left a complete description of Markie, but with the help of black and white photographs, a portrait painted by her father, letters, and diaries, we can develop a verbal picture. She was tall and slender with an oval face, even features, blue eyes, and long, brown hair worn in an upswept hairstyle. Mrs. George Washington Parke Custis described her as a "lively, warm girl…a Christian in name and deed." She was a devout Episcopalian with a deep sense of responsibility for her siblings and others she loved, was well read, wrote and recited poetry, played the piano, sang, and studied art -- drawing and painting. In this she was representative of many of the women of her time.

Markie's relatives and friends preserved a rich documentary record of her life; these documents are scattered in many public repositories and private collections. Brought together, they tell the story of this remarkable woman with a talent for friendship that should have a wide appeal to students of many facets of 19th century American history.

CHAPTER 1

FAMILY BACKGROUND AND EARLY LIFE

As Markie looked back on her life, she compared it to a chessboard: "So checkered, is it, with darkness and light."[1] This is of course a cliché, and can be applied to any life, but because of her temperament and the events of her life, for Markie it was particularly apt.

Markie (christened Martha Custis Williams – after her grandmother) was born into a distinguished family and comfortable circumstances. She was the first child of America Pinckney Peter and Willliam G. Williams. America was the beautiful daughter of Martha Parke Custis and Thomas Peter. Her father was the son of the first Mayor of Georgetown, Robert Peter, a very prosperous tobacco merchant and landowner. Her mother was Martha Washington's granddaughter and a Calvert of Maryland on her mother's side. Markie was born at her grandparents' house, Tudor Place, an elegant neoclassical mansion designed by William Thornton, the first architect of the United States Capitol.

Markie always considered Tudor Place her home and a frequent refuge. There she imbibed the traditions and history of the Custis-Washington family from her grandmother, who was very proud of her family connections. Martha Peter was the daughter of Eleanor Calvert and John Parke Custis. John (Jacky) was the son of Martha Dandridge (later, Mrs. George Washington) and Daniel Parke Custis, one of the richest men in Virginia. Eleanor was the daughter of Benedict Calvert and Elizabeth Calvert, both descendants of Lord Baltimore. Martha Peter named her children, especially the three daughters, to reflect her patriotic and family pride. Her eldest son was named George Washington Peter, and the daughters were Columbia Washington, America Pinckney, and Brittania Wellington.

Markie's parents had met in 1824 at Tudor Place, when the dashing William G. Williams, a recent West Point graduate, was invited to a reception the Peters were giving for General Lafayette. Williams had been appointed to the Corps of Topographical Engineers, then the most elite corps of the U.S. Army, and was destined for a brilliant career. His father came from England, his mother possibly from South Carolina, although little is known about her.[2]

America was much admired as one of the belles of Washington, and her proud name also made her stand out. When Josiah Quincy was presented to her, he could not avoid an awkward and yet comical consciousness of the august nationality which the lady in some sort symbolized. An introduction, followed by the usual sequences seemed almost such a desecration as one would be guilty of who proposed to shake hands with the Goddess of Liberty and entertain her with ballroom gossip.[3]

America had recently been ill when her aunt, Nelly Lewis,[*] wrote to a friend:

> Poor Mec will be united, in June, to Mr. Williams, they will come here two days after, I expect. She is in very delicate health, & much changed in her appearance. He is a genteel young man, has an affect[ionat]e grateful heart, but not at all remarkable I think for talents.... I hope it may turn out better than her friends anticipate.[4]

Williams was not from one of the families the Peters recognized as their peers, so they opposed the marriage. However, the young couple finally prevailed.

America Pinckney Peter and William George Williams were married in the west parlor of Tudor Place on June 27, 1826, by the Reverend Walter Addison of St. John's Church, Georgetown.[5] One of the wedding guests wrote to a friend:

> Did you [ever] hear of so singular and melancholy an affair? The scene was truly afflicting. It was like a funeral, all the family in tears and the bride almost in convulsions. It was very unexpected indeed, even to the bridegroom.[6]

However, by August Nelly Lewis could say that "My dear Mec & Williams are devoted to each other – her Parents are reconciled & she appears perfectly contented. He is very affect[ionat]e & generous to excess for his limited income."[7]

---

[*] Eleanor Parke Custis Lewis (1779-1852), Martha Peter's younger sister, adopted granddaughter of George Washington. She lived at Woodlawn Plantation, near Mount Vernon.

At first Lieutenant Williams was stationed in Washington, and Markie was born at Tudor Place on March 28, 1827. A month later, Nelly Lewis wrote: "My dear Mec has chills & fever & has lost her milk. Her Babe is fat & healthy & eats altogether I believe.... She [America] is with her Mother." In June, Nelly Lewis reported that "Dear Mec is very delicate, she has a sweet good Babe, but she is a helpless Mother, she cannot suckle it, & knows very little about the care of children."[8]

In rapid succession, despite her delicate health, America bore four more children by 1834: Columbia Wingfield, Margaret (who died as an infant), Laurence Abert, and Katherine Alicia. During this time the family continued to live in Georgetown, although Williams was often away on assignment, even spending time in Europe studying engineering works, collecting geological speciments, and studying art.

The passport issued to Lieutenant William G. Williams on June 1, 1830 gives us the only physical description of Markie's father: he was six feet tall, with a high forehead, blue eyes, brown hair, and an oval face. He was scheduled to sail the next day for England. He spent almost a year traveling in Europe, visiting England, France, and Italy.[9]

After his return, the couple's first son was born in January of 1833. Laurence Abert was named for Williams' brother, who was visiting the family from England, and for Williams' superior officer and friend, Colonel J.J. Abert.[10] In March, Nelly reported that:

> I...staid one day at my sister Peter's, & returned to take care of my dear niece America, & her sick children. Mr. Williams was sent to Alabama & Florida, on a survey, by the Topographical Department, & as Mec was obliged to shut up her house, she came to spend some weeks at her Birthplace. Her children had most severe colds, & as our good Doctor H was detained at home by unavoidable business, I could not leave them, & Mr. L[ewis], without any *medical* friend. Mec is again poor thing in a *progressive* state, & is often very complaining.[11]

In all, America Williams was to have 15 pregnancies in as many years, but only five children survived infancy. They were Martha (Markie), Columbia (Lum), Laurence (Lolo), Katherine (Kate), and William Orton (Bunny), born in 1839.

In 1838, William G. Williams was promoted to Captain and moved with most of his growing family to Buffalo, New York, where he had been given the important job of surveying the Great Lakes and supervising improvements to the Buffalo harbor.[12] Markie and Lum were left behind with their grandmother, Martha Peter, possibly in order to avoid disrupting their schooling.

By the middle of October, America reported that the family was comfortably situated at the American Hotel. She was very pleased with their new home, which had large residences, "furnished in a style of elegance that is scarcely imagined in the great City of Washington." America, whose health was always a concern, felt better than she had for many years, and walked every day, feeling braced by the cooler climate.[13] The next year, in July, America bore the baby of the family, William Orton Williams (Bunny). She wrote to her sister, Britannia: "[H]e has the most beautiful head of hair I ever saw light brown and curling all over his head…he has beautiful dark blue eyes but very bright and said to be very much like me and Kate…. I nurse him a little and feed him on cream and water." He was quite a pet among the ladies at the American Hotel, and received many handworked presents. For the first month of his life he had been very ill, but they had a wonderful Doctor, Austin Flint, who had brought him through the crisis.[14] Dr. Flint and his wife became close friends of the family, and especially close to Markie.

In the same letter, America apologized to her sister that Markie was complaining so much. Markie was evidently still at Tudor Place, the only one not to be reunited with her family, and probably was feeling lonely and left out.

The Williams family found a thriving society in Buffalo among the families of the garrison and the town. One of the ladies of the garrison wrote disapprovingly to her mother about the social life:

> Last Friday was New Years and a great day in this state. The Gentlemen all go out making calls and the ladies all stay at Home to receive them…. They commence calling about ten o'clock in the morning and the ladies offer cake and wine always and generally cold turkey, ham, chicken salad, punch, apple toddy, and eggnog so that the usually temperate, in some of their last calls toward evening, appear

extremely convivial and even unable to stand very firmly. This is not intended as a good story, but is sober fact and you will hear the next few days these things commented upon as capital jokes and mention of the most respectable gentlemen as being pretty well drunk. What a way to begin the New Year and yet they think it all very fine here.[15]

In the same letter, she mentions America: "Mrs. Williams is again, for the fifteenth time, as they say 'women wish to be.' She is said to have been very beautiful and fascinating and figured conspicuously in gay life at Washington, but her beauty is a near wreck and she looks prematurely old. She is not more than thirty-five." She was in fact 37, and her oldest daughter, Markie, almost 14, had finally joined the rest of the family in Buffalo and was now old enough to be a regular correspondent with her grandmother in Washington.

In February of 1841, Martha Custis Peter replied to a letter she had received from America and Markie:

I was much gratified my dear Martha by the receipt of the joint letter of you and your mother which came to hand yesterday. Your hand writing is much improved, and I hope you will take great pains to acquire a neat style of writing, as it is very pleasing to see a young lady neat in every thing that she does. I am pleased to find that your time is so occupied with study, and I hope you will derive great advantage from it.[16]

Mrs. Peter went on to tell the news of the week – the arrival of President-elect William Henry Harrison and the parade and festivities accompanying it. She told of his walking from the depot to City Hall without a hat in the terrible weather, but rather ironically notes: "He is quite a genteel good looking old man, who appears to have health, strength, and energy enough for the duties he is about to undertake and a much more honest countenance than Martin [Van Buren, the outgoing President]." In fact, Harrison died one month after the inauguration of pneumonia contracted that day.

Later in 1841, Markie was separated from her mother once again. Captain Williams was on duty at Mackinac Island, Michigan, and took America; the new baby, Toby; Laurence; Bunny; and his father with him. Why the three girls had to be left behind is unclear, but they stayed with a family friend, Mrs. Williams (not a relation). The climate at Mackinac was considered wonderful and Williams hoped it would improve America's delicate health. In planning for the trip, Williams wrote his wife from West Point on July 4:

> I have enjoyed myself here as well as I can any where without my dear Pinky.... I am more at home here than any place except my own peculiar home. Not in Washington St. but just where you and my dear children happen to be.... I anticipate so much pleasure in our excursion and I am sure it will be of importance to your health.... When will all your troubles in the way of children be over. I have never been enabled to enjoy the pleasure that I could enjoy if you were well enough to travel.[17]

By July 28, the family party was in Mackinac and America reported back to Markie that they had arrived after a delightful trip. America wrote "I am very much pleased with Mackinac it is not a Philadelphia or even a Buffalo in appearance but it presents a beautiful and picturesque aspect." [18] Markie's father added, in a more didactic vein:

> I hope you & all of you my dear Children attend to your duties and that Mrs. W. will give a good account of you on my return. You know [how] much interest we take in your education my dearest Mark – for it is that which will give you the stamp of gentility & refinement & without it you never can appear to advantage and inspire those who are interested in you with pride.[19]

During this separation, which lasted until late October, America wrote to Markie often. On August 15, she wrote that she was disappointed that Martha had not written. She wanted Mrs. Williams to insist that they all write every week, "as you know my anxiety about you...." Markie was admonished to practice the piano, "take pains with your French," take walks, visit friends, be obedient to Mrs. Williams and kind and affectionate to her sisters.[20]

On August 18, America was delighted to finally receive a letter and know that her daughters were well, but in the same sentence told Markie she must take more care in writing and spelling.[21] In another letter, she asked Markie to make a number of purchases for her, with the help of Mrs. Williams: gloves, handkerchiefs (pink silk), shoes for Bun, ribbon, etc. She hoped Markie was improving in music, industrious in rising, attending to her sisters' appearance and manners and setting a good example, "for nothing is more horrid than a careless young Lady." The girls should attend Church regularly and write to their grandmother very often.[22]

In her final letter from Mackinac, America reported the sad news of Toby's death:

> Alas my dear Child this is one of the many instances of the uncertainty of this life we are here to-day and to morrow we are no more he was indeed very very dear to us all and I flattered my-self that we should raise him but he is happier than if he were left to contend with the trials of this life he is an angel and I am now perfectly resigned to the will of God for he does all for the best.

She hoped to be with them soon after the first of October, and despite her grief, did not forget to compliment Markie on her selections in the shopping she had requested.[23] Williams and America lingered another month in Mackinac, then stopped off in Detroit to visit nine-year-old Laurence, who was now at school in Troy, Michigan.[24] Back at home, America did not outlive her last child by long. On April 25, 1842, she died in Buffalo.[25] Martha Peter wrote from Georgetown to her grandchildren:

> My dear Children, your kind friend Mrs. Gardener's letter has just come from the office, & you may easily conceive the distress I feel from the bad intelligence it contained – I have been very anxious about your dear Mother since the receipt of your dear Mother's last letter & feared to hear again – her distance from me has been doubly painful since her last illness – but yet I hoped as she had often been ill, & soon recovered, that Providence in his Mercy would have again restored her to us, but my dear children we must all remember that God is good, and wise, & orders every thing for some wise   purpose -- & we ought all to endeavor to live so that we may be prepared to die – as none knows who may be called next – I have heard it said, that the

manner – which we leave this world is a sure indication of our reception in the next – if so – you ought to feel great consolation, when you reflect how calm & sweetly your poor Mother sunk in the sleep of Death. I trust that she is now in heaven surrounded by those of her family who went before her and her little children as cherubs – fluttering around her -- & altho' she had much to endear her in this world – still pain & sorrow would often interrupt her enjoyment here – I hope you will all endeavor to exert yourselves on your father's account – that he will bring you to me, who will endeavor to supply your Mother's place to you, as long as I live.

Squares of dark and light indeed! Markie, just 15, and her siblings, bereft, would soon embark on a new phase of their life – their mother gone, they would also be separated from their father.

[1] Martha Custis Williams Carter, *Diary*, April 11, 1854, Arlington House Archives.
[2] Information about the Willliams family from Martha Custis Williams Carter, "About the Williams Family," n.d., Tudor Place Archives, MS-6 (3-27); and other references in the Tudor Place collection.
[3] Josiah Quincy, *Figures of the Past.* Boston: Roberts Brothers, 1883, p. 276.
[4] Ltr., Eleanor Parke Custis Lewis to Elizabeth Bordley Gibson, April 23, 1826, in Brady, Patricia, ed., *George Washington's Beautiful Nelly* (Columbia, University of South Carolina Press, 1991), p. 177.
[5] Britannia Wellington Peter Kennon, *Memoirs as told to Armistead Peter, Jr.* (1895), Tudor Place Archives, MS-14 (69-24). *National Intelligencer*, July 26, 1826.
[6] Ltr., Ann Shaaff to Harriet Addison, 1826, quoted in Guy Castle, "Life in Georgetown, 1819-1841, as Told in the Personal Correspondence of Anne Shaaff (1805-1862)," *Records of the Columbia Historical Society (1960-1962)*, pp. 82-83.
[7] Ltr., EPCL to EBG, August 3, 1826, in Brady, *G.W.'s Beautiful Nelly*, p. 182.
[8] Ltr., EPCL to EBG, June 24, 1826, in Brady, *Ibid.*, p. 191.
[9] Wendy Kail, "George Washington's Great-Granddaughter and the Topographical Engineer: The Life and Times of William G. Williams, Class of 1824," *West Point Assembly*, v. 58, no. 6 (July/Aug. 2000), pp. 35-39, 47.
[10] MCWC, "About the Williams Family," n.d., TP Archives, MS-6 (3-27).
[11] Ltr., ECPL to EBG, March 10, 1833, in Brady, *G.W.'s Beautiful Nelly*, p. 208.
[12] Ltr., William G. Williams to Mary Anna Fitzhugh Custis, October 14, 1838, Tudor Place Archives, MS-6 (3-9).
[13] Kail, Wendy,"Surveying Roads, Canals, and the Trail of Tears: The Life and Times of William G. Williams, Class of 1824," *West Point Assembly* (Nov./Dec. 2002), pp. 52-57.
[14] Ltr, APPW to BWP, August 3, 1839, TP Archives, MS-7 (1-1)
[15] Ltr., Helen Chapman to Emily Blair, December 27 and January 17, 1840, Center for American History, University of Texas at Austin, 401227HC.DOC. Transcript from Theodore Roosevelt House, Buffalo, NY.
[16] Ltr., Martha Custis Peter to Martha Custis Williams, February 13, 1841, TP Archives, MS-6 (1-5).
[17] Ltr., WGW to America Pinckney Peter Williams, July 4, 1841, TP Archives, MS-6 (3-9).
[18] Ltr., APPW to MCW, July 28, 1841, TP Archives, MS-6 (1-8).
[19] Ltr., WGW to MCW, July 28, 1841, TP Archives, MS-6 (1-8).
[20] Ltr., APPW to MCW, August 15, 1841, TP Archives, MS-6 (1-7).
[21] Ltr., APPW to MCW, August 18, 1841, TP Archives, MS-6 (1-7).
[22] Ltr., APPW to MCW, n.d., TP Archives, MS-6 (1-7).
[23] Ltr., APPW to MCW, September 15, 1841, TP Archives, MS-6 (1-7).
[24] Ltr., Laurence Williams to MCW, October 19, 1841, TP Archives, MS-6 (1-9).
[25] *Buffalo Commercial Advertiser*, Wednesday, April 27, 1842, v. 4, no. 100.

CHAPTER 2

BACK TO TUDOR PLACE (1842-1846)

Martha Peter's heartfelt offer to try "to supply a Mother's place" to her grandchildren was gratefully accepted by Captain Williams, who could not contemplate keeping five children, the youngest of whom was only three, with him in Buffalo. He took them to Tudor Place and by June 16, 1842, was back at his post. He wrote to Markie, often addressed as "dear Mark," that he missed them "Oh how much words can not speak."

> Dear Child I think of you with anxiety, nothing have I more at heart than your interests and I hope you will endeavor to improve – and make yourselves ornaments to society. Upon you dear Child a responsibility dwells for your sisters will look to you and you will give a tone and direction to their deportment and you will all have before you in your dear Aunt Britannia a model for the behavior of a young lady and in your affectionate Grandmother an advisor who constantly can never be too strictly attended to.

He also reported: "I have been out to the burial ground. The grave is covered with flowers and everything looks beautiful around it."[1]

Williams wrote Markie often and gave specific instructions for her schooling and that of her sisters: "I think it wd. be as well to keep the children at spelling and definitions entirely 3 lessons a day. They cannot improve too much in that branch. I hope you attend steadily to the school."[2] All three girls would eventually attend a regular school in Georgetown, but for now Markie was schoolmistress.

On July 8 Williams wrote that he had sent the piano so they could practice. In the same letter, there was an exciting piece of news. Williams' sister, Margaret Orton, had written from England begging him to bring Markie to her to finish her education.[3] Markie responded very enthusiastically to this proposal, but her father had to dampen her hopes: "Oh by the way do not think of going to England dear Mark it depends upon a great many contingencies. If my wish were consulted I shd. go. It is possible & that's all."[4]

Although none of Markie's letters to her father survive, a few that she wrote at this time to her Williams grandfather do. (Markie's Peter grandfather had died in 1834; she hardly knew him.) They are meticulously written, in beautiful penmanship, all the lines perfectly straight and the spelling almost perfect. In view of Captain Williams constant injunctions to Markie on these subjects over the years of their correspondence, her mistakes must have been due to carelessness and hurry. When she took pains, she did very well, and it annoyed her father that she did not always do so. However, throughout her life Markie was to be an indifferent speller.

Markie wrote enthusiastically to her grandfather about the arrival of some friends, the Gardners, from Buffalo, and their visits back and forth. She hoped to visit them at their new post in Annapolis, "as it is only *two hours* ride *from Washington* in the cars."* She and the rest of the family at Tudor Place also visited with the Abert family (Colonel Abert was her father's superior, the chief of the Topographical Department).

She told her grandfather, "My piano arrived safely last week and entirely uninjured it was put in good tune and I practice every day." She also reported that "dear little Bunny," the baby of the family, had just turned three and had been much pleased with his birthday party. "I think that Master Bun will become quite a distinguished philosopher *in time* everything that is said he must have a reason for and as soon as he gets one he is perfectly satisfied." Lum and Kate also had birthdays in July; they were now fourteen and eight respectively. Markie asked to be remembered to many friends in Buffalo and teasingly noted that now one of her father's colleagues, Mr. Woodruff, should be happy that office supplies, pens, and ink would last four times longer than formerly.[5]

Meantime, after his mother's death, Laurence had been moved from Mr. Hollister's school in Troy to West Point, with a Mr. Kinsley. He wrote to Markie that he liked this school much better, even though he was disappointed that West Point only had a ball for the Fourth of July (no fireworks, presumably, which would have been much more to the taste of a nine-year-old). However, other aspects of the school pleased him: bathing [swimming] over their heads, drilling after school, and as

---

* "The cars" refers to a rail service inaugurated in 1840 between Washington and Annapolis by the Annapolis and Elk Ridge RR Co., as a branch of the B&O main line between Baltimore and Washington (from *www.en.wikipedia.org*).

11

many cherries as they wanted afterwards. He noted "You said in your letter that you thought I had forgot you but indeed I have not for I would never forget such a good sister as you if I should be away all my life time."[6]

By September the girls were enrolled in school in Georgetown. This may have been the year that Markie attended the Convent of the Visitation (now called Georgetown Visitation Preparatory School). She referred to a year spent at that school later, while she was in Paris.[7] At this time, the school was at the forefront of women's education. Ahead of Harvard and other men's schools, the school had the most current scientific equipment and made laboratory science part of the curriculum. Although it was a Catholic school, run by the Visitation Sisters, an order founded by St. Francis de Sales and St. Jane Frances de Chantal, the school was popular with the social elite of Georgetown and Washington of any faith The education provided by the nuns was not just available to the wealthy, however. They also ran a Saturday charity school open to any young girl, including free blacks and slaves, even though teaching slaves to read was illegal at this time.[8]

The Williams sisters' aunt, Britannia Wellington Peter, had attended the school, and for Captain Williams, that was recommendation enough. He missed them sorely, but felt they were in the right place.

> Still you are well where you are and I could desire no better school for many of the spiritual qualities and above all that dignified reserve of character which makes the *charm* of a woman as it should be *her pride*. I know of no lady who in that respect I so much admire as your dear Aunt Britannia.[9]

It was an exciting fall at Tudor Place, for Aunt Britannia was now engaged to marry Captain Beverly Kennon, the Commandant of the Navy Yard. Laurence wrote from West Point that Cousin Mary Lee[†] had told him the great news, "but I don't think her choice is acceptable to me that is the Navy."[10] Captain Williams also wrote from Buffalo, "I suppose it is now the time of the wedding I wish I could be there to give my kind wishes to the parties in person but they must take the wish for the deed."[11] On the 21st of December Williams wrote in reply to a letter from Markie describing the wedding:

[†] Mary Custis Lee (1808-1873), daughter of George Washington Parke Custis and wife of Robert E. Lee.

I received your letter a day or two since giving me the acct of the marriage of Aunt Brit. I was quite amused and delighted or rather interested in the detail. I have no doubt it was very splendid, as it should be where the *principal* actor was so admirably calculated to impart elegance and dignity at the same time.

He had sent a check for $200 to Martha Peter, out of which she would provide for the children to buy Christmas presents. He chided Markie about her spelling:

Dear Mark you must turn over a new leaf in regard to your spelling. "Menny" is a queer way of spelling many. I have spoken of this carelessness several times my dear Mark but it seems to make no impression upon you. This surely is carelessness for you do know how to spell *many* I am sorry to complain but I fear that in this respect your teacher must be neglectful for your last letters are decidedly inferior to those I recd from you in the summer. Do not feel hurt for it is the interest I feel in you that urges me to speak. It is not an agreeable task and you say nothing about your music nor do I hear any thing of your improvement. I hope you practice a great deal for you must be aware that after the expenses for the education of you all from my income a mere support remains – but I am willing to sacrifice any thing to your education whilst I believe there is a feeling in you to appreciate it. Well enough of scolding.[12]

The family was separated for the Christmas of 1842, with Williams in Buffalo, Laurence at West Point, the rest at Tudor Place. Laurence, quite homesick, wrote forlornly on December 29, "Sister Martha I want to know why you do not write to me more often.... If you cant send me papers do send me letters and if you cant send me the latter do send me the former."[13]

In February 1843 Laurence was suffering from measles and staying with his father in Buffalo during the school vacation. He wrote to Markie that Papa was coming to Washington to visit them.[14] Whether because of the measles or some other reason, Laurence did not go back to

West Point, but remained in Buffalo with a Mr. Dennison for the next year and a half.

The exhortations from Williams to Markie on the subject of her education and that of her sisters and Bunnie continued unabated. He especially harped on music and French – wanting her to write to him in French.

In March a new concern arose. Markie wrote to him on the subject of religion, having evidently recently experienced a strong religious conversion. She wanted to be confirmed and join the church. The Peters had been members of St. John's Episcopal Church in Georgetown for many years, and Thomas Peter had been on the vestry. The advent of Clement Moore Butler as rector at St. John's in 1841 marked the beginning of a renaissance in a church that had been in decline for some time. Butler was an enthusiastic young preacher, and obviously inspired Markie. When he left in 1844, the vestry selected Alexander Shiras as the next rector. He was from Virginia, and a protégé of Bishop William Meade, a kinsman of Mary Lee Fitzhugh Custis, the wife of George Washington Parke Custis.[15] Meade had been one of the central figures in the Washington Group, young clergymen who started the evangelical movement in Virginia and Washington, DC about 1830. This movement, an "almost puritanical" reformation, frowned on all sorts of entertainment, including dancing, theater, horse racing, card playing, and other public amusements. George Washington Parke Custis, who loved the theater and wrote many plays with patriotic themes, wrote to his wife, knowing her attitude: "I have made a great mental effort lately. But I am sure you and the bishop [William Meade] will think my energies might have been better employed."[16]

By the early 1850s, the tide had turned once again, and St. John's gradually incorporated "high-church" forms of worship that had been introduced by the Anglican Oxford Movement. What Markie thought of this we have no record, but her Aunt Britannia was caught in the disagreement between the minister and the congregation on some of the new practices, including ornamenting the church with greens at Christmas. Britannia recalled that she made and mounted on the pulpit a homemade cross of pasteboard and boxwood clippings:

> I was so pleased with my pretty cross as I believe was
> the Reverend Mr. Tillinghast. But the next morning
> poor Mr. Tillinghast came to see me, at the request of
> the congregation, and asked me to take it down. He

told me that he had no objection to it and it was only in compliance with the request of the congregation that he requested it removed.

Captain Williams replied to Markie's sentiments, "I do most heartily concur in your wish my dear child and hope you will by your example produce a similar feeling in your dear sisters."[17] On April 14 he replied to her next letter:

I have just recd your most interesting letter my dear Mark of the 3rd of April. I hasten to reply to it, and oh my child! with what pleasure and with what pride! I was indeed gratified at the tempered tone and above all at the affectionate feeling that pervades the letter throughout. My feelings have been more touched and softened by your gentle letter my dearest child than by ought that has transpired for long months of tedium and gloom. I need not say how little I have had to awaken sympathy in my heart. I have been wrapped in my pursuits at home and altho' I have endeavoured to be cheerful and to dispel my depression by visiting with my friends I have not succeeded and I have of late scarcely found account to make the necessary effort to call upon any of my friends.

Dear Mark I would enter upon the subject of your letter which seems most to interest you but it opens such a vast volume of reflection that I can not enter upon it suffice it dear child to say that I heartily sympathize with you and I heartily pray that the beautiful sentiments may daily become more firmly rooted in your heart and that your dear sisters may follow in the same path under your kind and gentle guidance. But dear Mark let me advise in that, that you do not *importune* them on the subject the heart naturally revolts against constraint let silent example or an occasional hint be your principle of persuasion beware of appearing too rigid or make an ostentatious display of piety or religion. There is sometimes arrogance and ostentation even in the manifestation of charity nay in the manifestation of those very virtues that seem to be

15

the most kindred to humility and devotion. You must not get so far before the dear children as to throw them without the sphere of attraction. Tell dear grandmother that I am truly grateful to her for the affection she shows towards you all. Her care and kindness to you have been indeed a great source of happiness to me.[18]

This letter begins a new phase in the relationship of Captain Williams with his eldest daughter. Now, at 18, she became more and more his confidant, although the strict attention to her education also continued: "I have rcd your letter without date containing a page or two of French but as you begin by the words – *le* langue fran*cois* I concluded you had not paid much attention to my advice about the rules of the language."

> [M]y own dear child, it does make me uncomfortable that you seem so little addicted to the labor of life. In music as well nothing can be accomplished without labor, but this is my last *lecture*. You are at an age now when it becomes a painful task to one to do so, and I know so well that the very best mind, the best regulated feelings, do so wince under anything that sounds, like correction that I almost fear to make you love me less by undertaking to do so.[19]

Williams was especially lonely because his father had gone back to England, to visit his dying son Laurence, and was not to return until October. Williams was living at the American Hotel, and his only family company came on Sunday when his young son Laurence came from school to have dinner with him.[20]

This was a happy summer for Laurence. Both he and his father reported that he was getting along well in his studies, at the head of his class in Latin and doing well in French. There were fireworks on the Fourth of July this year, and he was excited about getting some new clothes. His father reported, "He is very neat in his dress and they say he is very handsome." [21]

Captain Williams was back and forth from Buffalo to Mackinac often and his life was so unsettled he felt he could not have his family with him. He wrote:

Dearest children my great anxiety is about you all –
and all my considerations of future plans turn upon
your happiness & prosperity. Oh that I could have you
all near me and in favorable auspices but how many
adverse circumstances are there to such a hope. It is
useless to speak on the subject.[22]

Again, a couple of weeks later:

I am still at Mackinac very much engaged with my
duties and have not much to say I think I mentioned
that I had received your several letters. I was indeed
glad to get them it is one of the few pleasures that I
have to hear from you and of your welfare. I enclose a
check of $100 which will meet immediate
contingencies if not pray write to me.[23]

The same letter enclosed a poem written to his daughters:

My Gentle Child: Very own my first born-child
  The word comes gushing from my heart
The years have passed; the hour when first you smiled
  From memory's darkened page may never part
That anxious hour of dread, of hope, of gladness
Gleams like a star through clouds of dreary sadness.

Along the roseate path of childhoods years
  We've watched and o'er thy infant joys have smiled
O'er thy sick pillow too have shed some tears
  And those hast well repaid that love my child
With more than childhoods wisdom, all its truth
Gentle thy ways have been from infancy to youth.

Life is a weary pilgrimage at best,
  To him 'tis doubly desolate and drear,
Whose household hearth has thus been blest,
  To feel at last no kindred spirit near.
But let not sorrow throw its cloud on thee
Thy fair young brow, unsorrowed yet should be.

Nor did I mean to touch so sad a strain,
  But my first thought did strike a mournful key.
Yet to recur to sorrows past is vain,

17

And now my thoughts shall turn from gloom to thee
To thee as now thou art – so formed to win
From my lone heart, the grief that lies within.

Nor must my yearning bosom cling to thee alone
    Columbia – generous child! Is cherished there
She who from fates rude grasp was scarcely won
    The feeble infancy to bless a mother's care
Graceful thou art and oh my child! I see
The promise of a noble heart in thee.

And Kate! My winning Kate! – whose looks recall
    A vision of the past. Mind, form, and face,
The gentle beaming eye, sweet smile, and all
    To leave upon the heart too fond a trace
A voice to me, like music from the wave
Mournful yet sweet – an echo from the grave.

Markie noted on one of her copies of the poem: "written by my dear Father when we had all gone to Tudor Place and he was alone in Buffalo after my dear Mother's death."[24]

Then he was silent until early October. Whether in the meantime he visited Washington is not clear, for he wrote, "I have been very busy and very much depressed when not so," and "You see I write to you darling Mark as a woman, not a child." Markie evidently had complained about being kept short of money. Her father replied:

> You say you "never have a cent in your pocket excepting what your Uncle Washington[‡] gives you." I am sure your Grandmama understands me fully to see that you have on my part all that an affectionate and discreet liberality should suggest. It has been my wish & I supposed it was so that you had been furnished with everything that was necessary to your happiness.[25]

But perhaps stung by his daughter's remark, in his next letter he said, "I send a gold piece in this letter & I wish you to get Bun a horse as a present from his dear Papa And the rest may be disposed of in some trifle for each of you."[26]

[‡] George Washington Peter (1801-1877), eldest son of Martha and Thomas Peter.

In November, Markie's Aunt Britannia had a daughter, another Martha Custis, also to be called Markie, just like her cousin. And in late December came news from Captain Williams that he would be with them soon, not in time for Christmas, but shortly thereafter, and Markie and her sisters had his company during January 1844.[27]

On January 1, 1844, Markie began a diary, the first in a series that she kept periodically throughout her life. New Year's Day was eventful:

> I spent New Years day and two preceeding days with Aunt Britannia. New Years I went to the levee at the Presidents, in company with Uncle Kennon, Miss Claiborn, Mrs. and Miss Kennon, and Mr. Wm. Kennon. We walked; it was a lovely day; and we arrived before the crowd had assembled. I was introduced to President Tyler.... I spent a very pleasant day, and a letter from Papa in the evening in which he mentioned his intention of visiting us in a few days, crowned the enjoyment of the day. On returning home in the carriage in the evening Bunnie observed that the stars were sublime. He went to Church for the first time the last day of the Year 1843, behaved admirably of course. He is now four years and six months of age.[28]

The next day, a Wednesday, was school as usual. Markie, Columbia and Kate were now at Miss Lydia English's Seminary at what is now 2029 N Street in Georgetown. Markie wrote in her diary about her friends at school, especially Louisa Abert, the daughter of her father's commanding officer, and Julia Nicholls, with whom she attended Bible class after school. These three girls often walked "down-town" together during recess (lunch-time) to do small errands and buy themselves good things to eat. On January 5, they each had a cent, so purchased three spice cakes, which "we three romantic young ladies ate ... on our way back to school."[29] The girls sound like typical teenagers, teasing each other about their boyfriends and writing each other long letters in French, probably to share secrets.

Besides Bible class during the week, Markie attended two church services on Sunday, at Mr. Gassaway's (Christ Church) in the morning and Mr. Butler's (St. John's) in the afternoon. These were the two principal Episcopal churches in Georgetown.

On January 12, a cousin brought word to school that Markie's father had arrived, so the girls hurried home. Despite a spell of horrible weather, the children were delighted to have their father's company. He was able to stay only a short time, for on January 17 Markie noted:

> Bunnie wanted very much to go to Buffalo with Papa so he went out, put on his hat and cloak, put up a bundle and bade every one good bye. At last however after much persuasion he took off his coat and decided that Buffalo was too cold for him and there would be no one there to take care of him. Poor little fellow burst into tears and said that he would stay here with Grandmama. When Papa had gone Bunnie said sister it seems as if Papa had not been here at all now. It cleared off in the afternoon and is a clear night but the wind is very high and bleak and I feel more gloomy than words can express.[30]

The diary entries are brief, always commenting on the weather, and noting the comings and going of the day. For example:

> Saturday Jan 20 1844
> A very pleasant day. Lum and Kate spent the day with Aunt Brit. I stayed at home with Grandmother. I went down town in the morning and took Bunnie to the toy store went to the Post Office and got an invitation to the Washington Assemblies.

> Thursday [Jan] 25 1844
> A very pleasant but cold day. Went to school. Louisa Abert, Julia Nicholls and myself went down town at recess, not however without providing ourselves with a roll of bread which we eat on our way. Louisa Abert went to Velards Jeweler's to get her bracelet mended. Bunnie is sweeter than ever. A lovely night.

There were often visits back and forth with the Aberts and Aunt Britannia, who now lived at the Navy Yard, where her husband was the Commandant. One evening they all attended a concert at the Assembly Rooms near the City Hall given by the ladies of Washington for the benefit of the poor. Markie continued her music lessons with Mr. Schaaf.

Friday, February 2, was the last day of the school term, but there were examinations all the next week. Markie was examined only in French. During the break, Markie visited her friend Louisa Abert in Washington, and attended another Levee at the White House: "We were all introduced to the President [John Tyler]. 'I could not dance that night.' I remained with Mrs. Abert, James, Charles, and the Col all the evening." Had Markie now decided that dancing was against her religious principles? Later in life she would eschew all parties and dancing and frivolity of any kind.

The next week the new school term began. On Monday Markie had a sore throat and did not go, but on Tuesday she was there and after school went home with Mary Abert to visit her friend Louisa, who had left school after the last term.

> I spent a delightful day. I had a bad headache but some
> carbonate of soda soon relieved me. When we were
> going to bed James told me that Louisa's arm was sore,
> and he had some ointment that he wished me to rub it
> with. I was very credulous on the subject and gravely
> posed it on my hand, to perform the operation but as
> soon as the disagreeable odour came in contact with
> my smelling faculties, I at once perceived the design,
> but too late. I washed my hands in *soap* and *water*, and
> cologne but the odour was perceptible for several days
> after.

That same week, Markie's father came again unexpectedly. February 22 was:

> A beautiful spring day. We all went to school as usual.
> At the fifteen minute recess, just before our french
> class I was walking on the portico with Maria Morris
> studying my french grammar, when one of the girls
> came and told me that Miss English wished to see me.
> I went and she told me to go to the parlour that some
> one wished to see me, and that she believed it was
> Papa. I ran to the parlour and to my surprise & delight
> found that it was he. We all went home in a hack. A

21

few minutes after we arrived Uncle Custis[§] came over; Grandmother had gone down to town and was of course very much astonished on her arrival to see the unexpected visitors. Pa went with Uncle Custis to the 22nd ball [an annual affair in honor of George Washington's birthday] in Washington. A beautiful night.

A few days later:

Papa took Bunnie and myself over to Washington. We stopped at Aunt Brit's where we remained until one oclock, then Papa took Bun and myself visiting we called on Mrs. Spencer, Mrs. Hunt, Mrs. Mitchel, Mrs. and Misses Scotts, Miss Worth, Miss Porter, Mrs. Wilkins & Miss Louisa Abert. All out except Mrs. Mitchel and Lou. We then returned to Uncle Kennon's and dined. I received a little package from dear Lizzie Gardner and a sweet note. About five o'clock we came back to Tudor Place where I found a note from Miss Emily Austin, and Miss Porters card.

The next day, February 27:

A very mild day. We all went to school. I was very glad to see the girls. We returned home at three oclock and found Papa and Aunt Brit here. Aunt Brit went home soon after dinner and Pa bid us good bye soon after, with the intention of leaving Washington to-morrow Oh! I feel so sorry.

To-morrow I anticipate going to Mount Vernon on board of the Princeton, but the wind is very high and I fear as usual, my hopes will be blighted.

February 28 started out well, but ended in tragedy:

The morning was beautiful, but a little windy. At nine oclock I left Tudor Place in Grandmother's carriage for

---

[§] George Washington Parke Custis (1781-1857), Martha Washington's grandson and brother of Martha Custis Peter, owner of Arlington House. He and William G. Williams were fellow artists.

the steamboat wharf, calling on the way for Aunt Brit, Miss Lucy, Mrs. and Miss Kennon. I waited at Aunt Britannia's until eleven oclock, then we left in two carriages, and stopped at the Navy Department for Uncle Kennon. We all anticipated much pleasure. The wharf was crowded with hacks and carriages, and about twelve oclock the little Steamboat Joseph Johnson awaited us. The river was calm and beautiful and although *very very* crowded, we had an agreeable trip down the river. I was with Miss Wickliff all the time, and Mrs. Reed, of Erie. We soon arrived at the Ship, which was laying off Alexandria, not however without being in great hazard of drowning or sinking. The U.S. Ship Princeton presented a most magnificent appearence, being completely manned, and Decorated with the flags of the different nations. The day passed delightfully the band played and the cannons were repeatedly fired until about three oclock. On our return from Mount Vernon and just past Fort Washington, the Great Gun was again fired. I was sitting on a little bench around the helm of the boat and saw the dreadful explosion. In a few moments we heard the shocking news of desolation. Aunt Britannia who was with me but we did not suspect our own cause of alarm until Miss Claiborne told us. I will not record the heartrending scene and universal sadness which pervaded the Ship. Enough, to have it enstamped on my memory. My Uncle Kennon fell a victim to the blow.[**]

Markie gave a fuller account to her Aunt Nelly Lewis, who wrote to a friend:

I received a letter from Martha—(poor Mecs eldest daughter) .... Martha was with her poor Aunt on board

---

[**] This was a famous incident in naval history. The voyage was intended to demonstrate to many dignitaries a new gun called the *Peacemaker*. All went well for several firings, but the last attempt ended in tragedy. Besides Commodore Kennon, several cabinet officers were killed, and President Tyler, who was on board, only escaped because he had remained behind in the cabin to entertain Julia Gardiner, the woman who later became his wife.

the Princeton, & by her presence of mind saved her poor Aunts life, or *reason* by concealing her knowledge of the dreadful effect on Captn. K, until they returned to W[ashingto]n & were sustained by poor Brits Mother & Brother.

.... When the explosion took place, she [Britannia] inquired for Captn. K, but had no idea that he had suffer'd, she was told that he was with Mr. Upshur [Abel Parker Upshur, the Secretary of State] who was badly wounded. She asked several of the officers to show her where Captn. K was, & permit her to go to him—but they assured her that she could not see him. At last Miss Claiborne (Captn. K's sister in law, rushed in, exclaiming "Brit Captn K. is wounded". She was near fainting, & insisted on going to him. Martha pacified her & went to make inquiries. She heard an officer say "Captn. K never breathed." Captn. Shubrick assured Brit that he was slightly wounded, & advised her to go home immediately & prepare to receive him—that he could not then leave Mr Upshur, & no one could be permitted to go where they were except the necessary attendants. This quieted her fears, & she returned to her house where her Mother was waiting with her infant. Brit said, "Mother they say that Captn. K is hurt, & I must fix his room to receive him" she went upstairs, & Martha then told my Sister "Poor Aunt Brit does not know it, but Uncle K is dead". Immediately they sent to G Town for Wash[ingto]n Peter who broke the dreadful intelligence as gently as he could. The effect on her was most distressing indeed, she kept her Bed several days & her grief was almost too much to bear. She insisted on knowing all the particulars, & Wash[ingto]n told her everything....

Martha writes me yesterday "Poor Aunt Brit is pretty well, of course very much distressed, but I think bears her affliction very well. She is now comfortably fixed at home. The Baby is the most lovely child I ever saw, & very lively & intelligent. On the 28th. March, being the day *one month* on which its poor Father was killed, Aunt Brit wished to have it christen'd...."[31]

For the next three weeks, Markie stayed with Bunnie at "Aunt Dick's"†† house in Georgetown. "I did not go to school during the time but remained with Bunnie my angel, *baby brother*. Nothing remarkable occurred."

At this point, Markie seemed to lose her enthusiasm for keeping a diary. On Saturday, March 2, she recorded the funeral of her Uncle:

> A cloudy gloomy day. The funeral of the unfortunate killed took place from the Presidents. All seemed to be mourning even the sky exchanged its azure hue for a dark and dismal shroud, more appropriate indeed.‡‡

After that, March is dismissed with one line: "Nothing happened worth recording" until her birthday, March 28, which passed "unnoticed by all except my dear Grandmother. Aunt Brit's baby was christened by Mr. Butler. I went to his Church in the afternoon, and he returned with me." A few entries at the beginning of April mark the end of this diary.

In the aftermath of the tragic death of Commodore Kennon, Markie seems to have been depressed. The diary ends, and she wanted to leave school, possibly also because her best friend, Louisa Abert, had finished in February. Her father wrote that he had no objection if Martha Peter thought it proper, but "I think that you might yet profitably continue a little longer."[32]

After some correspondence back and forth, Williams decided Markie should remain in school another year. "So be patient dearest child & do not be disappointed. We anticipate happiness in a change too often."[33]

Captain Williams had proposed a visit to Buffalo during the summer by Martha Peter, Britannia Kennon, and Markie (presumably bringing Bunny with them), leaving Kate and Lum at Miss English's, but found he must renege on the offer because he had a new assignment to survey all the harbors of the upper Great Lakes.[34] Reporting on a social event in Buffalo, he teased Markie: "The music & supper were quite delightful. Tho' you will think it not sentimental to place the 2 in the same category."[35]

---

†† Margaret Peter Dick (1776-1859), sister of Thomas Peter.
‡‡ Markie was so distracted by these tragic events that this entry in the diary is actually listed as February 31.

Markie was still determined to go to Buffalo. Her father said she could come if she could persuade the Aberts to escort her, but in the end Colonel Abert decided to go alone, so that plan fell through. Her grandfather Williams would have come to escort her, but for some reason, Williams would not allow that either. Then he fell ill with "intermittent fever" (malaria), saying he was confined to bed with illness for the first time in his life.[36]

By August, Markie, put off from a visit yet again, finally asserted her independence and found a way to get as far as Fort Hamilton, New York to visit with the Lees[§§], hoping from there to go on to Buffalo. She stayed with the Lees until the end of August. Then, escorted by Mr. and Mrs. Mahan,[***] she got as far as West Point, where she stayed at the home of her friend Blanche Berard, whose father, Claudius Berard, was the French instructor at West Point, and an old friend of William G. Williams. Blanche and Markie enjoyed a lifelong friendship. Along the way Williams sent Markie a check for $50 for her expenses, and a flurry of anxious letters.[37]

In mid-September, Markie was at Governor's Island in New York Harbor, hoping to depart within a few days for Buffalo, but her father put her off once again because he had to make another trip to the upper Great Lakes. Captain Williams was very troubled during 1844 by controversy over the best plan for improvements to Buffalo Harbor. "The truth is dear Mark I do not approve of a young lady of 17 setting out upon her travels."[38] At this point Markie gave up and went back to Fort Hamilton, where she stayed again with the Lee family until early October.[39] Markie had definitely asserted her independence. She evidently wrote her father complaining that he did not trust her, for he wrote back:

> You took too much to heart my remarks...no dear Child I have every confidence in your discreet and noble nature – you are my beloved child my pride & happiness – but I am sometimes fretted with business cares and I write just as the thought comes.

[§§] In New York harbor, where Lee was Captain of Engineering from 1841 to 1845.
[***] Mr. Mahan was Dennis Hart Mahan, professor of civil and military engineering at West Point, and the father of Alfred Thayer Mahan, the famous naval historian and strategic analyst.

I have been as sorry to relinquish the hope of seeing
you and having you with me as you can be to give up
the pleasure of the visit. I am delighted that you have
so pleasant a visit and I hope now you will return to
your home with satisfactory delight – do you not think
dear Mark another year of schooling wd be of use to
you.[40]

Although we have no definite proof, it appears from her father's
correspondence that Markie, on her return to Tudor Place, then attended
school for another year, probably at Miss English's Seminary. At about
the same time, Laurence arrived in Washington to attend Georgetown
College, which he entered on November 15, 1844 and stayed until
February 1847.[41] Georgetown at this time was more like a modern
preparatory school than a college. Laurence was only 11 years old.

Williams himself spent some time in Washington during the
Fall, possibly to get Laurence settled in school as well as on
Topographical Department business, but the main responsibility for Lolo,
now so close by, fell on Markie's shoulders. Laurence was a trial to
Markie and to his father. A little over a week after arriving at school, he
complained to Markie that his trunk had not yet arrived, and that he had
to send his letter by mail, because no boys lived near Tudor Place that he
could send it by (Tudor Place was and is approximately six blocks from
the College.) He had no clothes except the ones he was wearing and they
were torn.[42]

The trunk arrived with a "dear" note from Markie. He told her
he had been learning the ways of Georgetown boys, including swearing,
"because everyone does it." He said he was sorry he had been so
impolite to her while at home, and assured her that he said his prayers
every night. Both Markie and her father were worried about the bills
Laurence was running up for clothing; Laurence's answer was that he
was sorry he got so many clothes, but boys were allowed to get as many
as they chose. He was doing well in Latin and Greek, but not in Algebra
and French, which his father particularly wanted him to learn. "I mean
hereafter to tell you everything that will be to my good or bad."[43]

In answer to her next letter, he told Markie it was not possible to
find companions who didn't swear – there were none. He would not care
for his father to see his shoe bill – he got at least a pair a month and had
no idea how many he had.[44]

On the first of January 1845, Williams wrote to Markie about Lolo's latest school report: "he is indicted as deficient & inattentive – in all his studies.... Tell him from me *impressively that I must not have such another report.*"[45] Poor Laurence did not do well at Georgetown. In one of his reports he is 17th in a class of 26, in another, last in a class of 30.[46] His father was livid. Six months' board at the school cost $100, and the clothing bills were outrageous. Williams was so upset he would not write to Laurence himself, but let Markie act as intermediary.

In the same letter, Williams wrote to Markie: "You certainly do write very gracefully and I love to read yr letters but be careful my sweet child particularly when you write yr french letters." But, "I wd not have your letter criticized by others and am mentioning mistakes in the subject of spelling for the neglect of it makes the most agreeably written letter the subject of ridicule."

In this letter, Williams is full of praise for his commandant's wife: "I am glad you spent some time with Mrs. Abert. Do you not think she is very very perfect?"[47] He was soon to change his tune, however. During the next few months Williams and Colonel Abert were more and more at odds. Williams did not really know the cause, but after a visit to Washington in the Spring, he was relieved of his command of the Buffalo Harbor and Lake Survey project and reassigned to survey the border of Wisconsin and Michigan.[48] It seemed an especially cruel assignment for a man with as many family problems as Williams, which were well known to his commanding officer. By June he was in Green Bay for at least four months and quite depressed: "I shall endeavor to get a furlough after this campaign is over for the purpose of visiting you all & making some permanent arrangement for my family I can not live separated from my children for ever. I feel wretched & desolate a great portion of my time."[49] He did have the company of his nephew, John Orton, who had come from England to help with the survey, but his father had gone back to England at the beginning of the year and was in poor health.

By September, Captain Williams' break with Colonel Abert was complete:

> You must know dearest Mark that I have recd an order
> to remain here (Green Bay) or Milwaukie to complete
> my maps making it my head quarters for the winter.
> Now I shall talk to you no longer as a child but as to

one who can appreciate and sympathize in my vexations. I do not say my happiness for I have had so little of it lately that I begin to think it is a sentiment with which I have naught to do. You must know Marky that my former friend the Col. has of late shown a most vindictive feeling towards me which I can attribute to nothing but difference of opinion on professional matters or some mis-representation of which I can not name the source."[50]

Because of the break with Abert, Captain Williams was concerned about some of his paintings that had been sent from the National Academy of Design in care of Colonel Abert. He wanted Markie to find out if they had arrived and arrange for them to be stored at Tudor Place. Since one of the paintings was of James Abert, and he had promised it to the boy's mother, he wanted her to make sure she received it, but otherwise Markie should remain aloof from the Abert family:

[D]o you appreciate my object and sympathize in the views I take of this question dear Mark? Why should I compromise my personal respect by an attempt to deprecate the most unjust most contemptible persecution. You may feel in my thus making you the confidante of these circumstances how much I value your judgment and discretion. [D]o not refer to the matter to yr sisters or anyone, but treat with dignified reserve any invitation that may be given to you to visit the Aberts and make some excuse for your sisters should they be invited.[51]

This letter closes with the sad news of the death of Markie's grandfather Williams: "[H]e had arrived at more than the burial age of men. Still it throws a deep deep gloom upon my heart."

When Williams received Markie's reply to this letter he was established in his winter headquarters in Milwaukee.

I received your affectionate letter of condolence on the subject of your poor grandfathers death yesterday indeed my child it would have been a consolation to have you and your dear sisters with me, in many respects it wd be to me a great comfort.... You say in your letter Mark that you will let the Col. know that

29

you feel hurt. I wish you to do so my child *only* by not accepting the hospitality of his family or placing yourself in a position to appear to propitiate his good will, but by a dignified reserve.[52]

He was certainly calling on Markie to fulfill a most difficult role, caught between her family and friends, and having to be completely circumspect about it. They were also both still worried about Laurence:

I feel anxious about Laurence and am disposed to let him go to the school in Alexandria if you think it best. [I]t is difficult subject to determine. You know that I object to a school w[h]ere the boys have access to the streets. I know not what is for the best. As for the charges for clothes at his present school I do not understand them *from Nov. 15 to July 5*. There is a charge for 10 pr of pantaloons (3 Frock Coats & 1 Jacket) (5 vests) and yet Lolo writes me word that he is dreadfully in want of clothes and that he has *out-grown* all he has Really I expect to find him a very tall boy.[53]

In his next letter Williams had a lecture for Markie as well:

I am glad dearest Mark that you appear to take so much comfort in religious exercises and was pleased to find by Lums last letter that her thoughts were not entirely without bias of that kind. But Marky dearest you must not neglect your studies for I doubt whether you could reconcile this to a sense of what is due to religion itself. …do not consider this dearest Mark as personal in the least on the contrary you are my *beau ideal* of that which is morally good and beautiful….

I should think though I do not presume to advance my my opinions as orthodox dearest Mark that an hourspent in the assiduous and energetic endeavor to construct a sister or brother with all the sacrifice of patience and our natural disposition to indolence which it calls for, quite as acceptable in the eyes of the almighty as the same amt of time devoted to forms or ritual of Church exercises – the duties of life in my opinion enter more largely into what should be denominated true religion than is generally supposed.

He scolded her for neglecting her musical studies:

> You who have so fine a voice naturally who have
> excellent capacity and all the requisites to become
> a fine musician. Should yet plead indisposition to
> the drudgery necessary to acquire a proficiency –
> This you will think…quite different from the
> evangelical teaching of Mr. Shiras but Marky do not
> forget that however good a clergyman may be it is after
> all a profession.[54]

Although he had been trying for months to get a furlough to visit his family, Williams had been unable to do so, and so spent a lonely Christmas. In his first letter of the new year, Williams could not resist a dig at Markie regarding her spelling:

> [D]o you know my sweet Marky that both the girls are
> *ahead* of you in the matter of spelling. You do
> sometimes make the *funniest* mistakes in one of your
> later letters you wrote (no) for (know) a concise way of
> spelling the word certainly. The only way to correct
> this is by reading and by carefully examining your
> letters after they are written. Come Marky this last
> criticism that perhaps I shall even venture to make
> upon your letters goes rather hard with me. Your style
> is so excellent that you should not allow a defect in a
> subordinate branch of the art. You see my own darling
> child how anxious I am that you should be perfect and
> hence my observation which I fear you may feel hurt at
> but which nevertheless come[s] from the affections &
> love I bear you.[55]

Still bitter with Colonel Abert and concerned that Markie would try to be the conciliator, Williams wrote:

> [A]ll I hope is that you will not show any desire to
> propitiate him but keep as distant as you can I do not
> wish you to show resentment nor harbor any my
> dearest child   it is not in your nature and I am glad that
> it is so but I do not wish to compromise my proud

31

independence by conciliating one who has treated me so unworthily.... [E]xplain to your Grandmother my feelings or to your Aunt if you feel more unreserved in that relation.

This was really a most uncomfortable time, to say the least, for both Markie and her father. He summed it up well:

The mortification that I suffered my dearest child in consequence of the remarks that have been made –
relating to my having you all with me or remarks which imply that it wd. be desirable to Mrs. Peter is really very horrifying to my spirit. Assuredly I desire to have you with me and am prepared to make any sacrifice to do so. [B]ut what can I do at present I have no house – and am now if my furlough shd. be refused awaiting orders. I have never felt before my dependence for I never supposed that an officer commanding could act with such motives towards those whose movements he by the rule of service controls. [B]ut enough of that odious subject I shall await with patience until some change shall take place in the mean time keep yourself reserved nor make the slightest attempt to propitiate. I would rather it cd. be done with out wounding Mrs. Aberts feelings that you shd. have very little intercourse with the family – but keep these impulses within your own heart because the children might misconceive them and commit some indiscretion in conversation or by some remark. Give my affectionate love to your dear Grandmother & Aunt Brit and to the darling girls & dear Bun. I am glad to hear he has even made the attempt to speak french.[56]

On another subject that had been worrying Markie, Williams decreed that there should be no change in schools for Kate or Laurence. "It is the pupil that makes the difficulty at both Mrs. English & Mrs. Mercers," he said.

Frustration with his career led Williams to request a transfer out of the Topographical Engineers and into a different branch of the Army. By March Williams had evidently had a positive reply, and was able to come to Washington and Buffalo to make arrangements for his property

32

and visit his family.[57]   By early June, he was preparing to leave for Mexico, where war had begun in May. It is, we suppose, a measure of his extreme misery that Williams would leave his motherless children and go off to war, possibly hoping that it would soon be over and his career would be on a more prosperous track in the future.

Markie wrote to her friend, Blanche Berard:

> For some weeks I have been arranging dear Papas' clothes in anticipation of *orders*, which he received day before yesterday – *to join the Army in Texas* – since then, I have been "packing up" except on Sunday, when I gave my "sorrows leave to flow" and to-day, or this morning at 5 o'clock, he left us; so you may imagine how perfectly exhausted I am, both in mind and body.... Ah! Dearest Blanche, we all have trials in this lower world, *many, many,* have *I*, and yet when I see the innumerable blessings, I possess, to which others are strangers, I think perhaps the goods and ill of life are pretty equally divided – but that does not afford me much consolation. Some persons, however, are less affected by grief or joy than others, but for myself, I am *overwhelmed*, with either.

Although we have a lot of correspondence to Markie, and can read between the lines about her personality and the events and people that influenced her life, the few surviving letters from her to others, such as Blanche, are so much more directly revealing. Consider, for example, her attitude toward the Mexican War and her fears for those who did not have her strong religious faith:

> The difficulties in which our dear Country, has been so needlessly plunged, the situation of our *beloved Army*, (though *they* consider it favorable) and the danger to which many, *so many*, of my friends are exposed, without, that Shield, which can alone preserve them – weighs *heavily* upon my heart.

She thanked Blanche for her invitation to visit West Point, where they had many mutual friends, and reported that she also had invitations from the Lees at Ft. Hamilton and her dear friend Mrs. Pratt at Governor's Island, but did not see any possibility of leaving Tudor Place at that time.[58]

A few days later, Markie heard from Robert E. Lee, who was at Governor's Island, where the "smiling face of peace has been changed for the grim visage of war." He had come over from Fort Hamilton to see the troops that had been under his command off to the war. Mostly, his letter was a lighthearted account of the activities of all their mutual acquaintances. He even teased her about a certain Doctor:

> And now Markie I believe I have given you an account of every body, except the Dr. who is not yet married. His fine home is yet without a mistress & his fine daughters without a mother. How would such a responsible station suit you? Consult Bunnie on the subject.

But he also was feeling the weight of seeing his friends and colleagues go off to war:

> You will perhaps want to know how I came here. Feeling a little solitary & under the weather, I determined to refresh myself with a sight of the boys before their departure to Texas. I return to Ft. H. tomorrow.... [Y]ou must remember them in your orisons Markie, for it is no less certain that we neer shall look upon them all again.[59]

On June 16, Markie got a brief letter from her father, from Louisville, Kentucky:

> I have only time to write a few lines to you my own dear sweet child. And this letter is equally to dear Lum and to Kate and to Bun (William) he is too much of a man to be called "Bun" I have been reminded of you my darling child in the sweet rose leaves which you have scattered through my trunk with packing so careful have I been of them that when they fell upon the floor in taking out my clothes I have carefully gathered them up & replaced them. The perfume comes to me like the "breath of the sweet south" reminding me of happiness relinquished for I fear many a weary month – I am about to embark this even[in]g and have many things to attend to. God bless you all. I will write from N. Orleans.[60]

A week later, he had reached Galveston, Texas, after passing through New Orleans, where he had bought a horse, but it had jumped in the Mississippi River along the way. He did manage to catch it, but "a horse is rather a troublesome affair on board a Steamer as you may suppose."

> From all I can learn Genl. Taylor proposes to move towards Monterey on the 1st or in the beginning of July so that we shall be in time for that. I feel of course interested in the campaign it is something so new to me and I feel so much "esprit de Corps" that nothing but the love & affection I bear you all could make me [wish] to be elsewhere. I have been so much gratified by my own dear child in observing the   care   [and] interest which you showed in packing up my clothes. I never open my trunk that those rose leaves do not send a tender rapture upon my heart, my dear children & all the sweet associations that surround them come upon my mind with a gush of affectionate recollection.[61]

Williams was certainly not a father who ever had any problem expressing his affection for his children. Markie had been assured of his love from her earliest childhood.

The troublesome horse escaped for good at Port Isabel, Texas, and then another fine horse was stolen, irreplaceable at any price, but Williams finally received some letters from home in Matamoros, Mexico, *"dear affectionate letters"* that consoled him for all things. It was now time for Columbia to leave school: "[S]ay to her that I am willing she should leave school at the time appointed but I hope she will devote herself to reading and the improvement of her mind at home." He also addressed other problems at home. Laurence's college bills were still exorbitant: "[A]ttend to this matter of this schooling for L in a business like manner my darling Marky." And:

> Dear Marky I do not know what you can mean by a want of respect on my part towards your Grandmother, my cons cience fully acquits me of anything of the kind, the confirmed habit of your Grandmother toward myself is that of coldness and reserve. I feel no unkindness towards her however and have meant

35

nothing of disrespect in sending the checks to you, you know that I have requested to you to place the money entirely at your grandmothers disposal. My motive has assuredly been misconstrued in thus rendering the drafts subject to your endorsement instead of hers. I will however do as you wish. I only wish I had more to send in whatever shape it might be but I am woefully disappointed in my expectations of economy. The cost of living with the army is almost ruinous.[62]

On August 3, Williams was still in Matamoros, just over the Mexican border, but thought the army would move forward by land the next day. Once again caught in the middle of tension between her beloved Grandmother and Father, Markie had reported some comments her Grandmother made. Williams replied: "What you have said about the remarks of your Grandmother has given me pain but I can not help it and it is useless to refer to the subject."[63]

By mid-August, Williams had advanced up the Rio Grande to Camargo, from where he expected the army would go on to Monterey, where "it is quite uncertain…whether we shall meet with opposition."

I fear Marky the war is going to be protracted I do not judge from appearances that there is going to [be] an immediate termination to the contest.

On arrival in Camargo, Williams discovered that Markie had also been looking after his spiritual welfare in her careful packing of his trunks:

[I]t was only this morning upon getting a portion of my baggage which in the delightful casualty of war had been traveling the country in every direction but the right one since my arrival in the country that I found your little present for me with the accompanying letter. [I]t was an agreeable surprise and your sweet dear little letter was read by me with the greatest interest. I refer to the little bible which you put in my trunk.[64]

In his next letter, Williams thanked Markie for "your charming bouquet which although crushed was beautiful but more so to my heart as the evidence of my darling child's thoughtfulness, and of the delicacy of her taste which prompted so sweet a present." It was a welcome respite from the reality of war:

> Oh the bowers! The flowers! The shrubs, the showers, the tall trees and close cut verdant lawn, the smiles of affection. A thousand sweet things – where are they! At this instant a green lizard is looking me right in the face its track follows it upon the dust. A mule is braying hideously mixed with the sound of wagon chains and a cloud of dust is playing round them.
>
> The dust covers my writing case and the perspiration were it not for my pocket handkerchief would make a thousand mud puddles upon the paper.[65]

Still the army did not advance to Monterey. "The excitement of war forsooth – I have never been so devoured by ennui in my life." To ease the tedium, he was attempting to learn Spanish. Practical matters at home also engaged his attention. He sent Markie some papers relating to "the little property I possess in land" and then a long paragraph about expenses in general:

> By the way dear Mark I must speak and I wish it to be between ourselves. I am much annoyed in pecuniary matters that is my expenses are so great that I shall becompelled to suffer from wounded pride or economise my means more than seems to me possible. You can not imagine how expensive it is to live here and unless the greatest economy is used at home I shall not be enabled to send enough to have all that may be required – you must be especially careful in regard to Laurence – and prohibit any purchase whatever on his part without sanction – indeed it wd. be better that you shd. provide his clothes as you suggest in your letters. A portion of our allowance at home arises for an allowance for fuel, quarters, servant, and horses, -- in the field we have to be furnished with them and the allowance is entirely absorbed, this reduces the pay proper to very little, and the cost of every imaginable thing is here so great that I fear I shall not be enabled to send much home. What may come from my warehouse in Buffalo I fear will be very small indeed so that I shall have to enjoin the greatest economy, but

this dear Mark is between ourselves for it looks sordid to enter upon such matters – thus far only let my suggestions appear in what you may be enabled to influence.[66]

At last the army did advance, and Williams was sent ahead to scout the way to Monterey. The last letter Markie ever received from her father was written on September 17, 1846 from St. Marin, just outside Monterey.[67]

> We are just in the bustle of preparation. The whole column assembles here this evening and tomorrow morning we march toward Monterey. The next day will probably see our banners floating from the towers. When I tell you of our experiences for the last few days, you will not be anxious about me. You will see how little are the enemy to be dreaded.
>
> Approaching St. Marin,
>
> I was seized with the sudden thought that I should like to take possession of a place by myself and witness it in its desolation. Leaving the rest of the party I rode on deliberately, soon saw six men standing in the principal street. They seemed to be expecting us and I felt instinctively that there was no danger to be apprehended. I rode at once right among them extending my hand to them in token of peace. They all welcomed me with enthusiasm. They told me that the city was deserted, that the troops that had just left had driven them all from their homes and they wished to know whether they and their families might return to their homes. They were in transports of joy when I said they would be treated kindly and that no injury would be done them.

Unfortunately, Williams' luck did not hold. Four days later, he was dead, killed during the battle for Monterrey. According to witnesses, his last words were: "Tell them, I fell at the head of the column."[68]

[1] Ltr., WGW to MCW, June 16, 1842, Tudor Place Archives, MS-6 (2-6).

[2] Ltr., WGW to MCW, June 24, 1842, Tudor Place Archives, MS-6 (2-5).

[3] Ltr., WGW to KAW, July 8, 1842, Tudor Place Archives, MS-6 (2-6).

[4] Ltr., WGW to MCW, July 29, 1842, Tudor Place Archives, MS-6 (2-6).

[5] Ltr., MCW to WW, July 12, 1842, Tudor Place Archives, MS-6 (3-1).

[6] Ltr., Laurence Williams to MCW, July 22, 1842, Tudor Place Archives, MS-6 (2-10).

[7] Ltr., Laurence Williams to MCW, September 23, 1842, Tudor Place Archives, MS-6 (2-10).

[8] Georgetown Visitation Preparatory School website, www.visi.org.

[9] Ltr., WGW to MCW, September 2, 1842, Tudor Place Archives, MS-6 (2-7).

[10] Ltr., Laurence Williams to MCW, November 9, 1842, Tudor Place Archives, MS-6 (2-10).

[11] Ltr., WGW to MCW, December 1, 1842, Tudor Place Archives, MS-6 (2-7).

[12] Ltr., WGW to MCW, December 21, 1842, Tudor Place Archives, MS-6 (2-7).

[13] Ltr., Laurence Williams to MCW, December 29, 1842, MS-6, (2-10).

[14] Ltr., Laurence Williams to MCW, February 12, 1843, MS-6, (1-12).

[15] Frances Barbour Lumbard, *The Changing Face of St. John's: 200 Years in Georgetown*, Washington, DC, 1998, p. 46, 94-96.

[16] Murray H. Nelligan, *Arlington House: The Story of the Robert E. Lee Memorial*, Burke, VA: Chatelaine Press, 2001, pp. 181-82. George Washington Parke Custis, *Recollections and Private Memoirs of Washington*, Washington, DC: William H. Moore, 1859, p. 59 (Sept. 12, 1833).

[17] Ltr., WGW to MCW, March 9, 1843, MS-6 (2-8).

[18] Ltr., WGW to MCW, April 14, 1843, MS-6 (2-8).

[19] Ltr., WGW to MCW, June 11, 1843, MS-6 (2-8).

[20] Ltrs., WGW to MCW, June 5 and June 23, 1843, MS-6 (2-8, 2-3).

[21] Ltrs., Laurence Williams to MCW, June 11 and July 18, 1843, MS-6, (1-12).

[22] Ltr., WGW to MCW, August 1, 1843, MS-6 (2-9).

[23] Ltr., WGW to MCW, August 18, 1843, MS-6 (2-9).

[24] Note and poem in the Upshur-Brown papers, a family collection in Richmond, VA..

[25] Ltr., WGW to MCW, October 22, 1843, MS-6 (2-9).

[26] Ltr., WGW to MCW, October 26, 1843, MS-6 (2-9).

[27] Ltr., Laurence Williams to MCW, December 24, 1843, MS-6 (2-3).

[28] MCW Diary, 1844, Arlington House Archives, MCWC Papers, folder 15.

[29] *Ibid.*

[30] *Ibid.*

[31] Ltr., EPCL to EBG, April 5, 1844, in Brady, *G.W.'s Beautiful Nelly*, pp. 239-40.

[32] Ltr., WGW to MCW, March 17, 1844, Tudor Place Archives, MS-6 (2-10).

[33] Ltr., WGW to MCW, April 28, 1844, Tudor Place Archives, MS-6 (2-10).

[34] Ltrs., WGW to MCW, April 14 and 28, 1844, Tudor Place Archives, MS-6 (2-10).

[35] Ltr., WGW to MCW, April 14, 1844, Tudor Place Archives, MS-6 (2-10).

[36] Ltrs., WGW to MCW, June 24, July 12, 14, 20, 24, Aug. 2, 1844, Tudor Place Archives, MS-6 (2-11, 2-3).

[37] Ltrs., WGW to MCW, Aug. 19, 25, 26, 31, Sept. 2, 1844, Tudor Place Archives, MS-6 (2-11, 2-3). Ltr., R.E. Lee to MCW, Sept. 2, 1844, in Avery Craven, ed., *"To Markie"*, Cambridge, MA: Harvard Univ. Press, 1933, p. 3.

[38] Ltr., WGW to MCW, Sept. 11, 1844, Tudor Place Archives, MS-6 (2-12).

[39] Ltrs., R.E. Lee to MCW, Sept. 14 and 17, 1844, in Craven, *"To Markie"*, pp. 4-6. Ltr., WGW to MCW, Oct. 4, 1844, Tudor Place Archives, MS-6 (2-12).

[40] Ltr., WGW to MCW, Sept. 16, 1844, Tudor Place Archives, MS-6 (2-12).

[41] Ltr., WGW to MCW, Oct. 4, 1844, Tudor Place Archives, MS-6 (2-12); Georgetown College reports, Tudor Place Archives, MS-12, folder 7.
[42] Ltr., LAW to MCW, Nov. 23, 1844, Tudor Place Archives, MS-6 (2-14).
[43] Ltr., LAW to MCW, undated [Nov. 1844], Tudor Place Archives, MS-6 (2-14).
[44] Ltr., LAW to MCW, undated [Dec. 1844], Tudor Place Archives, MS-6 (2-14).
[45] Ltr., WGW to MCW, Jan. 1, 1845, Tudor Place Archives, MS-6 (2-13).
[46] Georgetown College reports, Tudor Place Archives, MS-12, folder 7.
[47] Ltr., WGW to MCW, Jan. 1, 1845, Tudor Place Archives, MS-6 (2-13).
[48] Ltr., WGW to MCW, April 11, 1845, Tudor Place Archives, MS-6 (2-14).
[49] Ltr., WGW to MCW, July 22, 1845, Tudor Place Archives, MS-6 (2-15).
[50] Ltr., WGW to MCW, Sept. 17, 1845, Tudor Place Archives, MS-6 (2-16).
[51] Ltr., WGW to MCW, Sept. 21, 1845, Tudor Place Archives, MS-6 (2-16).
[52] Ltr., WGW to MCW, Oct. 31, 1845, Tudor Place Archives, MS-6 (2-16).
[53] *Ibid.*
[54] Ltr., WGW to MCW, Dec. 5, 1845, Tudor Place Archives, MS-6 (2-17).
[55] Ltr., WGW to MCW, Jan. 9, 1846, Tudor Place Archives, MS-6 (2-18).
[56] Ltr., WGW to MCW, Feb. 18, 1846, Tudor Place Archives, MS-6 (2-18).
[57] Ltrs., WGW to MCW, March 9 and 17, 1846, Tudor Place Archives, MS-6 (2-18).
[58] Ltr., MCW to BB, June 3, 1846, Williams Family Collection, Eleanor S. Brockenbrough Library, The Museum of the Confederacy, Richmond, VA.
[59] Ltr, REL to MCW, June 7, 1846, in Craven, *To Markie*, pp. 17-20.
[60] Ltr., WGW to MCW, June 16, 1846, Tudor Place Archives, MS-6 (2-18).
[61] Ltr., WGW to MCW, June 23, 1846, Tudor Place Archives, MS-6 (2-18).
[62] Ltrs., WGW to MCW, July 10 and 23, 1846, Tudor Place Archives, MS-6 (2-18).
[63] Ltr., WGW to MCW, August 3, 1846, Tudor Place Archives, MS-6 (2-19).
[64] Ltr., WGW to MCW, August 16, 1846, Tudor Place Archives, MS-6 (2-19).
[65] Ltr., WGW to MCW, August 23, 1846, Tudor Place Archives, MS-6 (2-19).
[66] Ltr., WGW to MCW, August 3l, 1846, Tudor Place Archives, MS-6 (2-19).
[67] Ltr., WGW to MCW, Sept. 17, 1846, copy in MCWC hand, theUpshur-Brown papers, a family collection in Richmond, VA.
[68] Ltr., Lt. Daniel T. Chandler to his mother, copy in Tudor Place Collection; a variation of this is inscribed on his tombstone in Buffalo, NY: "His last message to his friends was 'I fell in the front of the column.'"

Self-portrait by
William G. Williams

America Peter Williams by
William G. Williams

Martha Custis Williams
"Markie"

Martha Custis Williams
"Markie"

All photos this page courtesy of Tudor Place Historic House and Garden

Tudor Place, ca. 1873
Photo courtesy of Tudor Place Historic House and Garden

Sketch of Arlington House by Martha Custis Williams
Courtesy of National Park Service, Arlington House,
The Robert E. Lee Memorial

Britannia Wellington Peter Kennon
"Aunt Brit"
Photo courtesy Tudor Place
Historic House and Garden

William Orton Williams
"Bunnie"
Photo courtesy Episcopal
High School Archives

William Orton Williams

Memorial hair brooch
with Markie's and Orton's
Initials

Both photos courtesy of Tudor Place Historic House and Garden

CHAPTER 3

FRIENDSHIP AND ROMANCE

Although Markie had an obsession about caring for her relatives, whom she referred to as "those I love," her life was not without friendships and romance. However, just when we think that her diaries will reveal secrets about a romance, we find that she has torn out pages, blackened them with ink or turned to a new subject, leaving us in suspense. Fortunately, she had a talent for making friends throughout her life, traveled more than most women did at the time, and had an exchange of correspondence with a number of friends and relatives who kept her letters. In her Catalogue of Addresses, she listed correspondents living in six foreign countries, 13 states, and the Territory of Utah.[*1] Reminiscent of her Grandmama Martha Washington, she burned many of her old letters - "Spent the day in looking over & burning old letters. It was a sad day & the past was so vividly recalled."[2] Although we wish we had the letters that she destroyed, her remaining letters and diaries give us an insight into the interesting life of this nineteenth century woman.

Those with whom she corresponded and mentioned most often in her diaries were a famous general, an eminent physician, a respected educator/author, and a Baltimore belle, known worldwide. These persons were General Robert E. Lee, Dr. Austin Flint, Sr., Blanche Berard and Elizabeth Patterson Bonaparte.

ROBERT E. LEE

Markie knew the Lee family most of her life. Her cousin, Mary Anna Randolph Custis, married their distant cousin, Lieutenant Robert E. Lee, at Arlington in 1831 when Markie was four years old. She was especially close to Mrs. Lee's mother[†] after her own mother died. After her father was killed in the Mexican War two years later, Robert E. Lee became a father figure to her and her siblings, often giving Markie advice about the education of her brothers. The Lees and Markie began

---

[*]When Markie was born, there were only 23 states in the Union. During her lifetime, an additional 21 states were admitted.

[†]Mrs. George Washington Parke Custis, nee Mary Lee Fitzhugh.

corresponding regularly after she visited the family at Fort Hamilton, New York, in 1844.

Markie visited the Lees often enough at Fort Hamilton that they referred to the bedroom which she used as "your little room." When Lee invited her to visit again, he wrote that "Rooney has appd it [your little room] as his study. It may therefore be considered vacant."[3] Through his letters to Markie, we learn that she was popular with men on the posts where he served, and that he sometimes attempted to play matchmaker. After visiting the Lees, Markie went to West Point, where she visited Blanche Berard and, incidentally, met Seaman Samuel P. Carter.

Lee, also a friend of the Berard's, wrote to Markie at West Point, "Mr. Chandler (Lt. Daniel T. Chandler) has a violent attack of the blues, brought on no doubt by his missing to escort you...."[4] The following year, she had a new interest. Lee wrote that he had been to Governor's Island and that "Neddy Townsend (2nd Lieutenant Edward D. Townsend), that God of War, was there - but without his Eve - looking as glorious as the May day Sun."[5]

In anticipation of leaving for Mexico, he wrote on June 7, 1846:

> I do not know where I could find a more appropriate place than this (Governor's Island) to write to my dear Markie. The Head quarters of her beloved 2nd & the Island of her associations. She would however be surprised to see how its smiling face of peace has been changed for the grim visage of war (Mexican War). There is nothing but preparations for battle.[6]

Soon afterward he advised, "Cheer up Markie, your favourite 2nd will return loaded with honors."

Captain Lee was Chief Engineer on the march toward Chihuahua; and he was at the siege of Vera Cruz. He was made Brevet Major for gallant and meritorious conduct in the battle of Cerro Gordo and Brevet Colonel for his conduct in the battle of Chapultepec. When Lee heard that Markie's father, Captain William G. Williams, had been killed in the capture of Monterey, he found his grave and retrieved his belt which he sent to Markie.

Two years later, (May 21, 1848) he wrote to her, from the City of Mexico, "We are all much exhilarated at the prospect of getting home again. So tell your Sweetheart you will keep him waiting no longer but are ready to give him 'indemnification for the past & security for the future.'"[7]

Markie and Lt. Townsend remained life-long friends, even during the Civil War, although he served in the Union Army and she was loyal to the South. It was Colonel Townsend to whom she wrote to get a permit to visit Arlington House, in the possession of Union troops."[8] He always responded to "My dear Miss Martha."

Lee took pleasure in teasing Markie about her forgetfulness. In reference to his horse, Traveller, he wrote, "I have never seen anything of the poem in his honour, & I confess I have never had any hope of his being immortalized except by your brush. That is my sure trust & I hope you will not forget to append his tail to his likeness." Three months later, he asked, "How are you progressing with Travellers portrait, Markie? He is getting old like his master, and looks in your pencil to hand him down to posterity. I am perfectly satisfied with what you have done for his rider."[9]

Lee's letters to Markie were not always lighthearted. None was more serious than the letter he wrote on January 22, 1861, concerning his fear of civil war. Part of that letter reads:

> I wish to live under no other government and there is
> no sacrifice I am not ready to make for the preservation
> of the union save that of honour. If a disruption takes
> place, I shall go back in sorrow to my people and share
> the misery of my native state.[10]

When Lee did not approve of her behavior, he let her know:

> You did not behave with your usual charity towards
> your escort from Lexington. His devoted attention
> entitled him to commendation, even if he was unable to
> please. Did you fear he was a widower Markie? You
> seem intuitively to recoil from their fascinations,
> though your eventual escape is so impossible. [11]

Although Robert E. Lee's letters are more available, the whole Lee family exchanged correspondence with Markie, even when they were at Arlington and she was just across the Potomac River at Tudor Place. Mrs. Lee wrote:

> My dear Markie: I thought this lovely weather would
> have tempted you over here. We had a very pleasant

visit today from old Rembrandt Peale[‡] with his wife....I have been very busy as usual cleaning up leaves & Robert has had the horses much occupied so that I have not been anywhere. Annie is going to write so I will conclude with much love. Yours affectionately, M. Lee.[12]

Markie always was willing to help the Lees and expected to be called upon when one of them was sick. In response to a letter from Annie Lee, she wrote, "My little Annita! I wish I had been with you when you were sick...It is my greatest pleasure to be enabled to minister to those I love."[13]

When Robert E. Lee died in 1870, Markie wrote from Philadelphia to "My darling little Agnes," about her father's death. "I am in a distant country as it were – in a strange boarding house pacing my little room – weeping alone & mourning without one responsive heart...I think so much of you all – your dear dear Mother – this is the overwhelming sorrow of her life..." She sent her sympathy, naming each member of the family. [14]

DR. AUSTIN FLINT

Markie often wrote about Dr. Flint, "one of the dearest friends I have on earth,"[15] usually without destroying pages. She first met Dr. Flint in Buffalo, New York, when she was twelve years old, at the time that he brought her new born brother, Orton, through a crisis. He and his wife became friends of the Williams family.[16] Dr. Flint was a brilliant, 27 year old doctor who had graduated from Harvard Medical School at age 21. He went on to achieve an outstanding reputation, was a pioneer of heart research and had great influence on the early course of medicine in the United States. He is known as one of the most eminent of nineteenth century physicians.[17] He was a gifted teacher, founder of two and professor in six medical schools, prolific writer and outstanding clinician. His longtime friend, Dr. Samuel D. Gross, recalled that he was: "Tall, handsome and of manly form, with well-modulated voice of great compass....He ranks especially high as a clinical instructor. As a diagnostician in diseases of the chest he has few equals."[18]

[‡] Rembrandt Peale followed in the steps of his father. Charles Wilson Peale, and became a prominent portraitist. He painted a portrait of George Washington from life and made numerous copies of it.

When her Mother died in 1842, Markie and three of her siblings left Buffalo to live with their grandmother at Tudor Place, but she kept in contact with the Flints through her brother, Laurence, who lived with the Flints while he finished his school semester. The first record of correspondence between Dr. Flint and Markie is his June 7, 1844, letter to "My dear Friend" with detailed instructions on how to treat sister Kate's ailment. He closed his letter "With best regards to Mrs. Peter and your sisters. With affectionate esteem, yours, Austin Flint."[19]

In March 1847, when Markie returned to Buffalo to attend her father's funeral, she stayed at the home of Dr. and Mrs. Flint. After the funeral, she and Dr. Flint visited Niagara Falls, and as was her custom, she kept pressed flowers in "Memory of my visit to Niagara Falls, April 10, 1847."[20] In her February 26, 1853, Paris diary entry she reminisced about this day, saying that the last day that she had spent at the falls, her heart was partly in the grave of her departed father, but that the one pleasurable remembrance was that her dearest friend on earth was by her side – "when this thought comes over me, the current of my feelings are unspeakably sweetened." On May 7, she wrote in her Paris diary, "This day last year, I wrote a long letter [at Tudor Place] to my dear friend the Doctor recalling to his memory and mine the fifth anniversary of this day sacred to the memory of our parting."[21] While in Paris, she often quoted advice from his letters to her.

In 1854, while at Arlington House, where she was caring for her Uncle Custis,[§] she wrote that after a week of "most anxious suspense," she had received a letter from Dr. Flint telling her that he could not arrange to visit her before he and his wife departed for Europe. She decided that "there were reasons contrary to the fulfillment of our wishes which we mutually acknowledged" and that she would not have had him "leave the path of duty, to follow that of inclination. He would not have done so. But, still, as long as there was the faintest ray of hope, I clung to that hope." Then she imagines his greeting her "as his sister" after seven long years.

> Oh! What ecstatic joy….And then, the pain of parting – Oh! Brother – I wish we had never met. We both reproach ourselves. But, thanks be to Providence, we have nothing, now, with which we can reproach ourselves. God bless thee, God bless thee, my dearest earthly friend – and she, to whom thou'rt bound by the most sacred of earthly ties.

[§] George Washington Parke Custis.

45

Orton "my darling little brother" sympathized with her, saying, "Sister don't look so sad. You can always cheer everybody but yourself." A few days later she wrote, "Today, my dearest earth friend will leave the shores of his Native land. In spirit, I go with him. . . . We dreamily enjoy the present – we think of much that has been left undone in the past – we reflect on the uncertain future." Her thoughts were interrupted by a servant (a slave) who brought the mail bag. In it, she found a letter, which diverted her thoughts for a time. "[It] would seem to assure me, that, although I am deprived of one friend, there is another who will by the warmth of his devotion, make amends; but, one friend cannot supply the place of another. . . ." Markie does not tell us who this friend was, but instead continues to write about Dr. Flint. "It is sad not to be loved, at all, but, to be loved by one, whose love, must not be reciprocated, is also sad. . . . How true, is it, that pain must ever follow earthly pleasures." Markie continued to seek Dr. Flint's advice, but she was not always pleased with his response. In a letter "from my dear friend, Adviser and Counselor, Dr. F....[He] does not seem favorable to my literary projects – fears I would have a great deal of labor and reap little pecuniary profit." She was terribly disappointed and thought about her many other friends who could and would encourage her, "but without his approbation, what are they all! My hands drop beside me, a blush of disappointment burns on my cheek – I feel now, the heavy chain of his friendship, & then, the freedom of being bound by no stronger ties – ties which might make submission to his suggestions a duty."[22] In spite of the doctor's advice, Markie did write an article, "The Family," published in the *Southern Churchman,* two months later.[23]

In 1860, perhaps with Dr. Flint's encouragement, Markie went to New York City to study painting at The Cooper Union for the Advancement of Science and Art.[24] Dr. Flint had left Buffalo Medical College, which he helped found, and was now in New York where he became a Professor of Pathology and Practical Medicine at Long Island College Hospital. In 1861, he again helped found a medical school, the Bellevue Hospital and Medical School in New York where he became the first Professor of the Principles and Practice of Medicine.[25] Markie was delighted to have this opportunity to pursue her study of art and to see her old friend. However, at times his busy career interfered with their plans.

> Dear Markie: I was obliged to go to Brooklyn professionally this morning & did not return till 3 P. M. I have engaged also to go tomorrow and may be detained all the forenoon. May I see you in the afternoon, & if the weather be fair, will you go to the

Cooper Institute & we will then arrange for Randall's Island. I shall try to see you this evening. Yours, A. F.[26]

For the first time, Markie celebrated her birthday with Dr. Flint. Among her keepsakes are pressed flowers with a note, "March 28th, 1861, Prof. Austin Flint. 263 Fourth Avenue, New York City, from a bouquet given me by my dear adopted brother."[27]

Two weeks later, the Nation was at war. Soon she learned that General Lee was with the Confederate army, his family had vacated Arlington House, and several regiments of Union troops occupied the Heights of Arlington. As much as she wanted to continue her studies, she was more concerned about retrieving her belongings, as well as those of the Lees, from Arlington. As soon as she was assured that she could travel safely, she returned to Washington, D. C.[28]

During the difficult war years, Markie and Dr. Flint continued corresponding, but the next record of their seeing each other was in 1867 when she was in New York with her deceased sister's children who were in her care. Robert E. Lee wrote to her in care of Professor Austin Flint, MD, 50 East 34th St., New York, saying that he was delighted to learn that she was well & pleasantly located in the beautiful town of Orange. "I am very glad you are able to enjoy the visits of Dr. Flint in your present retreat & I hope that he will be able to make them frequent during the summer....I feel much better satisfied, when you are near one of his goodness & friendship...."[29]

Markie was in New York in 1869 and 1870, but because she was not faithful to her diary for several years, we hear no more about her friendship with Dr. Flint. By this time, his son, Dr. Austin Flint, Jr., had joined the faculty at Long Island College Hospital,[30] and his grandson, Grover, the infant son of deceased daughter Susan, was in the care of the Flints.[31] In 1872, Dr. Flint was elected president of the New York Academy of Medicine; and in 1884, president of the American Medical Association. He was the principal orator at the International Congresses of Medicine held in Philadelphia in 1876, London in 1881, and Copenhagen in 1884. He had been invited to address the British Medical Association in 1886, the first American to be so honored, but his death prevented his fulfilling the engagement.[32] Except for a few small bequests, he left his estate to his invalid wife. The *New York Times* on March 14, 1886, the day after his death, published a full column on page two with the bold heading, "A GREAT PHYSICIAN DEAD."

BLANCHE BERARD

Blanche and Markie were childhood friends. Blanche's father was Claudius Berard, born in Bordeaux, France, and educated in his native land. He came to the United States at age 21 and soon afterward became a professor at Dickinson College where he remained until his appointment in 1815 as the first professor of French at the United States Military Academy at West Point where he spent the rest of his life.[33] When Cadet Robert E. Lee was one of his students, his class was first to use *A Grammar of the French Language* that Professor Berard had written.[34] While Markie's father was a student at West Point, he began a life-long friendship with Professor Berard. This association led to an even closer relationship between their daughters, Martha Custis and Augusta Blanche, born in West Point on October 29, 1824.[35] Their friendship eventually led to the happiest period of Markie's life.

Blanche became a teacher at Pelham Priory, an unconventional girls' seminary in Westchester County, New York. Its proprietor, the Reverend Robert Bolton, was an Episcopal clergyman who had studied for the ministry in England. He adapted the curriculum of an English boys' school to one for his school for young ladies with an intense religious atmosphere. The school took its name from the large house that Mr. Bolton had built in medieval English architectural style, suggested by Washington Irving. While Robert E. Lee was Superintendent of West Point, his daughter, Mary Custis, attended this relatively new school, not only because it was a favorite among Southern families, but because he knew the Berard family and Markie was a close friend of one its teachers.[36] Four years later, after the Lees had returned to Arlington House, Blanche spent a week with Markie who was living there. They had so many subjects to discuss and so many places to visit that "we feel overpowered at the mere thought of only a week, to do it all in." Blanche asked Markie to read aloud from her European diaries and encouraged her to write "a book of travels founded upon" her diaries. Markie was delighted. "Blanche has succeeded so well with her little History that I confess myself encouraged by her example."

Markie was referring to *School History of the United States,* published in 1855, under the name A. B. Berard. By today's standards, this is a small book – seven by four and one-half inches with 224 pages. The first paragraph reads: "The country whose history we are to study is called 'THE UNITED STATES OF AMERICA,' now consisting of thirty-one States and eight Territories." At the bottom of *each* page are questions about what the student should have learned on that page. The last paragraph reads: "Such is the beautiful country which God has given us for our heritage....let us remember, too, that only blessed is the people whose God is the Lord; and that His Word hath told us, that it is 'righteousness that exalteth a nation.' "[37] Berard's *School History of the United States* was reprinted numerous times between 1855 and 1878.[38] Later, she wrote *Child's History of the United States, School History of England,* and *Manual of Spanish Art and Literature.* She also edited history books written by other authors.[39]

Blanche was captivated with Arlington House, the beauty of the woods and fields, the spring wild flowers, and the slaves' church in the little school house where she, along with Mildred Lee and the slaves, worshiped the Sunday that she was at Arlington. She was equally fascinated with Mt. Vernon where she and Markie traveled by boat. Markie wrote a history of both houses for Blanche, as Uncle Custis had told it to her,[40] and Blanche included it in the letter to her mother that she had begun before she left Pelham Priory and added to daily. In 1949, this lengthy letter was published in the *Virginia Magazine of History and Biography* under the title "Arlington and Mount Vernon 1856 – As Described in a Letter of Augusta Blanche Berard." A footnote explained that this letter was recently found, among family papers, by Mrs. George Lyttleton Upshur, and sent to her niece, Mrs. Alexander G. Brown, Jr., who agreed to have it published. Kate Marion Upshur Brown was the granddaughter of Markie's sister, Kate.[41]

President Grant, a West Point graduate, appointed Blanche postmistress of West Point in 1873. President Cleveland removed her from office in 1884, but this feisty woman had no intention of giving up her job without a fight. She traveled to Washington to encourage her friends there to influence the President to reappoint her. The authorities in West Point and other influential persons across the United States sent petitions in her favor to the president. *The Washington Post* reported that the President was flooded with protests. They came from everywhere, and from the country's most distinguished men and women. "J. Pierpont Morgan, who is a personal friend of Miss Berard, it is said, went to Washington and saw the President in behalf of Miss Berard. The result was the withdrawal of the new appointment by the President." *The Washington Post* also reported:

> There is one office-holder in this country whose political existence is not at the mercy of spoils grabbers, and whose tenure of office depends not upon the exigencies of politics. She is Blanche Berard, the venerable postmistress of West Point, the home of the Military Academy.

Administrations come and go; one party succeeds another in control of the government, postmasters and postmistresses appear and disappear, but Blanche Berard remains in undisturbed possession of her office....

No woman in this country has so wide a personal acquaintance as Miss Berard.... She has a warm place in the affections of every man who claims West Point as his alma mater. Gen. Grant never visited West Point without paying his respects to the postmistress; the rugged Sherman was a bosom friend, and 'Little Phil' Sheridan...took delight in recalling cadet day reminiscences with this interesting character...it is no exaggeration to say that many an officer to-day wears his uniform because he heeded the advice and suggestions of Miss Berard.[42]

At the time that she resigned as Postmistress of West Point, a *New York Times* article claimed that Blanche was known to every living graduate of West Point and also reported her love story. As a young, exceedingly pretty girl, she had many admirers. Among them was a dashing cavalry officer who had been wounded while pursuing a band of Indians, and on that account was sent to West Point as an instructor. He "soon had sole charge of the pretty girl's affections, and they became engaged."

Detachments of cadets frequently rode through mountains, and the young officer was invariably in charge. One day, as the detachment rode rapidly down the steep side of Crow's Nest, a cadet's horse shied at something and ran full force into the officer, who lost his balance and was thrown headlong to the ground. He lived but a few days after the accident, and Miss Berard still mourns for her lover's untimely death.

She resigned from the post office in March 1897, which "was heard with regret by all who are acquainted with the venerable woman."[43]

Blanche lived the last years of her life in Hackensack, New Jersey, to be near her four sisters. She died from a stroke in 1901, two years after Markie's death. Her body was accompanied by a nephew, Major Vogdes, from Hackensack to West Point where it was borne by a detail from the West Point Cavalry detachment, with members of the Academic Board acting as honorary pall-bearers, and interned in the Post Cemetery with the service of her beloved Episcopal Church.[44]

ELIZABETH PATTERSON BONAPARTE

"Madame Bonaparte is certainly one of the most remarkable women I have ever met." Markie wrote these words in her 1875 diary while she and Madame Elizabeth Patterson Bonaparte were living at Miss Gwinn's, 84 Cathedral Street in Baltimore. Markie was living at the boarding house to be near sister Lum and her husband, Abel B. Upshur, and because it was all that she could afford. Madame Bonaparte had been living there for several years because she chose to deny comforts for herself so that she could use her fortune to benefit her grandsons, Jerome Napoleon Bonaparte II and Charles Joseph Bonaparte.

Markie and Madame became acquainted in Miss Gwinn's parlor where boarders gathered in the evening. Their friendship deepened when Madame invited Markie to her room to see a portrait of herself as a beautiful young woman wearing a lovely, yellow dress. She said that in the past she always had a yellow dress in her wardrobe because it suited her dark hair and eyes. Markie was impressed with her youthful beauty and asked permission to copy the painting, "but Madame Bonaparte would not allow it." She also refused to have her picture taken or to give an autograph because she was ashamed of her "decrepit handwriting."[45]

Elizabeth Patterson was born on February 6, 1785, to Dorcus Spear and William Patterson, a prominent, wealthy Baltimore businessman. In September 1803 she met and immediately fell in love with the handsome, charming Jerome Bonaparte, who was visiting in Baltimore. He was the youngest brother of Napoleon Bonaparte. In October Jerome applied for a marriage license. Mr. Patterson, who was furious, sent Betsy to Virginia and forbade her to see suitor. Betsy fled from her Virginia captivity, and returned to Baltimore and into the arms of Jerome. Willful, beautiful Betsy, as usual, had her way. On the following Christmas Eve, eighteen year old Betsy and nineteen old Jerome were married in the Patterson parlor. Because her Presbyterian father foresaw trouble from Catholic Napoleon, he had a special marriage contract drawn up and arranged for a Catholic ceremony to be performed by the Archbishop of Baltimore, Monsignor Carroll.

Napoleon refused to recognize the marriage and ordered Jerome to return to Paris, alone. However, the young couple was having a delightful time, being entertained in Baltimore, Washington, D.C., Philadelphia and New York. Finally, two years later, Jerome and Betsy sailed for Europe, but when they arrived in Lisbon, they learned that

51

Napoleon had forbidden Betsy to enter Europe. Jerome continued on to Paris where he intended to convince Napoleon to recognize their marriage. Betsy sailed to England where her son, Jerome Napoleon Bonaparte, was born on July 7, 1805. Her husband wrote romantic letters, professing his love for her, but as demanded by Napoleon, he became King of Westphalia and married Princess Catherine of Wurttemburg.

The Imperial Council of France issued a divorce decree, but Pope Pius VII refused to invalidate Betsy and Jerome's marriage. Therefore, Napoleon offered Betsy an annual income of 60,000 francs on the condition that she not use the Bonaparte name and that she live in the United States.

A disheartened Betsy reluctantly accepted his offer and returned to Baltimore, but when Napoleon's empire crumbled, she and son Bo (Jerome Napoleon Bonaparte) returned to Europe, using the Bonaparte name. She wanted Bo to attend school in Europe and eventually marry European royalty. He missed his Grandfather Patterson and wanted to attend school in the United States. Betsy finally allowed him to return, but she remained in Europe, hoping that she could arrange a royal marriage for him.

Betsy was proud of Bo for graduating from Harvard College in 1826, but she was crushed when she learned that he had married an American woman, Susan May Williams. Her last attempt to make her son eligible for succession to the French throne was the failed lawsuit to obtain part of the estate of King Jerome, who died in 1860, and recognition of his and Betsy's son as his legitimate heir.

With her beauty, wit, and brilliant conversation, Betsy was popular in Europe and continued to live there off and on until the summer of 1834 when she returned to Baltimore. Her father, who died the following February, left her only a relatively small part of his property, saying:

> The conduct of my daughter Betsy has through life been so disobedient that in no instance has she ever consulted my opinions or feelings, indeed she has caused me more anxiety and trouble than all my other children put together, and her folly and misconduct have occasioned me a train of expense that first and last has cost me much money. Under these

circumstances it would not be reasonable just or fitting that at my death she should inherit an equal part of my estate as the other children.

Her inheritance was four small houses. She chose to live in the one that had been her parent's first home; and with the other houses initiated a real estate business that, along with her ability to make wise investments, made her a wealthy woman.[46]

While Markie lived at Miss Gwinn's, she devoted most of her diary to recording her almost daily conversations with Madame Bonaparte. "Madame B. does not seem at all to object to my taking notes of what she says & on one occasion, [I] asked her if I might write down something & she said yes, certainly & then dictated as I wrote." Markie described her room:

> Her room is the largest in the house and an east room without carpet or papering on the wall. Simply a white washed wall. She says this is in accordance with health – She will not have even a rug or a piece of carpet under her feet – an air tight wood stove – no gas. An inch stump of a candle....Three large black arm chairs, two wardrobes, a bed & a cabinet & a table compose the rest of the furniture. In one of the armchairs sits Madame Bonaparte – a little old lady now almost as broad as she is long with her nice little feet in a pair of tight fitting leather slippers.

Madame Bonaparte and Markie, who were more than forty years apart in age, with diverse backgrounds and personalities, developed a friendship that prevailed until death intervened. Markie was drawn to older people, perhaps because of her love for Grandmother Martha Custis Peter with whom she lived after her parents died. She cherished the memory of Aunt Custis (Mrs. George Washington Parke Custis) with whom she shared a love of flowers, books and poetry; and she happily lived at Arlington with venerable Uncle Custis in his waning years as he reminisced about his life and that of his grandmother and step-grandfather, Martha and George Washington. When she was in Paris, she became friends with aged Madame la Baron de la Morondiere who "quite wins my heart" and reminded her of "dear Grandmother."

Elderly Mme. Bonaparte was delighted to have a well-educated, cheerful friend who visited her almost daily, was sincerely interested in hearing about Madame's adventures, and enjoyed reading and discussing newspaper articles and books with her.

Markie took pleasure in "listening to her delightful letters" and "her account of her first trip to Europe." When she read to Mme. Bonaparte, she thought that "She is very interesting in her comments." She asked Markie to read the morning newspapers to her because she wanted to hear world news and especially news about royalty. She was delighted when Markie read about the Martha Washington Charity Ball in New York City where "the Grand Dukes Alexis & Constantine were present." However, what she wanted to hear first was the Baltimore stock market news. Markie read it if she had not time for anything else. "Nothing could be more uninteresting to me than that, but I duly read it." Madame said that she invested in a great number of different stocks and "thanked God for the capacity that he had given her to make money."

Madame Bonaparte's son, Jerome, died in 1870; now she doted on his two sons. Grandson Charles Bonaparte, regularly visited her, often to discuss her investments. Her other grandson, Jerome II, had been living in Europe for a number of years. Markie never mentioned that he had visited his mother. However, it was he whom Madame referred to when she said, "My grandson who married the widow Edgar is the idol of my heart." She was determined that he should have the advantages of wealth. "I give him five thousand dollars** per year all of which I made by economy....I will not wait to give it to him."[47] She was pleased that, unlike his father, her grandson, Jerome II, was fascinated with France and the Bonaparte family. He was in the West Point Class of 1852, as was Markie's brother, Laurence, who wrote to his grandmother that "I have an excellent tent mate. He is a nephew of Napoleon Bonaparte – and a very nice person."[48] Six year old Robert E. Lee, Jr. liked Jerome, too. He and his father accompanied Custis Lee when he entered West Point in June, 1850. The little boy wrote to his mother that Jerome and Laurence had been especially nice to him.[49] After graduating from West Point, Jerome served on the Texas frontier until August 16, 1854, when he resigned from the United States Army because Napoleon III summoned him to Paris to commission him into the French Army.[50] Superintendent of West Point, Robert E. Lee, a friend of his father, wrote, "I hope Jerome [the young West Pointer, then serving with the French in the Crimea] will never have cause to regret his leaving us, and [I] feel sure of his adding to the luster of his name and distinction of his family." Jerome II distinguished himself in the Crimean War and the

---

**$100,000 at today's value.

Franco-Prussian War and became a colonel. To Madame Bonaparte's disappointment, he did not marry European nobility, but returned to the United States and married Mrs. Caroline Leroy Edgar, granddaughter of Daniel Webster, whom he had met in Paris.

Charles Joseph Bonaparte, who was twenty-one years younger than his brother, graduated from Harvard Law School. He cared nothing about royalty or France, never traveled outside the United States, and was happy to live in Baltimore with his wife Ellen Channing Day. However, he became interested in better government, and served in Theodore Roosevelt's cabinet as Secretary of the Navy and later as Attorney General. He was also a prominent Roman Catholic layman in Baltimore.[51] As Attorney General, he led the Department in landmark antitrust investigations, argued over 50 Supreme Court Cases, and founded a unit that became the Federal Bureau of Investigation. All his life he was active in civil service reform, assisted in founding the National Civil Service Reform League and was president of the National Municipal League.[52]

Madame B. always looked forward to Charles's visits. On December 20, 1876, Markie wrote, "Made a longer visit than usual to my friend Madame B. this morning for it was cold & dreary & she looked so pitiful & desolate as she said, 'Oh! Come in; I am glad to see you – my grandson (Charles) will not be here today. I am dreadfully low-spirited.'" Markie thought that "I might possibly interest her in the Bible from which in her desolation she might derive consolation. She refused to allow me to read the Bible to her – said she hated the mention of religion – she knew the Bible by heart." Nevertheless, she "knows there is a God because a fool must know that the world could not make itself." She said "most emphatically" that she believed in the Presbyterian Doctrine of original sin. However, she "brought up her child and grandsons to be Roman Catholics" because it was the religion of royalty. She did let Markie read the hymn, *Abide With Me*, which made her wonder "which dresses we would appear in [in] heaven & if we would live in houses."

Markie read books to Madame B. that she thought would interest her and prompt her to tell about events in her life which Madame delighted in relating. "This morning I read a great deal to Madame Bonaparte in Fox's *Mission to Russia*." She was pleased that Markie was going to read about her friend, Prince Gotchakoff, an attaché at the Russian Embassy in Florence, with whom she flirted and became friends. When she read *The National Portrait Gallery* by Count Mirabeau, a book that had belonged to "Grandmama" Martha Washington,[††] Madame B. "was delighted with the sarcasms." Markie told her that she did not like it, to which Madame replied, "Oh, it is so witty." Markie thought that it was "those bons mots that delighted her." Madame Bonaparte always thanked Markie "with a great deal of feeling" for reading to her. Markie wrote that she was truly glad "to soothe the declining days of one who like myself has had a sad & unfortunate life." In fact, she considered it but obeying the golden rule "to do unto others as I would have others do unto me. I am glad that God has given me this little work to do for Him."

The book that she read from most often was *The Memoirs of Madame Vigée Le Brun*. Marie Louise Elisabeth Vigée was a famous female artist of the eighteenth century who traveled throughout Europe. Hearing about her experiences encouraged Madame B. to happily reminiscence about her own experiences in European society. When Markie appeared with the memoirs, Madame Bonaparte would say, "Ah, you have Madame le Brun – come, I want to hear it." As Markie read about Florence, Madame B. recalled that she was escorted through "the beautiful galleries there by the Duke of Birmingham." At the mention of Paris, she recalled that she had spent many evenings at the home of the Duke of Wellington. "She says her passion was for society & for courts." She described dresses and hats that she wore on special occasions. She claimed that she might have been the mistress of kings, but, "that was not my game – I had not the slightest idea of going down in History as a prostitute." Thanks to Napoleon, she said that she had "entrée into society of Europe and the means to make herself comfortable." When Markie read about Madame Le Brun's sketch of Lafayette, Madame B. said that she "had no predilection" for Lafayette. Markie told her that she had a great deal of admiration for him – that it was at a Ball given by her grandmother honoring General Lafayette "when my father first met my mother….I spoke of George Lafayette's [son of General Lafayette] having been an admirer of my Aunt Lewis (Eleanor Custis Lewis), but that Gen. Washington objected to American ladies marrying foreigners."

On another occasion, Markie wrote about a conversation that they had in the parlor.

[††] This book is in the Pierpont Morgan Library collection. The former owners were Martha Washington, Mary Lee Fitzhugh Custis, and Martha Custis Williams. It has a presentation inscription from Mrs. Custis to Markie dated 1852, the year that she went to Paris.

As I sat by her she took my hand & said as she frequently does, 'You have a most beautiful hand – such aristocratic hand. It is soft & flexible & the coloring so beautiful. How Lord Byron wd have admired it. He adored beauty. I remonstrated with Madame & said I thought she was too complimentary. 'Not at all,' she said, 'It is far more beautiful than mine ever was & mine was admired all over Europe.' I thanked her.

When she "examined my ring given me by my dear friend & cousin General Lee," she was reminded of a watch chain given her by Princess Borghése, Napoleon's sister, Pauline.

Markie's life was not entirely devoted to Madame Bonaparte. She regularly visited sister Lum and occasionally brother Lolo as well as her many friends in Baltimore, and she entertained visitors. She also devoted time to her painting and correspondence, although she often neglected them to be with Madame Bonaparte. When she attended weekly lectures given by Dr. Lord, she kept notes to use in discussing his topic with Mme. B. On one of her visits with General McClellan and his wife, she told the General that she had read his articles in Scribner's Magazine to Madame Bonaparte, who said to tell him how much she admired his style of writing. "General & Mrs. McClellan asked [for] an introduction to Mme. B." Madame Bonaparte was delighted. Before they visited, Markie thoughtfully suggested "some very agreeable topics upon which she (Madame Bonaparte) conversed with them."

In addition to her many conversations with Madame B. about religion, which "all end unsatisfactorily," Markie expressed a few other disappointments. When Markie had a visit from a "poor old colored woman asking for charity," she gave her "75c & my very nice pet water proof cloak, which it was a great sacrifice to give away, but [I] pray that it may comfort the poor creature who is more miserable than I." However, when a blind man came to Madame Bonaparte, she refused to help him. Markie tried to arouse her pity, saying that she wished she could help him, but had not the means. "Just now, I have not twenty-five cents." Madame B. commented, "Well, I made all the money I have & am not going to distribute it around to beggars." Markie noted, "I was very much shocked with this phase of Madame Bonaparte's character. I had heard that she was hard & cold but in all my intercourse with her, I had failed to see this."

On a Sunday, as Markie stood at the window, she remarked on "all of the people going into Emmanuel Church. Mme. B. said she wished there were as many good people in the world as there are churches." Markie replied that she thought there were many more. "She looked at me in a very surprised way & said, 'you retain your innocence of human-nature a long time.'" Markie was startled when Madame said, "I cannot tell you how perfectly absurd it seems to me all this going to Church. In Europe no one ever thinks of such a thing." Markie gently remonstrated, "So much the worse for you & them."

An admirer of Madame Bonaparte sent her a box of camellias which Markie exclaimed over, "but Mme. B. was not impressed....Mme. said she never had a taste for the beauties of Nature. 'You lose a great deal I said, because those things are a happiness when there is no other happiness.'" Although Madame did not take pleasure in flowers, she did enjoy animals. She thought it was "terrible that animals have to be killed for food." When she walked to dinner, leaning on Markie's arm, she stopped to talk to Jack, Miss Gwinn's little black terrier.

On February 6, 1877, Markie wrote in her diary, "This is Madame Bonaparte's birthday. She is ninety two....Mme B. is always saying, 'What a terrible thing it is to grow old'....[and] said with a sigh the last asylum of human dejection is a Baltimore Boarding house." When she reflected on her happy, but brief life with Prince Jerome, she came alive. She liked to remember the $6,000 worth of clothes that he bought for her wedding gift and their beautiful wedding on Christmas Eve in her parents' parlor. She said that her mother opposed the marriage, but that her father was pleased. "Mme. B made a resume of her life to-day as she often does & said, 'Was it not singular that I always carried out the line of my intentions never wavered – I determined to keep my character – I determined never to step down after having put my foot on so high a round of the ladder.'" Nevertheless, Markie quoted her as saying several times, "I was never happy in my life. I suppose no one ever lived who was more ambitious than I was unless it might have been Napoleon & Alexander the Great."

During one of Markie's last evenings at Miss Gwinn's, she sat in the parlor with Madame Bonaparte.

> This evening she [Madame Bonaparte] said to me, 'I often say to Charles, when I was young I had everything but money – now I have nothing but money.' I said to her with sincerity that she still had the

power of making herself very agreeable and interesting to others. I told her that her society had been a great charm to me this winter. She looked so pleased & thanked me.[53]

Although Markie left the boarding house, she continued to visit Madame Bonaparte until her death in 1879. She was always delighted to see Markie, greeting her cheerfully.[54]

Elizabeth Patterson Bonaparte, age 94, died April 4, 1879, at Miss Gwinn's boarding house. Grandsons Jerome II, who had returned from France a few days earlier, and Charles, were at her bedside when she died. Her coffin was taken to the home of daughter-in-law Susan where her funeral was held with only the family in attendance. As she had requested, her funeral was delayed several days because she was terrified of being buried alive. Her marble gravestone at Greenmount Cemetery was engraved with her name and words that she chose:

After the fever of a stormy life she has found rest.[55]

[1] Catalogue of Addresses, Martha Custis Williams, TP Archives, MS-6 (5-3).

[2] MCW Diary E, June 23, 1862, TP Archives, MS-6 (4-4).

[3] Avery Craven, ed., *To Markie, The Letters of Robert E. Lee to Martha Custis Williams,* Cambridge, MA: Harvard Univ. Press, 1933.

[4] *Ibid.*

[5] *Ibid.*

[6] *Ibid.*

[7] *Ibid.*

[8] Ltr., MCW to MACL, July 13, 1861, *Lee Family Papers,* VHS.

[9] Craven, *To Markie.*

[10] *Ibid.*

[11] Ltr., REL to MCW, 3 November 1866, MA1045 (1) Pierpont Morgan Library, NY.

[12] Ltr., MACL to MCW, undated c. 1858, TP Archives, MS-10.

[13] Ltr., MCW to Anne Carter Lee (Annie), November 17, 1860, *Lee Family Papers*, VHS.

[14] Ltr., MCW to Agnes Lee, October 15, 1870,Lee *Family Papers,* VHS.

[15] MCW Diary A, September 29-December 14, 1852, TP Archives, MS-6 (3-27).

[16] Ltr., APPW to BWP, August 3, 1839, TP Archives, MS-7 (1-1).

[17] Biography: Austin Flint, (www.whonamedit.com/doctor.cfm/1476.html).

[18] Nirav J.Mehta,MD, Rajal N. Mehta,MD,and Ijaz A.Khan,MD,*Austin Flint: Clinician, Teacher, and Visionary,* Texas Heart Institute, Houston, TX.

[19] Ltr., Dr. Austin Flint to MCW, June 7, 1844, TP Achives, MS-6 (3-1).

[20] Pressed flowers, Dr. Austin Flint to MCW, April 10, 1847, TP Archives, MS-6 (5-2).

[21] MCW Diary C, March – May, 1853, TP Archives, MS-6 (4-2).

[22] MCW Diary, March 17, 1857, Arlington House Archives, folder 5.

[23] Martha Custis Williams, "The Family," *Southern Churchman,* Friday, May 15, 1857, V. 23 #19, p. 76.

[24] Mary P. Coulling, *The Lee Girls,* Winston-Salem, NC: John F. Blair, 1987.

[25] Mehta *et al., Austin Flint.*

[26] Ltr., Dr. Austin Flint, Sr. to MCW,1861, TP Archives, MS-6 (1-1).

[27] Pressed flowers, Dr. Austin Flint to MCW, March 28, 1861, TP Archives, MS-6 (5-2).

[28] Ltr., L. Thomas to MCW, May 24, 1861, TP Archives, MS-6 (1-3).

[29] Craven, *To Markie.*

[30] Mehta *et al., Austin Flint.*

[31] 1870 United States Census, NYC (Dr. Austin Flint, Sr.)

[32] Mehta *et al., Austin Flint.*

[33] Biography of Claudius Berard, Virtual American Biographies (http://famousamericans.net/claudiusberard/).

[34] Douglas Southall Freeman, *R. E. Lee, A Biography,* Volume I. N.Y., Charles Scribner's Sons, 1942.

[35] *Ibid.*

[36] Coulling, *Lee Girls.*

[37] A.B. Berard, *School History of the United States*, Philadelphia, PA. H. Cowperthwait & Co, 1860.

[38] University of Pittsburgh Libraries (http://pittcat.pitt.edu)

[39] Virtual Biography, Berard.

[40] MCW Diary, January 1854-1856, Arlington House Archives, folders 5 and 8.

[41] Augusta Blanche Berard, "Arlington and Mount Vernon 1856,"*Virginia Magazine of History and Biography,* v. 57, No. 2 (April 1949), pp. 140-175.

[42] *The Washington Post,* March 9, 1896, p. 7, from the *New York Journal.*
[43] *The New York Times,* May 29, 1888, p. 3; and March 15, 1897, p. 4.
[44] Augusta Blanche Berard, "Arlington and Mount Vernon 1856."
[45] MCW Diaries, 1875-1877, MA 1045 (1) Pierpont Morgan Library, NY.
[46] S. Mitchell, *A Family Lawsuit – The Romantic Story of Elisabeth Patterson and Jerome Bonaparte,* Farrar, N. Y., Straus and Cudahy, 1958.
[47] MCW Diaries, 1875-1877, (MA 1045(1) Pierpont Morgan Library, NY.
[48] Ltr., LAW to MCP, July 30, 1848, TP Archives, MS-2, Box 1- f.5.
[49] Ltr., REL, Jr. to MCL, June 22 1850, TP Archives, MS-5, Box 5.
[50] Francis B.Heitman, *Historical Register and Dictionary of the U. S. Army,* Washington:GPO,1903; rpt., Urbana: University of Illinois Press, 1965
[51] S. Mitchell, *A Family Lawsuit.*
[52]Remarks, *Charles J. Bonaparte, Founder of the Federal Bureau of Investigation,* Arthur Gajarsa, Judge, U. S. Court of Appeals of the Federal Circuit, Delivered at the Grand Hall of the Department of Justice, June 26, 1998.
[53] MCW Diaries, 1875-1877, (MA 1045(1), Pierpont Morgan Library, NY.
[54] MCW Diary F (1878), TP Archives, MS-6 (1-6).
[55] Claude Bourguignon-Frasetto, *Betsy Bonaparte – The Belle of Baltimore,* Baltimore, Maryland, Maryland Historical Society, 1988, 2003.

CHAPTER 4

THE ORPHANS (1846-1852)

"May you never know how dreadfully desolate it is, to be an Orphan," Markie wrote to her good friend Blanche Berard.

> To unburden to you my heart's grief, would be impossible, for volumes could not reveal the world of different feelings, which agitate my mind. Now, my thoughts are riveted upon the past – upon yesterday's sunshine. Now, the awful present comes to my view. It dims my sight and I almost gasp for breath; and then the dark uncertain future!, but amidst all this, my God has not left me comfortless.[1]

Markie's letter pouring out her grief provides a wonderful insight into her character. It is dramatic – Markie's feelings and her expression of them were always extreme. It is eloquent and articulate – she knows how to say what she feels: "In the garden of the convent of San Francisco, where his lifeless form's entombed, my heart lays bleeding while my spirit soars Heavenward and seeks in God, a balm, distilled not from earthly plants." It reveals her close relationship with her father:

> He has, from my earliest Childhood, claimed so much of my love, so much of my confidence and undeviating affection and bestowed so much on me, that I have painted no dream without him. I never thought, what life would ever [be] without the sunshine of his smile.

It shows the importance of religion in her life: "You know my dear Father made no outward profession of religion, but from the tenor of his mind and from the excellence of his principles, I hope he thought more of God & Heaven, than we could know." It also shows the importance to her of her friends, and the sentimentality she felt for anything associated with her loved ones. West Point is "hallowed" to her because her father loved it and she loved Blanche "for his sake" long before she had actually met her.

Markie would go on with life, however, devoted to her remaining family: "My dear little Bunnie is a great comfort to me now and Lolo, I hope will realize all my hope."

A month later, Markie wrote again to her friend, thanking her for her interest in "the welfare of one, whose heart has been so crushed. . . . I do not say that I shall never be happy again, tho' at times I feel <u>dreadfully</u> desolate."[2] But her faith in God sustained her:

> Earthly friends are sweet indeed, and they may by their affection & friendship & sympathy, help us bear our burdens, but the promised <u>rest</u>, comes alone from <u>Heaven</u> & leads our minds to contemplate a happy home, where there shall be no more weeping.

Markie was "shocked" that Blanche had shown Markie's previous letter to her pastor, who had sent messages of sympathy, because of the very personal nature of the letter, but trusted her friend's judgment. Invited to visit West Point the following summer, Markie said:

> I feel that I never can leave Georgetown and I can never leave Bunnie for among the last words my dearest Father said to me was "Take Bunnie, wherever you go, dearest Markie." He has always been a great pet with me, but <u>now</u>, he seems a <u>sacred charge.</u> To take him with me, on a visit, would not be practicable, but nevertheless, I will <u>hope</u> that fate's decree will be, that we shall <u>meet again</u> on earth.

Not until February of 1847 did Markie receive a letter of condolence from her great-aunt, Nellie Custis Lewis, who was living at Audley in northern Virginia, the home of her son, Lorenzo. Lorenzo died in 1847, perhaps explaining the delay. She wrote to Markie of her father that he "was ever to your dear mother the kindest the most truly excellent & devoted husband I have ever known." She urged Markie to "try to be all he would have wished you to be, an example to your young Sisters & Brothers – a comfort to your aged Grandmother who like myself cannot expect to remain long with her children."[3]

In October Markie finally heard from Robert E. Lee:

> I have thought of you so often since I have been in this Country. I have seen so many of your <u>Army</u> friends.

63

I have talked to them so much about you. I could not write to you. My letter now will be a sad one. It has been to me a melancholy pleasure to listen to the accounts of the gallant conduct of your dear father at Monterey. You know the whole story. You feel the certainty of your loss. I could say nothing to diminish the intensity of your grief. I have however thought that something from him, something attached to him on that fatal day would be precious to you. I send you what I believe to have been his sword belt. If so, you will probably recognize it, & it will be the more endeared to you by being stained by his life blood.[4]

The next April Markie replied that she had received the belt and recognized it as her father's.[5] Someone also sent her a leaf from a tree in Monterrey, which Markie and her descendants kept as "a precious memento from a tree, upon the spot where my beloved Father fell at Monterey Mexico." In the same collection there is also a small piece of stone, enclosed in a note in Markie's hand that reads: "A stone from the grave of my much loved precious Father who was killed at Monterey Sep. 21st 1847."[6]

Markie's father had been buried in Mexico "in the garden of the convent of San Francisco" but a committee of citizens of Buffalo made arrangements early in 1847 to have his body returned so that he could be buried with his wife, America. Markie attended the funeral in March, staying with Dr. Austin Flint and his wife. Among her keepsakes was a copy of the sermon preached by the Reverend Dr. Melton. Attached to it is a note in Dr. Flint's handwriting, "The foregoing address is copied for Miss Martha C. Williams by her devotedly attached friend A.F., Buffalo, April 16, 1847."[7]

Markie was the only one in the family to go to Buffalo for the funeral. Perhaps it was a money problem, for her grandmother, Martha Peter, wrote:

I rejoice my dear Child that it was in our power to afford you this great gratification. Be assured it will always afford your Aunt, & myself pleasure to add to your happiness. I regret poor Lum, & Kate could not have gone with you – but you know it was not in my power to send them.[8]

Markie managed to linger in Buffalo until the beginning of May. She stayed on when her escort to Buffalo returned to Washington, and young ladies did not travel alone in those days. Her host, Dr. Flint, was expecting to go to a meeting in Baltimore, and she might come home then. Years later, Markie noted that on April 10 she spent the day at Niagara Falls with "one of the dearest friends I have on earth" and May 7 was noted as "this day sacred to our parting."[9]

Meanwhile, financial considerations were to become even more important. Captain Williams had already been worried about all the expenditures for Laurence's schooling and kept urging Markie to economize. Now Markie and her grandmother would be forced to even greater economy. The U.S. Army would pay $25.00 per month for five years to the minor (under 16) male children, Laurence and Orton. Kate was also still a minor, but no provision seems to have been made for females. Martha Peter was named guardian and received the pension payments every six months from the U.S. Treasury.[10] Other than that, Captain Williams had some investments in Buffalo and in western land, which would bring in some income to Markie and her siblings over the years.

Martha Peter was not a wealthy woman – her husband's wealth had been mostly tied up in land, and much of that was now in the hands of her sons, or sold over the years. Concerned over the future of her orphaned grandchildren, she provided in her will that one-third of the eight-acre Tudor Place parcel would be sold after her death to support them.[11]

Laurence continued at Georgetown College until February of 1847 and then transferred to Benjamin Hallowell's Alexandria boarding school, where he stayed until May 1848. There he did much better than at Georgetown – perhaps his father's death sobered and matured him. He went from last in his class at Georgetown to second in Alexandria.[12]

Benjamin Hallowell was a Quaker, who encouraged the boys to call him and his wife, Margaret, by their first names. Laurence reported that he liked the new school much better than Georgetown College. He seems to have had much more opportunity to see family and friends in Alexandria, attending Christ Church each Sunday. During the summer of 1847, he went to visit his aunt, Eleanor Custis Lewis, at Audley.[13] Back at school in the fall, Laurence showed an impatient streak in his letters to Markie:

No wonder I always write to you for something for I have to wait so long for things it is two weeks since I wrote to you for my toothbrush and I have not seen it yet.

He also complained of being very cold and having nothing to wear.[14] In the spring, after being home for Easter at Tudor Place, he was studying hard for the entrance examination for West Point. Mr. Hallowell had been hearing his arithmetic lesson every evening. "Pretty sure of passing the first examination," he asked Markie if he could have his father's watch before he went. It would be of great use and "I will have one thing that was formerly my dear Fathers."[15]

In June 1848, at the tender age of 15, Lolo went off to West Point. In a letter to Markie, Robert E. Lee summed up the great expectations that everyone had for Laurence:

Do impress upon him the necessity of application & strict attention to duty & the regulations. It will be a great distress to us all if his fathers son does not acquit himself worthy of the expectations we are entitled to form of him, & do credit to the Institution he so much loved. I shall watch his course with much anxiety.[16]

Lolo was quite a correspondent from West Point. He wrote to his grandmother, his Aunt Britannia, his sisters, and his uncles. On June 3, he wrote to his grandmother:

I am at last here safely housed in the Barracks – and undergoing the duties of a Plebe, which are not particularly inviting especially the drilling part. Yesterday I spent a very unpleasant day as another boy and myself were put in a room with nothing in it at all except our trunks which we used as chairs, but now I am very well situated as we went to the store yesterday and procured our Beding – a [table] & two chairs.[17]

Laurence also reported to Markie on how he was settling in. He had seen their friend Blanche Berard and most of the plebes had now arrived. He was to be with three others in a room about as big "as that closet by your room." He thought it would be very hard to live on his cadet's pay ($40 a month). They had charged him $15 for a bed, basin, broom, and some pens and ink. He was homesick, but as he wrote quite sadly, "I have not been at home quite enough to know the charms as expressed in 'Home Sweet Home.'"

> I suppose Old Tudor looks quite beautiful – I very often think of the flowers I planted for you, and when I come back in 2 years, I hope to see the rose bush "grown up."[18]

After settling in, the first summer at West Point was spent in camp. Lolo wrote:

> Being in rather a home-sick mood occasioned by a little indisposition I thought I could write you a long letter and am now sitting down in my tent with a large dictionary on my knee which answers the purpose of a desk writing to my dear little sister Markie, and thinking how I should like to be with you all at old Tudor. You know you used to tell me I would miss "Sister" some of these days and I now realize the fact. Camp is very dull indeed and we are not allowed to visit without a special permit only on Saturdays I always spend the evening with Miss Blanche who is the same enthusiastic and interesting person.[19]

He sent love to all the family and urged them all to write. He looked forward to getting into the Barracks in about a month and looked back longingly at other summers spent at Montevideo.* "I should like to go through the happy days there again. They seem to be the brightest and most joyful I ever spent."[20] Lolo seems to have been very fond of fruit. In his letters, he often bemoans the lack of fruit at West Point and in this one remarks that peaches must be in abundance at Tudor just now. He also tells Markie proudly that her next letter may be addressed to "Cadet Williams." He had passed the entrance examinations and his title was now official.

To his grandmother he wrote at the end of July that he had been in the hospital but was now back on duty in camp with a swollen neck. "I shall be very glad indeed to get in Barracks and I think I can study hard – we have only four months to determine whether we will stay here or not and I am going to make the most of them.... There is one

---

* Home of his uncle, John Parke Custis Peter, on the Potomac River in Seneca, MD, where the family liked to spend at least part of every summer.

consolation at least in camp – and that is that I have an excellent tent mate. He is a nephew of Napoleon Bonaparte – and a very nice person."[21] Jerome Napoleon Bonaparte II was in fact the grandson of Elizabeth Patterson Bonaparte and Jerome Bonaparte, and therefore the great-nephew of Napoleon.

At this time, cadets at West Point were not given leave for the first two years, so Lolo depended on letters from home, always urging Markie and the others to write more often. He kept his promise to study hard. By September, he had risen from 65th in his class to 12th and on February 18, 1849, Laurence reported that he had taken the oath of allegiance before the Academic Board and was now a "genuine" cadet.[22]

Lolo had been urging Markie to have her daguerreotype (he called it "Dog-ra-type") taken and was glad to hear from her that she finally had the money to do it. He urged her to have it taken in the dress she looked "sweetest" in, and would she also send him a copy of their father's portrait.[23]

Money was a problem for Lolo also. He asked Markie to send him spending money, as the $40 monthly allotment from West Point was kept in an account from which purchases were subtracted. He had to have some cash to take care of any items or services not available through the Academy, such as having his clothes mended.[24]

Meanwhile, both Columbia and Kate had continued at Miss English's Seminary for a time after their father's death. In May of 1849 Kate, only 15, became engaged to a young naval officer, John Henry Upshur. Lolo wrote that he hoped to come to her wedding the following summer if he could get leave (she was actually married in February of 1851). Hearing from Markie that their aunt, Eleanor Custis Lewis, was in Washington visiting the new President (Zachary Taylor), he proposed that maybe she could use her influence on his behalf. He also was still complaining about the state of his clothing – it was much worn and washed. Markie was evidently still providing his clothing, because he proposed that she send him money instead so he could buy his own shirts.[25]

In June, no longer a lowly plebe, Laurence was pleased to be able to order a new plebe to pitch his tent for him. He was still homesick, especially the evening he heard the band play "Home Sweet Home" and "Auld Lang Syne."[26] In July, West Point was very gay with social life and Lolo reported to Markie on all their friends. He bragged of meeting many young ladies and teased Markie about receiving an invitation to be his "bridesmaid."[27] In September he wrote to Markie, who was visiting her uncle George Washington Peter in Charlestown (now West Virginia), that there was cholera at West Point and he was taking every precaution to avoid getting it.[28]

By now the youngest child, Orton, was in boarding school in Alexandria, Virginia, probably with the Quaker Benjamin Hallowell, giving Markie more freedom to travel[29]. By January 1850 Laurence had finally received the long-awaited daguerreotype of his sister, possibly as a Christmas present.[30] In March, replying to Markie, who had spoken disparagingly of someone who danced the polka, Lolo wrote that he danced polkas, waltzes, and other dances as well.[31] There are no more letters from West Point, although Laurence did not graduate until 1852.

Markie must have seen him the following November, when she went to West Point for the funeral of her friend Blanche Berard's brother.[32] Whether Laurence was able to come home for Kate's wedding in February of 1851 we do not know. Just before the wedding, in January, Markie and Kate visited their grandmother's old friend, Anna Maria Thornton, widow of the architect of the Capitol and Tudor Place. Mrs. Thornton gave Kate a lace collar and cuffs for a wedding present.[33] We have no first hand account of Kate's wedding, but it must have been a simple affair. Markie wrote to Robert E. Lee in February describing the affair. Her letter does not survive, but in his reply he referred to "the disappointments of the young gallants on the Wedding mor[nin]g...at their lack of breakfast."

In the same letter, we see evidence of the close and playful relationship between Lee and Markie. He begins:

> You have not written to me for nearly three months.
> And I believe it is equally as long since I have written
> to you. On paper Markie, I mean, on paper. But oh,
> what lengthy epistles have I indited to you in my mind!
> Had I any means to send them, you would see how
> constantly I think of you. I have followed you in your
> pleasures, & your duties, in the house & in the streets,
> & accompanied you in your walks to Arlington, & in
> your search after flowers.

Lee, writing from his current post in Baltimore, reported that he had been to West Point, where he saw Laurence.

He was looking very handsome & well, & with the exception of his inattention which caused him demerit, was doing well. He assured me he would not overrun the awful 200, & I do not think he will, though he is coming rather too near, & has reached the respectable number of 195. Still I think he will not exceed the limit. He will commence upon another year at the close of this month, & begin a clean sheet. Can't you persuade him, as it will be his last, to keep it so. He will graduate a year from next month, & will return to you much improved in every way.

Lee had no demerits during his four years at West Point, so he showed remarkable restraint in discussing Lolo's total. Still teasing Markie about real or imagined suitors, Lee told about a young couple who had been separated almost since the beginning of their married life, because of military duties, and said "Take warning, Markie."[34]

Sometime during the spring or early summer of 1852, Markie suffered a fall from horseback returning to Tudor Place after a visit to Arlington, injured her back, and was "from that time for two or three months...an invalid confined much of the time to my bed."[35] This accident, together with the fact that her brothers and sisters were now more or less independent and well taken care of, persuaded Markie to accept a long-standing invitation from her aunt, Margaret Orton, to visit her in Paris. She received great encouragement from Lee, who wrote:

I shall be too sorry dearest Markie if I should not be able to get to New York before your departure to say "good bye." I shall endeavour to do so, but I cannot leave the Point[†] at this time.... You will carry with you my earnest prayers & warmest wishes for a prosperous voyage & happy meeting with all your kind relatives beyond the big water. ... You must not be cast down at the prospect of your departure Markie. Kind friends await your approach & warm hearts will gladden at your arrival. Those you leave behind, though saddened by your absence will hold you as close & dear as if you were present. Then cheer up Markie & carry a brave as

---

[†] Lee had become Superintendent of the U.S. Military Academy on September 1, 1852.

well as true heart for every occasion of life.... I am very sorry that you are still suffering from your back, I hope the voyage will entirely restore you.[36]

And so Markie set out on her great adventure.

[1] Letter, MCW to BB, November 20, 1846, Eleanor S. Brockenbrough Library, The Museum of the Confederacy, Richmond, VA.

[2] Letter, MCW to BB, December [23], 1846, Eleanor S. Brockenbrough Library, The Museum of the Confederacy, Richmond, VA.

[3] Letter, ECL to MCW, February 4, 1847, Tudor Place Archives, MS-6 (4-12).

[4] Letter, REL to MCW, October 28, 1846, Lee Papers, Virginia Historical Society, MSS 21 (575a.34).

[5] Letter, REL to MCW, May 21, 1848, in *To Markie*.

[6] Both items in the Upshur-Brown papers, a family collection in Richmond, VA. Markie must have written the notes much later, for her father actually died in 1846.

[7] *Ibid.*

[8] Letter, MCP to MCW, March 25, 1847, Tudor Place Archives, MS-6 (1-5).

[9] MCW Diary, April 10, 1853, Arlington House Archives.

[10] We are indebted for this information to a chronology compiled by Wendy Kail in the Tudor Place files. The information is from the National Archives, Record Group 217, Entry 724.

[11] Will of Martha Custis Peter, Tudor Place Archives, MS-2.

[12] Correspondence, LW to MCW, March 1, 1847-April 18, 1848, TP Archives, MS-6 (1-15,16).

[13] Correspondence, LW to MCW, March 1, 1847-July 10, 1847, TP Archives, MS-6 (1-15).

[14] Ltr., LW to MCW, Oct. 28, 1847, TP Archives, MS-6 (1-15).

[15] Ltr., LW to MCW, April 18, 1847, TP Archives, MS-6 (1-16).

[16] Ltr, REL to MCW, May 21, 1847, in *To Markie*.

[17] Ltr, LW to MCP, June 3, 1848, TP Archives, MS-2 (1-5).

[18] Ltr, LW to MCW, June ?, 1848, TP Archives, MS-6 (1-16).

[19] Ltr, LW to MCW, July 18, 1848, TP Archives, MS-6 (1-16).

[20] Ibid.

[21] Ltr., LW to MCP, July 30, 1848, TP Archives, MS-2 (1-5).

[22] Ltrs., LW to MCW, Sept. 18, 1848 and Feb. 18, 1849, TP Archives, MS-6 (1-17).

[23] Ltr., LW to MCW, Feb. 18, 1849, TP Archives, MS-6, (1-17).

[24] Ltr., LW to MCW, April 16, 1849, TP Archives, MS-6,(1-18).

[25] Ltr., LW to MCW, May 18, 1849, TP Archives, MS-6,(1-18).

[26] Ltr., LW to MCW, June 24, 1849, TP Archives, MS-6 ((1-18).

[27] Ltr., LW to MCW, July 23 , 1849, TP Archives, MS-6 (1-18).

[28] Ltr., LW to MCW, Sept. 6, 1849, TP Archives, MS-6 (1-18).

[29] Ltr., LW to MCW, Nov. 1, 1849, TP Archives, MS-6 (1-18).

[30] Ltr., LW to MCW, Feb. 14, 1850, TP Archives, MS-6 (1-19).

[31] Ltr., LW to MCW, March 16, 1850, TP Archives, MS-6 (1-19).

[32] Ltr., Eleanor Custis Lewis to MCW, Nov. 29, 1850, TP Archives, MS-6 (4-12).

[33] Ltr., Eleanor Custis Lewis to MCW, Feb. 6, 1851, TP Archives, MS-6 (4-12); A.M. Thornton's Diary, William Thornton Papers, Library of Congress.

[34] Ltr., REL to MCW, May 10, 1851, in *To Markie*.

[35] MCW Diary, Oct. 23, 1853, Arlington House Archives.

[36] Ltr., REL to MCW, Oct. 8, 1852, in *To Markie*.

CHAPTER 5

ADVENTURE IN EUROPE (1852-1853)

"God, in his infinite goodness, has given me a brave heart and courage to bear the bitter trial of parting from my country and friends," wrote Markie in her diary, October 16, 1852, the day that she sailed on the *Atlantic* for England, armed with a passport signed by the Secretary of State, Daniel Webster[1]. She considered herself an invalid because of her back injury, but with family encouragement she had agreed to visit Aunt Margaret Orton in Paris.[2] Nevertheless, while Markie was in New York, she received a letter from her Grandmother telling her that "We had prayers for you in both Churches," and that she was delighted to learn that "your prospects were so good for protection the rest of your journey," but suggesting that she return to Tudor Place if she could not find a desirable person to serve as her traveling companion.[3]

Brother Lolo had accompanied Markie from Washington to New York and to her stateroom. He looked for Mr. and Mrs. Rogers, whom she referred to as strangers and her future protectors, but he did not find them. He came back with Stewardess Annie who faithfully promised to do anything in her power for Markie. Two English friends of Lolo also promised every kind of attention. In the evening one of them, Mr. Bright, invited her on deck to see the sunset, and they walked until long after the moon had risen, "talking of dear America" and gazing "upon the dashing waves and the clear moon-lit sky."

The next morning and for several days she was seasick, but there was always someone to look after her. "Often did my heart fill with emotions of gratitude to God for giving me so many friends to care for me." She enjoyed most the time spent with Mr. Bright who was acquainted with American authors and knew Lolo and her cousin, Robert E. Lee. They often walked or read to each other. While they were on deck to see the coast of England, she finally met Mr. and Mrs. Rogers who had been seasick the entire trip. When they disembarked at Liverpool after their ten-day voyage, they accompanied Markie on the train [from Liverpool] to London and went to the Mosely Hotel where Mrs. Fisher, a friend of Aunt Margaret, called to take Markie to her home.

The following morning, Mrs. Fisher took Markie sightseeing. She was delighted to visit Westminster Abbey and hoped that on her next visit to London she could spend a whole week at the Abbey with Washington Irving's description before her. His "The Sketchbook of Geoffrey Crayon," a short story collection, includes his impressions of England. He began his story of the Abbey, "On one of those sober and rather melancholy days....I passed several hours in rambling about Westminster Abbey....as I passed its threshold it seemed like stepping back into the regions of antiquity and losing myself among the shades of former ages."

Markie had looked forward to visiting St. Paul's Cathedral, but it was being prepared for the funeral of the Duke of Wellington. They drove past the Cathedral and Apsley House which had long been his residence. She purchased an engraving of the "old Duke"* by way of "being very loyal" to her Grandmother Peter who was an admirer of this famous man – she named her daughter Britannia Wellington in honor of him.

The next day when Mr. Fisher took her to the train station, he said to a nice looking old gentleman, "If you are going to Paris, sir, you will oblige me very much by taking this young lady under your charge." Although he was not going to Paris, he said that his son would be happy to take charge of Markie. She found her seat "in first class, of course," removed an umbrella on the back of the seat and sat down next to the window. In walked the old English gentleman who said, "That is my son's seat, if you please, Miss." With him was "a strapping, bouncing, ruddy" adult. Markie was indignant. "What American," she wrote, "would have asked a *Lady* to remove to a less comfortable seat – and I, an invalid, too!" However, after this first unfavorable encounter, she found her traveling companion to be "a person of considerable cultivation," and they discussed many interesting subjects during the whole journey. He asked her if she had read *"Uncle Tom's Cabin,"* by Harriet Beecher Stowe. When she said that she had not, he handed a copy to her, saying, "You ought to read it. You will be very much pleased with it."

> Not feeling disposed to discuss the abolition subject
> with an Englishman, I merely looked over the book,
> observed that I believed the authoress to be a person of
> a good deal of merit & returned it with a bow of

---

*An engraving of the Duke of Wellington still hangs at Tudor Place.

thanks. The English are quite crazy about *Uncle Tom's Cabin.* I observed at the Pantheon Bazaar [that there were] Engravings of all of the principal scenes in it – also songs and pieces of music entitled from this celebrated book.

It is dramatized in every book store and at every railway station.... The fact is, I had looked over the book in Washington, several times with the intention of reading it, but having ascertained its character, I laid it aside, having a particular aversion to reading horrors.

When they arrived at Folkestone to board the ship, "my gallant escort took my cloak and my pillow on one arm and myself on the other and so we walked from the cars to the boat.... My English friend as I must call him (never having known his name, nor he mine)...after arranging me comfortably on deck," left. Soon she was seasick and went down to the cabin where a number of seasick women were lying on every available surface. When the movement of the boat threw her to the floor, she continued to lie beside a little Italian girl until the steward announced that they had arrived in the harbor of Boulogne. Markie expected to see her English companion, but he did not appear.

How they would have laughed at home, could they have seen me bundled up to my chin, with a large, heavy cloak in one arm and a work-basket and a bouquet of flowers in the other with a group of Italians, French, German and English, all seasick and dismal, plodding up from the boat to the Custom House, in the rain without umbrellas....

She joined her little Italian friend with her father (the "Mudies") who agreed to stop at the Bedford Hotel where Markie had reservations. Early the next morning they went to the train station with Mr. Mudie taking charge of her luggage. They arrived that evening in Paris where Markie met her aunt and said goodbye to her Italian friends.

As she and Aunt Margaret rode through the streets of Paris, Markie was impressed with the gas lights and thought that Paris might be the most beautiful city in the world. When they arrived at the apartment, little Cousin Phillie came dancing to meet Markie, kissing her on both cheeks and saying, "My dear Cousin, I am so glad to see you.... Why, how large you are – how tall – I expected to see you as small as myself." (Markie and Phillie were about the same age.) Her aunt introduced her to

Uncle Thomas Orton whom she described as an old gentleman, rather tall, very thin and pale.

During her first week in Paris, Markie saw sights that she had read about so often, the Garden of the Tuileries, Place de la Concorde, and the Champs Elysées, which she noted did not disappoint her. She and Aunt Margaret visited the American Embassy where they left cards and Markie's letter of introduction to Mrs. Rives, the wife of the Minister.*

Because Markie was in severe pain on Sunday, she did not accompany the family to church, but instead spent the time reading her Bible. Her aunt and uncle had insisted on her being measured for a corset, but when the Femme de Corsets came on Sunday, Markie was horrified. She indignantly announced that she could not have measurements on the Sabbath. Soon the valet appeared with hammer and nails to festoon the draperies only to learn that he, too, must return another day. "I was reminded that I was not in my own dear Country where the Sabbath is so sacredly kept." The day had another surprise: a visit by Monsieur L'Abbe Auger, a Jesuit, who had taught French to her father, a student in Paris over 30 years ago. "Notwithstanding my horror of Jesuits, I was glad to see one who had so long ago known my dear Father."

On December 1, Markie was excited about seeing Napoleon III's procession on the Champs Elysées. Aunt Margaret had rented a window in a building from where Markie could see the procession, but to her disappointment the police would not allow anyone to stand in front of a window. The city was still tense because Napoleon III had assumed dictatorial powers a year ago. Aunt Margaret bought Markie an engraving of the Emperor to console her.

That evening, she copied in French a newspaper article about the events of the day and wrote in her diary:

> I have just sent Frederika into the parlor to get my engraving of the Emperor which I have put in my drawer with the blank side uppermost, lest one of the

---

* William Cabell Rives (1793-1868), twice U. S. Minister to France, U. S. Congressman and twice U. S. Senator from Virginia, and Confederate Congressman. He and his wife, Judith Walker Rives, an author, had a home, Castle Hill, in Albemarle County, Virginia.

Red Republicans should break in and consider a likeness of the Emperor as a demonstration of our principles. These are days when one must not express an opinion in politics. Dear Aunt has cautioned Uncle not to let a sentiment fall from his lips for or against the Emperor.

The next day, she went with her aunt and cousin to the palace where people gathered to see the Emperor. Again she was disappointed. They had just missed seeing Napoleon III who had made an appearance on the balcony. She finally saw the Emperor the following March from Place de la Concorde. "I gained a pretty good view of their Imperial Highnesses. The Empress...very pale & thin...bent forward in the carriage, smiled & bowed. The emperor maintained his dignified position...."

Aunt Margaret took Markie to one of the most celebrated homeopathic physicians in Paris to consult about her painful back. He prescribed simple, light meals with meat and plenty of wine, the habit of early to bed and early to rise, and two long walks every day. In the morning Aunt Margaret accompanied her on her first, long walk. After some distance, they saw an omnibus with an inscription on the side, "Père La Chaise" (a large cemetery). Markie wrote an enthusiastic description of the colorful bus and their tour. She and her aunt were "handed in by the polite conductor" who wore an outfit with a red collar and a blue cap with a red tassel. She was pleased to learn that she could travel all over Paris for three sous. At length they arrived at *Place de la Bastille* where they transferred to another omnibus going to the cemetery. Almost the whole street to Pére La Chaise was lined on either side with little shops that sold items used in the cemetery: wreaths, crosses, artificial flowers as well as fresh flowers, and plaster statues of the Savior, the Virgin Mary and the saints. They entered an immense stone, arched gateway and saw a chapel with a large cross, situated on a hill over a broad, ascending avenue. On either side of the avenue, Markie saw what reminded her of sentry boxes. Actually, they were vaults with open worked, iron doors, and inside were tombstones that served as altars adorned with statues, wreaths, crucifixes, holy water or flowers. She was fascinated by a child's tomb of pure white marble as were all of the decorations on its altar. Just below it, a large doll was standing, dressed in pure white muslin, a white sash and a little *bouquet de corsage*, and hanging gracefully over her head was a long, white veil. On one side of the doll was a bag of sugar plums and on the other side little playthings. Markie was delighted to see so many flowers on the tombs. When she spied one that she had never seen previously, she wanted to pick it, but decided that taking it would desecrate the grave. She was impressed with the attractive, well-kept cemetery and thought that the unremitting attention to the tombs of their departed ones was a beautiful trait in the French character.

The last stop for the now fatigued Markie and Aunt Margaret was a small chapel. At the door within sat an old woman with a long brush in her hand which she dipped in a basin of holy water and besprinkled anyone who looked wistfully at her, hoping for a few sous. "It was with a feeling of pity that I looked at the poor old creature" moving her lips in prayer. "Oh, that the omniscient God may illuminate her beclouded vision!"

We do not know how Markie and the Ortons spent Christmas, because the diaries for this period do not survive or have not been found. Her diary resumes on February 13, 1853.

When Uncle Orton's niece, Madame de Monbeison, and her husband, Comte de Monbeison, visited the family, Markie noted in her diary that counts and countesses were very much like other people. She was not prepared, however, when the count, speaking in French, asked, "Mademoiselle, do you think of marrying in France or in the United States?" She was "so astonished that I could not believe that I had understood rightly." Aunt Margaret came to her rescue, saying, "I believe she does not think about it." The Countess added, "Marriages are not conducted in America as they are here." Markie remained speechless as she wondered why people, even her family and friends at home, were so concerned about her marital status. She had recently received a letter from "my very dear friend, Dr. Flint," who wrote that he hoped she would not marry an Englishman or a Frenchman. "How little fear there is of this! I feel that I could never marry other than one of my own countrymen."

The next day she and Phillie took a long walk and stopped at a picture shop on the Rue de Rivoli where she purchased a colored engraving of "Murillo's Conception" for "dear Cousin Mary Lee" (Mrs. Robert E. Lee) and a French history book for "darling Bunnie." She and Aunt Margaret attended a reception given by Mrs. Rives, the American Minister's wife, at their residence, 30 Rue de Ville L'éveque. Markie thought that Mrs. Rives was a true specimen of an American lady and that she and her daughter showed the hospitality of Virginians. "February 22nd, the Birthday of 'the Father of his Country!' I must not forget it, tho' in a foreign land, to bless the God that gave us a Washington."

The family had to vacate the apartment at 28 rue du Monthalor before Aunt Margaret was able to rent another apartment to accommodate all of them. She rented rooms for herself and Markie in a pension, on the rue du Faubourg St. Honoré that they referred to as "the convent." Uncle Orton and Phillie would go to Vendôme in the Loire Valley. He "subscribed for the *Galignanis Messenger*† which we are to receive daily when we are at the 'convent'.... I am quite delighted with the idea." After a day of packing, Markie wrote, "Wearied & worn out with fatigue, I was sitting by the fire indulging in the most pleasing reminiscences of past hours with which were associated my very dear friend, Dr. Flint," when her Aunt handed her a letter from him, "I seized it with indescribable pleasure."

Markie wondered what sort of place this "convent" would be – 20 ladies and no gentlemen. She felt sure that she would meet some congenial spirit, and quoted "my favorite, Tupper‡ - 'some more and some less, but, truly all may boast a little and one may travel through the world and see it thick with friendship.' " She thought about the many good things that had happened since she had been living in this building, but she never had left a place with less regret and hoped the future would be happier. "As the dear Dr. most justly said in his last, sweet letter, 'So it is, we are anxious to hurry on through the journey of life, always anticipating with prospective events which shorten with each succession the distance to the tomb.' "

While waiting to move, Markie and Uncle Orton visited the Louvre to see Le Musée des Souvraines, a suite of apartments reopened by Emperor Napoleon III within the past fortnight. Another day they went in search of a French and English phrase book and she bought a little book by Lamartine§ entitled *Graziella*. "This author's translations into English have always delighted me...it will be a good exercise for me and I am sure it cannot be bad if it is Lamartine's." The last evening, "Aunt presented me with a miniature of my dear Mother, painted on ivory by my precious Father...I shall love to keep it as his painting."**

---

† Giovanni Antonio Galignani, born in Italy, lived in London for some time and then went to Paris where he published a daily newspaper, *Galignanis Messenger,* printed in English.
‡ Martin Farquhar Tupper(1810-1889), English writer of verse and prose.
§ Alphonse Marie Louis de Lamartine (1790-1869), French poet, writer and statesman.
** This miniature is in the Tudor Place collection.

Because the rooms at the pension were not ready, the family stayed for two days at the Hotel de France in the Rue St. Honoré. Markie was especially delighted by their visit to École Imperial Polytechnic because it was here that "my dear Father passed a year during his West Point vacation or after he had been two years at West Point…dear Aunt, too, retains vivid recollections of this period. She was at Madame de Pages Pension on the Rue Notre Dame des Champs…." When a young officer appeared, Aunt Margaret asked if they might see the building to which he replied that there was nothing to see. In the courtyard, Markie saw some little flowers and asked if she might have one, whereupon the young officer pulled some and presented them to her. She thanked him kindly for indeed she was most happy to possess some "memento of the place where dear Father had been so long ago." She put one in her diary and noted that it was the first primrose that she had ever seen.

A friend of Aunt Margaret, Miss Andoc, took them on a tour of the Convent Mont Sion, the only English Convent in Paris that was not disturbed during the Revolution of 1789.

> Passing through the vineyard, I espied over the walls an Old Dome. 'What building is that?' said I. 'An old convent,' she replied, 'formerly the Convent of the Nuns of the Visitation….' 'Ah!' said I, 'I was a year in school at a Convent of the Visitation in America.' 'What part?' she said. On replying Georgetown, she remarked, 'Oh, yes! I remember when two or three nuns were sent from this convent to establish the one in Georgetown.' I looked at the Old Dome with renewed interest.

On March 1, Aunt Margaret and Markie moved into their rooms at the "convent." After their first dinner in the pension dining room, Markie wrote, "I never was less fascinated with dinner company than on the present occasion. The ladies, with two or three exceptions, all seemed of a *certain age*…." She described most of the women in unflattering terms and added that they ate fish and everything else with the same knives and forks. She had heard that there was another American at the table and asked the woman next to her if she were the woman with delicate features.

> 'No,' said the person I asked, 'there is the American – that great fat lady at the end of the table with red

ribbons on her cap....' What was my mortification when I looked up to behold in the representative of America the most common, vulgar looking person I ever saw one who, if possible, eclipsed all the rest.... I could not help wishing that America had a better specimen than either of us, but I really think to the eyes of a stranger, I was the better of the two.

By March 7, Markie was becoming more accustomed to her new abode. She was pleased that everyone spoke French at the table and in the parlor where she and Aunt Margaret went during the evening to visit and read the newspaper. On this day, an article about Emperor Francis Joseph I of Austria, recovering from being shot, made her think about home. "How happy and fortunate has my own country been so far. I was in Washington in spirit on the 4th of March, bestowing on our new President (Franklin Pierce) my ardent wishes for his success and prosperity and that of our dear country...."

On March 10, she read an "interesting paragraph about the Jews" in the *Galignani Messenger:*

A remarkable change it is said is in progress among the Jews – in almost every country. Rabbinism, which has enslaved the minds of the people so many ages, is rapidly losing its influence. Multitudes are turning aside the Mishnah [first section of Talmud] and the Talmud [Rabbinic writings, basis of authority for Judaism] and betaking themselves to study of Moses and the prophets. Among the Jews in London there is at the present time great demand for copies of the Old Testament. The subject of their restoration to Palestine and the Nature of the promises on which the expedition is founded are extensively engaging their attention. In examining these matters they have obtained considerable assistance from a Continental Rabbi,who has lately arrived among them and exhibited a manuscript in which he has endeavored to prove from Scripture, that the time has come when the Jews must set about making preparations for returning to the land of their fathers. The said manuscript has been formed to further the movement proposed by the learned Rabbi.

Markie was always willing to go sightseeing. During the second week of March, she accompanied her Uncle to the Louvre and then went with Aunt Margaret and Phillie on a walk through the Barrière de l'Etoile.

> It is a magnificent structure. It is called 'Arc de Triomphe de L'Etoile.' The idea of this monument, says *Galignani*, originated with Napoleon le grand who decreed its erection in 1806.... On the marriage of the Emperor with Maria Louisa and her triumphal entry into the Capital [1810], there was an immense model in wood & canvas of this temporarily & brilliantly illuminated.[††]

Markie wrote that she was getting along admirably with the mademoiselles and that she and the deaf Scottish lady were great friends. She had taught Markie sign language so that she could "converse with her fluently...she always greets me with a smile, and so does the poor nervous lady who is in perpetual motion." However, when new arrivals, an English mother and daughter, criticized a letter defending slavery that Mrs. Tyler, the former President's wife, had written in response to a letter written by the Duchess of Sutherland, Markie was incensed. The woman exclaimed, "What an impertinent thing...it was for her to write in this way." Indeed, she did not believe that Mrs. Tyler wrote it because the style was so masculine, but thought that it could have been written by Harriet Beecher Stowe.

> By this time, I am sure that my face was a little pinkish and my feeling very much the same hue. With my best effort at dignity, I said in defense of my country – 'Women, I am sorry I have not read the letter, but from what I have heard, I should think it was an excellent piece of composition. It was not written by Mrs. Stowe, however...as her sentiments are diametrically opposite...from Mrs. Tyler.... I should think any highly educated American Lady was capable of doing such a thing.'

The woman's response was, "The Colonies of England were once trammeled by slavery – we saw the evil of it and the government purchased the slaves and set them free." Markie replied:

[††] The monument was finished in 1836.

But, as to the government of the United States buying the slaves & setting them free, it would be perfectly impossible; for you must know that our Legislature is composed of Slave-holders and free-Soilers – two strong parties – entirely opposed to each other – hence, on that subject they could never agree. Besides, the comparative hand-full of slaves, which you speak of, in your colonies, is a very different thing from the overpowering population in our southern states....It is impossible for you, or the Duchess of Sutherland, or any other person, living at the distance of four thousand miles from a country, to form any correct judgment on this subject. I am far from approving slavery – in the abstract and would do anything in my power to further the cause of colonization.

When Markie made it clear that the slaves were not native Americans, the English woman replied, "Well, then, how dreadful to think of these American traders going to Africa and tearing them away from their families." Markie responded defiantly that the Africans themselves sold their own people. "Dear Aunt said, 'I quite agree with my niece that slaves in America are not as bad off as white servants in England,' and thus, the conversation ended. The English lady before we parted, expressed herself with the greatest admiration for America and the ladies, and I retired from the field and from the parlor."

A few days later, Mrs. Miller called to Markie from across the room, "Mademoiselle Williams, here is a compatriot of yours, an American." When Markie discovered that the newcomer did not speak English, she spoke to her in French and learned that she was from Guatemala. Markie wrote that she had become accustomed to the ignorance of foreigners on the subject of America. She had been asked "trying questions..., 'Do Indians speak French or English?' Seeing a picture of an Indian chief, an English lady asked, 'Is that the way the gentlemen dress in America?' An Irish lady asked me if monkeys were not often seen in trees in America."

Apparently, by March 28th, Markie's birthday, all had been forgiven between her and the English ladies, because they, "Miss and Mrs. Robinson," invited her and Aunt Margaret to accompany them to Notre Dame Cathedral. Having made two unsuccessful attempts to see the cathedral, Markie was delighted. "I should never be tired of gazing on the towers of Notre Dame – they are so beautiful. The extreme antiquity of this church makes it more interesting to me than any church in Paris." When they arrived at the cathedral, they stood where they could view the procession of a number of priests as well as little boys and youths in gorgeous robes. "While I stood there a little flight of robins flew across the congregation.... I thought what a theme it would have been for a poet's pen.... I was enchanted with them."

On the way back to the pension, she saw the École de Médicament which "has an inexpressible charm for me [and] my countenance so brightened up.... I was so glad to see it on my *Birth Day!* What a delightful faculty of the mind is that of *association*. What hidden treasures of joy does it give to those who are wont to exercise it."

Markie continued to expand her circle of friends and joined them in sightseeing trips. When they went to the zoo, one of the women called out, "Here's a countryman of yours, Miss W.," pointing to a bear. Markie looked at the sign over the cage and saw that it was from Brazil and replied that she was not from South America. When she saw a bear from Louisiana, she said, "*Here* is a countryman of mine." They visited the "far famed Manufacture Nationale des Gobelins," and Markie wrote several pages exclaiming about it because she knew Aunt Lewis (Eleanor Custis Lewis) would enjoy hearing about it. She learned that this was where dyers of wool had been established since the 14th century. Here was the celebrated carpet manufactory that was made a royal establishment in 1604 by Maria de Medici in favor of Pierre DuPont who invented the process of finishing carpets. The tapestries hanging on the walls were so perfect that they appeared to be oil paintings. "I was enchanted beyond all description with my visit to the Gobelins."

On April 7 she wrote, "Madame la Baron de la Morondiere...has become quite a friend of mine.... The dear old Baroness and I have a tête-à-tête every evening and often play chess." The women's sobriquet for Markie was "La petite religieuse" because she would not attend their parties, the theater or dances. To her amusement, one evening in the parlor, she surprised all of them. Madame de la Morondiere showed the women a daguerreotype of Markie's brother, Laurence, saying that it was her nephew for whom she was going to choose a wife.

They crowded around to look at it and passed many compliments on his personal appearance.... I sat still and said not a word...one of the ladies said, 'Oh,

Mademoiselle W, you have not seen it....' 'Oh! yes I
have.... I am perfectly in love with him.'.... I seized
the portrait and pressed it to my lips to the utter
amazement of the whole party. Some of the ladies sat
aghast at the indiscretion, while Mrs. Miller...clasped
her hands, rolled her eyes, and told Madame de la
Morondiere in the greatest excitement,
....'Mademoiselle Williams l'a baisaient.' 'Est il
possible?' said Madame Morondiere, arising from her
chair and approaching me, 'Il faut l'epouser – il faut
l'epouser!' and I perfectly convulsed with laughter,
sank down in my chair amidst the astonishment of the
whole party.... My Aunt, much mortified at my
having been so indiscrete as to kiss the portrait of a
gentleman, whom I had never seen, in that public
manner...at length came to look at the wonderful
picture. As soon as she saw it she was but too happy to
acquit me of Mrs. Miller's scandal.... 'It is *my* nephew
– her own brother!' There was for a moment a dead
pause and then a burst of laughter. Mrs. Miller declared
she never had been more deceived...certainly, she
never had thought Miss W capable of doing what her
own eyes seemed to assure her she had done.

A few nights later when Madame La Baron de la Morondiere
visited her, Markie wrote, "There is something to me exceedingly
interesting in that old Lady – she quite wins my heart.... She is the first
friend I have made in Paris and I prize her kind attentions greatly." She
reminded Markie of her "dear Grandmother." They discussed religion,
history, current events and their own lives, and Markie often read to her.
This night from a French newspaper they learned that Harriet Beecher
Stowe had arrived in England and that "our celebrated author," Nathaniel
Hawthorne, had been appointed Consul at Liverpool.

In just three days, April 20, "in the evening we take our final
departure from the Pension and Mademoiselle Content for that of
Madame Gilbert, rue du Chateaubriand, where we join Uncle and Phillie
from whom we have been so long separated.... I had just begun to feel at
home and to make a few friends here – and now I must leave them." The
women and the staff at the pension expressed their regret at the departure
of Markie and Aunt Margaret. "My kind friend Mrs. Boadea has sent me
two volumes of the 'Life of Thomas Dermody' written by her father,
James Grant Raymond." Madame de la Morondiere revealed that at one

85

time she wrote articles for a French newspaper, and she presented some of her writing to Markie.

The Robinsons and Miss Fannie Woods invited Markie and Phillie to join them on a visit to the Palace of Versailles on their last day at the pension. Markie especially enjoyed the gardens and fastened a sprig of yew and flowers to a page in her diary. "I saw among [the flowers], here and there, my favorite little star flower, the dandelion, which is so sweetly associated in my mind with the dear old lawn at Tudor.... How delighted dear Aunt Custis (Mrs. George Washington Park Custis) would have been to revel among the cowslips." In the palace, she sat in the chair at the desk of the secretary of Louis XIV and wrote a paragraph in her notebook. She also sat in one of the chairs in the boudoir of Marie Antoinette and took a thread of green silk from the arm for a keepsake. In another room, she noticed the likeness of the Compte de Custine "who I heard grandmother say sent the beautiful set of Sèvres China, now in the drawing room at Tudor Place, to General and Grandmama Washington." When the women saw the painting, "A Siege of Yorktown, Generals Rochambeau and Washington Giving the Last Orders for Attack," they all at once asked, "Which is Washington?" Markie proudly pointed to General Washington.

That evening, the family moved to the new apartment at Miss Gilbert's on rue Chateaubriant. Markie was pleased with the new quarters, writing that the gem of her room was a writing table. She enjoyed her dinner companions and immediately made friends. She was invited to go on walks and sightseeing, but when the first party was held, she again explained that she did not approve of parties, theaters, dancing or card playing. She was disgusted with a young clergyman who amused the group with card tricks. However, when she and Phillie went with Monsieur and Madame Mollard to see an exhibition of Mesmerism[‡‡] in the Palais, Markie commented that "it fills me with wonder and amazement." After "the Mesmeriser had given a lecture...he cast his eyes around the room and asked who would like to try its effect...presently, to my utter amazement, he asked me. No Monsieur! I said most emphatically." She was shocked by the ladies who accepted. "I suffered agonies looking at them. My face was one continued blush."

[‡‡] Franz Friedrich Anton Mesmer, an 18th century Austrian physician, was known for inducing a trancelike state, called mesmerism, an early forerunner of hypnosis.

May 7, "This day last year, I wrote a long letter to my dear friend the Doctor recalling to his memory and mine the fifth anniversary of this day sacred to the memory of our parting. How vividly do I recall the letter that I wrote as I sat in the dining room at dear old Tudor with a little vase of Lilly of the Valleys before me...." May 14, "This is perhaps the last Saturday evening we shall spend in Paris. Oh, it is not possible. I cannot bear to think of it." Except for weekly parties, Markie had thoroughly enjoyed her stay at Miss Gilbert's. Her companions had helped her with French, invited her to go sightseeing, were interesting conversationalists, and did special favors for her such as her next door neighbors who put fresh flowers in front of her door each day. Her aunt and uncle couldn't have been more considerate. "Dear Phillie and I have been so happy together – she is so *ever bright*! She reminds me of a little 'Butter Cup.'" A few days later,

> My heart has been crushed by the sudden and mournful intelligence of the death of my dear, dear Aunt Custis (Mrs. George Washington Parke Custis of Arlington House) – it is utterly impossible for me to realize it.... Her Christian example was a Beacon Light to me.... We loved the same books – we dearly loved flowers, we loved them passionately as others love them not...with her I always felt at home.... In her last letter, she wrote, 'Shall I be here to see you, when you return....' Alas! how ominous, but God's will be done.

The next we hear from Markie, she has departed France from La Havre and arrived in London, England. A loose page dated June 20, 1853, is titled, "A Day At Hampton Court."[4] Her friend, Mrs. Skinner, whose husband had been killed at Waterloo, had an apartment there, and invited Markie to stay a week in Henry VIII's favorite palace. She regretted that she could stay only one day having already booked her passage to the United States. After seeing the galleries and gardens, she and Mrs. Skinner had a dinner that Markie recorded: a joint of mutton, the finest ham, a dish of potatoes, cauliflower with celery, gooseberry tart, Cheshire cheese, with the most tempting little crackers, and ginger wine. She was struck with the simplicity of everything, the style of serving that could not have been exceeded, and the excellence of the food prepared in a kitchen with shelves filled with copper, there for generations. "That day was charming and one ever to be remembered."

The next diary that we have begins on July 13, aboard the ship *Northumberland.*

In a day or two we shall have been three weeks at sea....How on earth – or on sea – I have ever existed as long as I have, in the midst of such utter uncongeniality is to me an indefinable fact.... I am sure after this voyage, I shall feel equal to anything. I might get up a 'Sir John Franklin expedition'[§§] all by myself. Most of the time has been spent by poor Mrs. Harris and me in the quiet seclusion of our berths. When I've been well enough,   Mr. Weigel has kindly assisted me on deck where we would   walk or sit and study French together or he would teach me German. I retain at this moment the very same opinion of every one which I formed at first.

A week later, for two days and nights, dreadful storms of wind and rain, with unabated fury, caused the ship to toss and roll. When the storm subsided on the third day, Markie and her constant companion, Mr. Weigel, joined other passengers in the veranda and sat in the stern of the ship. They looked out at the foaming billows which bounded mountain high, all the time holding fast to the side of the ship to keep their seats. They passed the afternoon singing *Cheer Boys Cheer* and other songs. "I even consented for the benefit of our homesick, heartsick party to give them *'Love Not'*[***] and *'Oft In the Stilly Night.'*"[†††]

On July 24, she wrote:

Our Fourth Sunday at Sea – 'Tis a lovely sunny day. The benches and chairs were placed in congregation attitude on deck, and the Star Spangled Banner was thrown over the Capstan, beside which Mr. Crane stood with head uncovered.... Mrs. Crane, Mrs. Woods and myself...formed the principal part of the Choir.... The grouping of emigrants with heads uncovered and all standing in an attitude of respect, presented a scene most interesting. Young mothers with babies at their breast and little children standing around together with

---

[§§] Sir John Franklin was a British Rear Admiral who organized expeditions to explore the Artic and the Northwest Passage.
[***] Caroline Elizabeth Sarah Norton (1808-1877), English writer.
[†††] *National Airs* (1815), Thomas Moore (1779-1852), Irish poet.

old men and women formed altogether a picture replete with beauty, to an artistic eye.

In the evening when Markie and Mr. Weigel walked on deck, she admired the view.

> The ocean is so beautifully calm and the stars vie with each other in their brilliancy. I recall the sweet lines of Byron 'Blue the sky spreads like an ocean, hung on high....' As I counted over the constellations so familiar to my eyes, my mind went back to the days of childhood when I traced them out upon the maps and to later days when the heart was as much engaged as the eyes in finding out their beauties.... They seemed a link, how beautiful and bright a link, between my native land and me. The emigrants sang many pretty sacred choruses which greatly enhanced the agreeableness of the evening.

July 27, "A dense fog for the past two days and nights – the alarm bell ringing constantly.... Captain Lord is in a terrible humor – says there must be a Jonah on board." The sea was dreadfully rough the next afternoon. Markie sat on the sofa in the dining room with Mr. Weigel learning the German alphabet. She began reading the *History of the Huguenots*, having finished reading *Uncle Tom's Cabin* by Harriet Beecher Stowe and *The Spy* by James Fennimore Cooper. She felt that some of the characters in *Uncle Tom's Cabin* were remarkably well drawn, especially the Negro characters. Some of them, however, she thought were overdrawn. Some pages in it made her love Mrs. Stowe. "Others made me convulsed with laughter and some I could not read and only felt like throwing from my hand never to see them again." It is indicative of the length and tediousness of the voyage that Markie finally read this book.

Markie's health required that she walk daily, and Mr. Weigel always appeared immediately after breakfast to accompany her. Afterwards they taught each other languages or translated and read *Graziella*. But she enjoyed more conversing with Mr. Crane on various subjects of mutual interest. She found him reading Goldsmith's poems and they read together several pieces, commenting on their beauty. "It was delightful for me to see a Book of Poems, and I read *The Traveller*[‡‡‡] as I would have greeted an old friend. How truly applicable now are the lines which were once quoted to me by one most dearly loved."

My heart untravelled fondly turns to home
To thee 'my Brother' turns with ceaseless pain,
And drags at each remove a lengthening chain.

[My heart untravel'd fondly turns to thee;
Still to my brother turns with ceaseless pain,
And drags at each remove a lengthening chain.]

"How much more pleasant and profitable my interview this evening than ordinarily…. " She recorded that Mr.Crane said that in the time of William the Conqueror, the law was to put out all the fires at eight o'clock. William, being a French King, the words were couvrefeu [covering of the fire], hence the origin of the English word curfew.

This has been a day (August 6) of interesting incidents; the first of which was the appearance of a butterfly on deck. Oh! Sweet harbinger of land, never did thy soft wings seem to me so beautiful – stay with us tiny insect of the air, for thou art come from my loved, my native land that land I so long to see again. Henceforth, butterflies shall hold a place in my affections which they never possessed before….

About eleven o'clock, a dismasted ship was seen, and the Captain said it was a ship in distress. As soon as the boat came along side, the Captain asked what was the matter to which a young Scotsman replied that he needed provisions. The passengers aboard the *Northumberland* were touched with compassion, but the Captain said that he could give them only lard, matches and medicines because his ship would be out of provisions if a storm arose. "We looked at the poor *Julia* as long as she was in our sight and gave her our warm, compassionate wishes in lieu of something more substantial."

Markie went to the dining room expecting a Church service, but finding none, she joined Mr. and Mrs. Crane. Together, they read from

---

[‡‡‡] *The Traveller, A Prospect of Society,*(1765) by Oliver Goldsmith (1730-1874), Anglo-Irish playwright, novelist, poet and essayist.

90

her prayer book. "Certainly, the most congenial hours I have passed on board this ship have been in their society. I lent them my book of extracts to read Mrs. Sigourney's lines on Arlington House."[§§§]

When it was announced that passengers were invited to see a Portuguese Man of War, Markie, not having heard the term before, took it literally. "Oh! Captain, suppose it should be an American man of war and my Brother Harrie (brother-in-law, John Henry Upshur) should be on board.... The Captain laughed heartily, and I saw there was something wrong, but did not dream of the extent of my ignorance until" she saw one being exhibited on deck. "I roared (as Kate would say) at my droll mistake and allowed those around me to enjoy the joke."

> The Captain...availed himself of the opportunity to enter upon a conversation, the text of which was German passengers or what he called 'Dutchmen.' He wished me to understand that Germans were deceitful.... As for Mr. W., he thought it was very likely pitch and toss whether he would be a second class or a steerage passenger. He was very certain he would not have been an associate of mine on land and he wondered what my friends would think of him. I said, 'Captain, I am much indebted for your warning as I suppose you mean it as such. Mr. W. always conducts himself genteelly in my society and I hear nothing to the contrary.... He is intelligent and exceedingly kind to me, and although I have perception enough to see that he does not move in the circle of society that I do, I shall still be kind to him and not discourage altogether his attentions.'

As she meditated in her berth on the evening's conversation, she reproached herself for encouraging Mr. Weigel, but she felt it would be cruel for her to avoid him. She reminisced about what a source of pleasure her painting had been. "I amused myself taking the likeness of Mr. W. at his particular request. What pains did he always bestow on his toilette the days I devoted to painting...and then that new crimson vest which the Captain used to laugh at" and tell him he was mistaken if he

---

[§§§] Lydia Huntley Sigourney (1791-1865), American poet, friend of Markie's great uncle, George Washington Parke Custis, who built Arlington House.

thought it would win her heart. "And then the London Tower Beefeaters that I used to amuse them all by painting!"

On August 9, at about 4:00 o'clock in the morning, Markie was awakened by Mr. Crane's shouting, "The Pilot! The Pilot!" She hurriedly dressed and ran up on deck where the Captain assisted her up the steps behind the Wheel House. The pilot at this moment sprang on board and soon joined the Captain, Mr. and Mrs. Crane and Markie behind the Wheel House. They learned that there was a great deal of yellow fever in New York, that the weather was intensely warm, and that hundreds were dying in the streets from the heat.

The next morning, Markie arose in time to see the sunrise and was inspired to write what she called a *collection of words*:

> Sunrise at Sea
> First, golden tinted clouds appeared
> As t'were to form a starry diadem
> For the Monarch of the Day,
> Who gently merged from the blue Sea
> To win his crown.
> The sapphire orb eclipsed
> The tiny shadowy clouds,
> In his refulgent glory,
> And burst in glittering radiance
> On the ocean world.

A pilot boat came along side of the ship and sent up New York newspapers. "As I looked over the political news, I felt as Rip Van Winkle must have felt." The administration had changed, and she did not see any names familiar to her. An article about the sale of Mount Vernon to speculators grieved her. The same article deprecated the State of Virginia for the want of respect shown to her great men. "We are wont to follow the example of Europeans in most things; why not in this admirable trait?"

> August 11, Just seven weeks today since we left London and not yet in sight of land...as I looked around on all the familiar faces with whom I had been so long associated and the old ship which has borne us safely over so many thousand of miles...the little   sea birds in our course, the infinitely spacious ocean, and

the glorious sunset, I could not but breathe a sigh of regret.

> I never said the word farewell
> But with an utterance faint and broken
> A heartsick longing for the time
> When it should never more be spoken.

Markie wrote the first part of her diary for August 12 while sitting on deck. "The last shades of evening are departing and I think I perceive a misty bank of clouds. 'Yes!' said the Pilot, 'that is land' and he gave orders to the sailors to throw out the lead line." For fully an hour "if not two" Markie sat with her face toward the light as if spellbound. When the ship arrived at the Sandy Hook Light House it anchored. Later, she wrote that when she noticed that all of the other women had left, she immediately arose to leave. "Mr. W. implored me to stay...threw himself at my feet, seizing passionately my hand, pressing it to his lips. I am sure the Captain at least saw him. I was really provoked and walked in silence to my room, he accompanying and bidding me good night."

> This morning, (August 13) we awoke in full view of the green
> shore of New Jersey and the Hills of Navesink.^{****}
> Never shall I forget the joyous impression as I stepped
> on deck and once more, in the full light of day and a
> brilliant sun, beheld my Native Land. My heart rose in
> gratitude to God, and these expressive lines of Walter
> Scott burst from my lips,

> > Breathes there a man, with soul so dead,
> > Who never to himself hath said,
> > *This is my own, my native Land!*

She turned to Mr. Weigel and asked, "How do you like America?" Then she asked the same question of other passengers. "They all said it was a beautiful country." A pilot boat soon came along the side of *Northumberland* and towed it into the New York harbor. Markie wrote that she did not feel "that rapture I thought I should feel. I wondered who would meet me...what would be the news from home...what should I do

---

^{****} *Twin Lights of the Navesink Highlands, New Jersey,* once the brightest lighthouse on the Atlantic Coast, was built in 1828.

with Mr. Weigel?" In a melancholy mood, she took a seat by Mr. and Mrs. Crane who gave her consolation and advice with regard to Mr. W. and expressed sympathy for him. Although she avoided looking at Mr. W., he caught her eye and immediately took a seat beside her. However, there was a reserve and he scarcely spoke.

"Thus passed the day – While sitting on the bench in front of the Wheel House, I saw a little German woman come out all dressed in one of her national costumes all ready to Land." Markie thought that there was something so quaint about her, that she sketched her likeness which Mrs. Crane admired. Markie gave it to her as a souvenir, and then sketched another for herself. Finally, the Health Officer came aboard.

> This over, we departed for the Haven where we would be. New York looked so new after coming from the old countries. The Harbor was filled with steamboats and ships. How beautiful the green grass and the trees looked. I thought that I could never see enough of them, and how strange to see so many objects in one view. How we will appreciate our blessings after such a respite.

---

[1] The Upshur-Brown family papers, a private collection in Richmond, VA.

[2] Unless otherwise noted, information in this chapter came from MCW Diaries A, B, C, or D, September 13, 1852, to August 13, 1853, Tudor Place Archives, MS-6. When necessary for clarity of quotations, spelling and punctuation have been corrected.

[3] Ltr., MCP to MCW, October 4, 1852, TP Archives, MS-6(1-6).

[4] Loose diary page titled, "A Day at Hampton Court, June 20, 1853, Martha Custis Williams Collection, MA 1045(1), The Pierpont Morgan Library, New York.

Katherine Alicia Williams Upshur
"Kate"

John Henry Upshur

Robert E. Lee

Columbia Williams Upshur
"Lum"

All photos this page courtesy of Tudor Place Historic House and Garden

Laurence Abert Williams
"Lolo"

Sarah Law Williams
"Sallie"

Markie with nieces Kate and
Gertrude Upshur

Engagement brooch that
Laurence gave Sallie

All photos this page courtesy of Tudor Place Historic House and Garden

Samuel Powhatan Carter
Photo courtesy of
Roger D. Hunt Coll.
U.S. Army Military
History Insititute

Martha Custis Williams
Photo courtesy of
Tudor Place Historic
House and Garden

Martha Custis Williams Carter

Samuel Powhatan Carter

At about the time of their marriage
Photos courtesy of Tudor Place Historic House and Garden

CHAPTER 6

WITH GEORGE WASHINGTON PARKE CUSTIS

Newly arrived home after her year in Europe, Markie hoped to pursue the study of art. A letter from Robert E. Lee in early September probably changed her course. After the death of his wife in May, George Washington Parke Custis had gone to West Point to stay with the Lee family. Lee, who was Superintendent of the Military Academy, wrote to Markie:

> You are aware that your Uncle C_____ is now with us. You will be pleased to learn I know that his health is quite restored, & that he seems cheered & interested by the new scenes around him. I fear however that he will soon tire of the monotony of our life & wish to return to his home. I cannot bear the idea of his living there alone & yet can do nothing to remedy it.[1]

Whoever first proposed that Markie should go to live with her great-uncle, whether Markie herself or some other member of the family, she felt she must.

> I feel it my duty to stay with dear Uncle if he desires it, tho' it entirely frustrates my plans for this winter. I had quite set my heart on taking painting lessons or drawing, but it would be impossible to get a teacher to come so far from Town to give them to me. I will put it off till a more convenient season.[2]

On October 27, the Arlington carriage came to Tudor Place for Markie and proceeded to a bookstore in Washington where Mr. Custis was waiting for her. Meeting for the first time since her return from Europe, she and her great-uncle discussed all that had happened since they were last together, getting more and more depressed. As they approached the house, Markie's tears started to fall, and when she entered the parlor, she "gave vent in bitter tears and sobs."[3] Everything in the house reminded her of her beloved great-aunt – the old green-covered Bible, her chair, her servants.

> When I went down stairs and took her seat at the table – when the evening candles were lit & the cheerful fire blazed and her vacant chair was before me the tears

came fast in my eyes, but, I felt that I ought to be cheerful, and I banished my mind to foreign Lands and talked of what I had there seen & of my adventures by land & sea. Uncle seemed interested. He listened with fixed attention & ever & anon interrupted me by questions. I was glad to have succeeded in diverting his mind & I felt happier.[4]

A few days later, Markie set out to visit her great-aunt's grave:

I had not yet been to the grave – I had only an idea of what direction it was in, by the motion of Nurse's hand as she spoke of it. It was a lovely day – such a day as my dear Aunt would have been in the garden with her flowers. I had not been in the garden – though I had seen the bright crysanthemums peeping through the fence & I wondered how they could be so bright now. But, I could hesitate no longer, I walked slowly toward the old black gate, wh opens to that Labyrinth of roses, Ivy & jessamin – and as I plucked the roses to strew upon her grave her living image came before me and I wept. I went around & looked on all the familiar flowers. I felt that I was greeting a circle of old friends some of whom had departed. They were all cast down. It seemed right they should be, for the one who had supported them with her care was no longer there to sustain them. I wended my way with my sweet tokens of love along the road until seeing a little path leading out of the main road in the direction where I supposed the grave to be I flowed its course. It conducted me to that hallowed spot – with a little wreath of Immortel in one hand and some lovely flowers loosely gathered in the other I stood and wept beside the green mound wh marked the last resting place [of] one of my best & dearest friends. I wept & did not refrain from weeping for I thought tears were but a small tribute of my deep affection. They were selfish tears I know. I did not weep for her, for I knew that her gentle spirit had fled to a sphere far more congenial than the one it had occupied. I knew that in her Savior's arms she rested. But, I wept for myself and those who loved her as I did.[5]

Markie's love of flowers and sentimentality were always intertwined. One early June day, she put down these thoughts:

> No fairer day ever dawned than this one – though I felt languid & unlike exertion, I was tempted to go into the garden and gather a bouquet of flowers. Among damask roses and Ivy Leaves, I lose all consciousness of self and I remained for a long time, enjoying these "precious relics of a lost Eden" & then came to the House, to decorate the glasses in the parlor. What a pure, exalted pleasure it is to arrange flowers! I sometimes wonder how some persons can pass through this dreary world, without the joy which flowers bring. I never regret the moments I spend, in culling & arranging them. I am the happier for it! Flowers seem to me like <u>friends</u>; and there are times, when I feel as if they were the only things on earth with wh I find congeniality. I plucked a white rose and took it out to my dear Aunt Custis' grave.[6]

She and Mrs. Custis had shared this interest along with their strong religious faith, and it was a great bond between them.

> Another time, strolling with a young man:

> ...we saw the blue forget-me-not – that sweet little wild-flower, wh I love so much ... stooped to pluck them & very naturally, offered what we had, to each other – making them more valuable, by means of <u>exchange</u>. This little piece of sentiment ere we had proceeded twenty paces from the House, was only the commencement of a series of delicate little attentions during the Promenade. After our return to the Hill, I went with him in the garden & made him a pretty bouquet as a Trophy of Arlington which he seemed to prize beyond measure.[7]

And again: "Mr. P. transferred to my hand, a little bouquet of Trailing Arbutus, which he had been all the while holding, and which he told me he had gathered for me in the woods. This most favorite wildflower, presented by a favorite friend, charmed me. ...Mr. P. says he likes to see me on the subject of flowers for then I <u>wake up</u>."[8]

For the next four years, Markie would spend most of her time at Arlington, although she did return frequently to Tudor Place for long visits. At the same time she was still supervising her brother Orton's education. She had consulted Robert E. Lee about where to send him, and hearing good reports about the Episcopal High School, near Alexandria, enrolled him there. Thus he was able to visit her often at Arlington.[9]

The diary that Markie kept while at Arlington, she said, was designed "principally to put down the sayings & doings of my much loved & admired Uncle, wh in after days when he is gone, may be referred to with pleasure."[10] Regarding Mr. Custis' daily routine, Markie noted:

> Uncle is pretty regular in his movements. He reads & talks for some time after breakfast – then goes in his painting room where I generally go & sit with him some time. Then, he goes to the farm & returns about 1 o'clock. After dinner he takes his coffee goes in to the painting room & then to the farm again. When he returns he smokes a segar & then comes in the parlor for the evening.[11]

Mr. Custis often regaled Markie and his visitors with historical tales and reminiscences of George Washington, which Markie faithfully recorded, sometimes noting that she had now heard the story in question many times. They also discussed current affairs, taking note of the arrival in Japan of the Perry expedition (which Markie's brother-in-law, John Henry Upshur, was a member of), and the looming Crimean War. In time, Markie would note the safe return of Upshur, grateful "for my poor Sister's return of happiness." Regarding the Crimean War, she noted:

> Another article from the London Times, describes in heart-rending language the sufferings of the British Troops in the Crimea and all it appears owing to mismanagement and reckless conduct, of the "Higher Powers."

> So, do monarchal [sic] governments, trample down the rights of their fellow men. How does this contrast with the humanity of our own government from its primeval date, in times of war.[12]

But Markie's main preoccupation during her stay at Arlington was the state of her great-uncle's soul. When she first arrived, she was especially sad because she missed her great-aunt's custom of having morning and evening prayers for the assembled household. "Uncle said nothing about my undertaking this duty and I did not like to propose it."[13] Not until March 1854 did she work up the courage to propose them.

> During all my sojourn here, I have not had morning & evening prayers. In the first place, when I first came, the recollection of my dearest Aunt was so vivid, that I did not feel as if I could conduct the service. Then, I felt that if it was agreeable to Uncle he would ask me to do so, especially, as I had so often had Prayers, when dear Aunt was ill, at her request. Morning & evening have I looked longingly at the Books, and my conscience has at times smote me for neglecting this duty, but, then, a feeling of delicacy prevented my making any suggestion. For several days past I have been meditating how I should broach the subject. To-night, just as I was coming to bed, while arranging the Books, it again occurred to me – Shall I ask now, I thought, or put it off till a more convenient season? The answer came to me 'Put not off for to-morrow what can be done to-day.' The impulse was strong and I knew it was good & I obeyed. Uncle, I said, I miss our morning & evening prayers – won't you have Prayers as we used to have? He sighed and said 'Ah, my dear, I do not feel like doing anything of that kind. I'm in no spirits for that – or anything else – but, I have no objection to your having them.' 'Well, may I commence to-morrow? I said. I think as to-morrow [is] Saturday, you had better wait till Sunday. You ought never to commence anything on the last of the week. I could not help smiling at the originality of the idea & yet it was a sad smile, for it convinced me that he looked upon it only as a <u>duty</u> & not a pleasure. Ah! I thought, Uncle, we may not live till Sunday. We may put off other things, but not God's bidding. But, I only answered – very well, then, Uncle, <u>Sunday morning</u>! And giving him a kiss on his venerable Head, said good night & retired with a light conscience. Oh! That I had done this sooner. This now my self-reproach.

<u>Procrastination</u> thou art my crying sin! God forgive me
and bless my future efforts.[14]

Although Mr. Custis was certainly a believer, attended church,
and often had Markie read from the Bible or other works such as books
of sermons on Sunday, he was not the Christian that Markie's high
standards expected. He often fell asleep during her readings, to her great
consternation. In her usual way, any small interest he showed in the
"improving" literature she placed before him caused her extreme
happiness. Then, when he didn't show the piety she expected, especially
on Sundays, she was in the depths of depression. One Sunday she wrote:

> I have this evening made a resolution to retire to my
> room every evening at twilight to pray especially for
> his conversion. It grieves my heart to see him going
> down to the grave without a saving belief in his Savior.
> Often, too, I think of my Brothers & other members of
> our dear family who are yet without our Holy
> Communion. They too, shall have my warm, my
> fervent prayers.[15]

Markie was keen to record details about her great-uncle's habits
and personality.

> Hereafter, when dear Uncle shall have passed away
> from our midst, as in the course of nature he must do –
> tho' even the thought of so sad an event bring a <u>tear</u> –
> with what pleasure, shall those of his nearest relatives
> who remain, peruse these little portraitures wh bring
> his life-like image before them.

> Recording as I am all that is remarkable, in the daily
> life & conversation of my dear Uncle Custis, whose
> talents & virtues & social position, are so distinguished
> in the world, I must not omit to note a striking
> characteristic:

> Upon my return to Arlington a week or two since…I
> saw upon the centre table a large collection of little
> bundles of business papers, with loose bills &e
> scattered all about them. What is all this, said I, Uncle?
> "Oh! Those my dear, he replied, are some very
> valuable papers – <u>exceedingly valuable</u>. I had a visit

100

the other day, from Mr. Nelson, from my lower estates
& these are the papers he brought me." There they had
been laying for several days – <u>two</u>, at least. If they are
so valuable, I said, Uncle, had you not better put them
away – "Yes, my dear, he said I wish you would take
them up in your room & keep them for me – I am
going to send them to Robert Lee."

This utter carelessness of business matters, was so
perfectly characteristic.[16]

Mr. Custis had many visitors who came to talk to him about his
distinguished grandparents.   On occasion, if distinguished visitors were
expected, there would be great preparations.   One day, Lord and Lady
Napier* were expected. Although they never came,

> ...from an early hour a grand revolution was going on
> downstairs with Cousin Mary [Mrs. Robert E. Lee] at
> their head. Henry & Percy & Billy & George & Mary
> Anne & Agnes & Marselina were all stirring about with
> scrubbing brushes, brooms &e &e. I dressed my pretty
> little hanging basket with flowers & suspended it in the
> parlor window and arranged the books & pictures.
>
> Uncle's toilette was immense – that is, he put on a
> clean shirt out of the regular time – assumed his new
> coast vest & pants & consented at my request to wear a
> black silk cravat.   I trimmed his moustache on the
> occasion....
>
> Cousin Mary also, made great exertions in the dressing
> line & I am sure felt herself <u>en grande toilette</u>, when
> she put on her little Paris cap & threw around her, her
> Mexican scarf, wh suited well with her black silk dress
> – but, still I don't think it would ever have occurred to
> Lady Napier than any <u>effort</u> had been expended on her
> costume.[17]

---

* Francis, 10th Lord Napier (1819-1898) was a Scottish diplomat and the
British Minister to the United States from 1857 to 1859. From
www.wikipedia.org.

Mr. Custis was always delighted to reminisce about life at Mount Vernon and in New York and Philadelphia during the Washington presidency. He was also always eager to show off his grand paintings of Revolutionary scenes. This rather embarrassed Markie:

> [W]e went into the Studio and stood before that grand effort of genius which Uncle is now executing – the Battle of Trenton. Dear Uncle! It is wonderful to see how deluded he can be, about his pictures. He told Mr. B this evening, that the horse in Powell's Picture of the discovery of the Mississippi was not to be compared with his horses, &e &e. Praised his own genius and industry stood before the Picture with all the pride and pleasure of a most accomplished artist. Sometimes I feel almost tempted to tell Uncle that every one does not think of his pictures as he does, but, then, I remember his age and think it is all very well, if it is a source of gratification to him.[18]

A frequent visitor to Arlington was Benjamin Perley Poore, who was a popular newspaper correspondent, editor, and author. At this time, 1854, he was newly arrived in Washington as a correspondent for a Boston newspaper. Still in his 30s, he had already published lives of Louis Phillippe and Napoleon Bonaparte. As a student of history, he enjoyed coming to Arlington and talking to Mr. Custis about his memories of the great figures of the Revolution. Markie also enjoyed his company:

> This evening Mr. Ben Perley Poore ... brought us his life of Napoleon. We had a charming conversation about Paris &e &e.... [H]e agreed, before he left, to come over & take breakfast with us one morning ere long – and when he left, he begged me to remember the Poore, wh I told him I would be charitable enough to do.[19]

Markie's sojourn at Arlington provides some insights into the development of her thoughts on slavery. Although she never mentioned it specifically, these years just before the Civil War were a time of great national debate about the issue. At Arlington, the issue was close and personal. George Washington Parke Custis had about 70 slaves (at Arlington – he had more on other plantations) at this time, many of whom had little or no occupation, as he no longer farmed his land much.

Markie had close contact with many of the "servants," as she tried to continue her great-aunt's duties toward all the residents of Arlington.

It had been Mrs. Custis' habit to educate the slaves at least in religion – to read to them from the Bible and even to teach the younger slaves to read so that they could read it for themselves. As Mr. Custis noted to Markie, this was technically against the law:

> Do you know, said he in a half serious half playful manner, that it is my duty [to] confine you a month in jail, in accordance with the laws of the state? – but, surely, he continued, it can never be wrong to teach them that Holy Book. No, Markie, I won't put you in jail. I want you here with me too much. I am sure I could not spare you.[20]

While in Europe, Markie often defended slavery against the criticism of the Europeans, but now at Arlington she was quite taken aback by some of her great-uncle's opinions:

> To-day, Uncle was speaking of the ignorance of Irish Overseers & said when his overseer first came here, "he looked upon & associated with the Negroes as if they were quite on a par with himself." Yes, said he, "he was really as ignorant as that." I could not help smiling at the innocence with wh Uncle made this remark wh would in Europe have been thought quite criminal. I mentally answered I do not at all doubt the fact that he was on a par with them. Evidently, the difference was not in education unless it preponderated on the side of the Blacks – doubtless, the soul of one is not more valuable in God's eyes than the other – then, where do they so materially differ except in the tint & texture of their complection? But, I was not disposed for argument.[21]

On another occasion, Abel Upshur (who later married Markie's sister Columbia) came to visit and "riveted" Markie with descriptions of his visit to a "slave warehouse" in Richmond,

> where the poor slaves were brought up & sold like horses or cattle – made to walk up and down to show the strength of their limbs &e &e and the women too

103

treated with quite as little delicacy.... I said Mrs. Stowe's pen could not be employed too severely on this despicable inhumane practice. Uncle also agreed that it was very offensive. Alas! Alas! The evils of slavery. Where will they cease?[22]

Markie wrote a piece on slavery, perhaps intended for publication, in which she expanded some of her thoughts, ending up, however, with the conclusion that slavery was an insoluble problem. She started out with an anecdote about a freedman in Philadelphia who was asked whether a recently freed slave would get along well there. He said yes, because he knew the person to be well brought up, polite, and would not aim to something she could not attain. From there she went on, rather illogically, to a homily to slaves to be content with their lot.

> My dear people, I full well know, that you have not everything in this world wh you may desire.... You are aware, that you are but one, out of a hundred or more, who all have to be provided for out of your master's purse.... It is a great charge! It is an awful responsibility! Think of it! Just reflect on it a little while and tell me if you have no sympathy for your master – and if you would not rather be in your own position, humble and dependent as it is – though not without its comforts and its little pleasures, if you would but acknowledge and make the best of them – than in his. Why! Remember – he is to be sure, in one respect, a master, but, in another and a far more comprehensive sense, he is a slave – a slave to your interests....

> You may ask, why, then, if slavery is such a curse to the slave-holder – why if it is considered as such an evil, do you continue to keep us in bondage – why do you not set us free?

Here Markie falls back on an economic argument, that most slaveholders had inherited their slaves, and if they gave them up would put themselves in a state of poverty, and surprisingly, manages to say, "While we live in this world, it is the maxim of the world to be just to ourselves, that is where injustice to others, is not thus involved, which in this instance we do not believe is the case." Also, freeing slaves without provision for their upkeep would be irresponsible to the community.

No, it is my firm conviction that slaves had better remain in a state of slavery. I speak not in reference to their masters, for I believe it is never to their advantage or to their comfort or pleasure, that it shd be so – but, as far as the Slave is concerned I really do think, it is infinitely better for him, temporally & spiritually, to remain in a state of bondage – that is, of course, if they are cared for as servants ought to be.[23]

In keeping with her very strict ideas of what was proper to do on a Sunday, Markie often visited the slave cabins to read the Bible or other improving works to them. Soon after her arrival at Arlington in October 1853 she went to see Mammy and Aunt Ellenor. Mammy (whose real name was Judy) was about 75 and very feeble. She missed Mrs. Custis very much, so she and Markie commiserated on their loss. Markie contrasted the two servants: Aunt Ellenor (also called Nurse) was "the personification of pomposity" whereas Mammy was "the picture of humility & meekness." Aunt Ellenor:

...received me with a great deal of air & manner & putting a chair to the fire begged me to sit down – she was very glad to see me – she wanted to tell me all about Mistress [Mrs. Custis].... Sadly & with tearful eyes I listened. She told me, that only two days before her death, she had gone in the garden to have some flowers planted...[Nurse] had gone to [re]monstrate with her on the impropriety of staying there.... Coming from anybody but Nurse this would have seemed a very dictatorial tone for a servant to assume towards her Mistress, but, Nurse was a privileged character and always prided herself on her superior wisdom and the right she possessed of speaking just as she chose to any of the family. The Queen of Ethiopia could not display more pompous dignity in her mien than did said "Nurse."[24]

Every day, when she was able, Markie visited some of the older or ailing slaves.

This sunny, calm day, rendered my walk of duty this morning, more agreeable than the same exercise yesterday. I had intended to make my daily visit to poor "Uncle Gid," but, the ground being frozen & the walking better than it has been for a long time, I decided to wend my way first to the farm, where I have not been for a long time. So bundling myself up in a shawl & a cloak, furs & head wrapping, with my brown straw hat & black veil to crown all (equipped, as Cousin Mary says, for a tour to Noverzembla [Novaya Zemlya, Russia] I started forth prayer-book & tracts in hand & made my first visit to old Austin Grey.[25]

On Sunday afternoon, services were held in the old schoolhouse at Arlington, mostly for the slaves, but others attended as well. Almost always, Markie and Mr. Custis were there. These services were run by young theological students from the nearby Episcopal Seminary, which had been founded by Mrs. Custis' cousin, Bishop Meade, during the great revival of the 1830s.

On the first Sunday after her return to Arlington, Markie rode to the schoolhouse with a large contingent to take care of her, for it was the first time she had been on a horse since her bad riding accident before going to Europe.

[D]ear Orton walked beside me all the way expressing great care & anxiety lest I should fall. Uncle flanked off by himself on foot and my cortege was formed of a troop of black boys among whom were Perry & George my especial escorts. Arrived at the old School House, Bunnie seemed quite proud of the manly assistance he rendered me in dismounting. I was glad on entering to find the colored congregation (made up almost entirely of Uncle's Negroes) so large.... I felt that my soul might be more benefited there, than in the gorgeous edifices of Paris. I could but compare the probable amount of good done in this very very humble room, to that effected in the Church of St. Genevieve the exquisite structure & decorations of wh cost $5,000,000.[26]

The slaves remembered Markie as well. Two of the daughters of Thornton and Selina Gray, who were very young at the time of Markie's residence, remembered her as "a very pretty and attractive girl." One of them said she used to imitate Markie and the way she rolled her eyes when she came down in the morning, skirts billowing out, and said

"Good morning, Cousin Robbie" to General Lee. The Lee sons saw the young slave girl doing this imitation, and afterwards often came to her and asked: "Annie, show us how Miss Martha Williams rolls her eyes when she says 'Good morning, Cousin Robbie.'"[27]

Markie developed the idea during her sojourn with George Washington Parke Custis that perhaps she might make some money by writing for publication, like her friend Blanche Berard. Blanche, who came to visit her at Arlington in April of 1856, had encouraged Markie to do something of the sort with her journal from Europe. The following year, Markie asked her good friend Dr. Flint's advice. He discouraged her, saying that it would be difficult and she would not make much from it. This really depressed her, but nevertheless, she determined to try her luck. Early in May, she sent a short piece to the *Southern Churchman*, and was delighted when it was published (anonymously) on May 15.

> On my return home, it occurred to me to ask for the "Southern Churchman." It contained the first piece I ever wrote for publication, addressed to "The Mothers of our community."… I had it put in my hand & the very first thing that met my eye, at the very head of the page was – my first essay – I beheld it as <u>calmly & emotionless</u>, as if it had been <u>my last</u>.

While Markie was reading the article, a cousin, Florence Marshall, came into the room and asked what she was reading. Markie rather disingenuously replied, "A piece to <u>mothers</u>…<u>you</u> ought to read it." The article was read aloud and everyone remarked that it was an excellent article. "I was glad they thought so and I hoped it might do good."[28]

Strange that Markie's first essay should be on a subject that on the surface she was quite unqualified to attempt. But she did have experience – she had been a mother to her siblings, more or less, since she was half the age she was now. In the article, she quoted *Proverbs*: "The rod and reproof give wisdom, but a child left to himself bringeth his mother to shame." She went on to say: "Parental neglect is the universal sin of the age, and I doubt not, but, that half the crimes committed in the world might be traced back, link by link, to this fashionable folly." It took a great deal of time and attention to keep a watchful eye on children, but "Crush little sins in the bud and they will not grow to great ones." Above all, mothers should be firm and decisive, so that the child "will see at once that you *mean what you say*, and intend to enforce it by punishment if milder measures fail."[29] Unfortunately, we have no record of any further publications by Markie.

During the first two years that Markie was at Arlington, life was very quiet; both Markie and Mr. Custis were in mourning for his wife, and in 1854, after the Lees came home to Arlington from West Point for a stay, Markie went home to Tudor Place and stayed for five months. During that time she nursed her grandmother, Martha Custis Peter, in her last illness. When she died in June, Markie wrote, "The vital spark has gone out – so gently did it cease to burn, that we could scarcely mark its extinction."[30] Mourning again deeply, she stayed with her Aunt Britannia and Cousin Martha Kennon until October. When she returned to Arlington, she noted: "I have drunk deeply of the cup of human sorrow – my beloved Grandmother, whose Parental care and whose interesting character, I had begun, more than ever to appreciate has gone forever, from my earthly vision."[31]

Returning for a visit to Tudor Place in November, she paid tribute to her grandmother:

> The dear familiar face of my beloved Grandmother, was not there to greet me with a hearty welcome & press me, when we parted, soon to come again. I so sadly missed her, that I burst into tears, when I entered the dining-room & it was fully an hour, before I could compose myself. Even now, ever & anon, I cast my eyes upon the old chairs, where, with her Bible under her head, she used to lie & doze, after the toils of the day were over. I say the toils, because, she did toil, in mind and Body for others' weal. Such an example of sincere devotedness, to those she loved & of whole hearted zeal, in any cause which she espoused, I never met before. Such spending and being spent of self!!! Alas! Is it indeed so, that she is gone from the earth forever?[32]

Later visits to Tudor Place would bring memories of her "dear Grandmother" back poignantly: "I looked around and everything seemed to recall the past & those quiet happy days when my highest pleasure, was derived from being dutiful."[33]

Back at Arlington, Markie's life resumed its quiet flow of activities: receiving visitors to George Washington Parke Custis, attending church services in Alexandria and at the Old Schoolhouse on the plantation, visiting and teaching the slaves.

The following year, however, Markie's social life began to pick up. At the end of February, Mr. Custis was to speak at the Smithsonian Institution and invited Markie to come with him. "I felt very much gratified by hearing dear Uncle express this wish for me to go with him; for I have had a great desire to do so; but, hesitated to speak of it, lest it should be inconvenient or otherwise, not agreeable."[34]

> Although my heart was too sad, to enjoy very much, the idea of being present at a crowded assembly, I accepted with a feeling of pleasure, dear Uncle's invitation to accompany him. As a general thing, he prefers going alone, to such places and has never, on any previous occasion, expressed a desire for my company – therefore, I felt it to be more complimentary, on this account.

Markie proceeded to make a full day of it.

> Leaving Uncle at the Smithsonian, I went to call on my friends, the Aberts & to leave a note, for Custis [Lee], making arrangements for our meeting & going together, to the Smithsonian. I then called at Mrs. Tayloe's – dined at the Aberts' and after dinner, went with Thayer [Abert], to Church at St. Johns'. (this, was an unexpected pleasure.)

> From thence, we walked to Mrs. Thornton's Dear Mrs. Thornton, I feel towards her as a very near relative, from the intimacy which has always existed, between my dear Grandmama & herself. I yielded to her persusasions to go down to Tea & scarcely had we reached her rooms on our return, when Custis was announced. After sitting a few minutes, I made ready to depart, and we wended our way, by the light of a clear and beautiful moon, to our place of destination – thinking it very bad taste to ride, when the evening was so delightful for a walk.

Markie wrote a full account of the evening, starting with the music played as the speakers arrived on the rostrum. *"Hail Columbia ...*

inspired a most lovely sensation of Patriotism."[35] Her dear uncle "looked so well, so venerable, so like a gentleman of the olden time." Mr. Custis was introduced as the adopted son of George Washington and the Farmer of Arlington (for this was a meeting of the Agricultural Society). His discourse consisted of anecdotes about Washington, "in his domestic, civil & military character & then as a Farmer." He then read an ode he had composed in honor of the centennial of Washington's birth. Afterwards the whole party went to Professor Henry's private room and visited for a while.   Joseph Henry, a famous scientist, was the first Secretary (Director) of the Smithsonian Institution. Back at Arlington by ten, they had tea and talked about the day, "then I read in the Bible to Uncle, had Prayers as usual and retired at 12 o'clock to my room."[36]

Another outing to the Smithsonian the next year was to hear Edward Everett speak on the *Character of Washington.* Mr. Custis had been personally invited by the speaker, but could not make up his mind to go until the last minute, "for nothing else that I could see, but, because he was not in the habit of doing such things – especially with Ladies, wh he seemed to consider a very awkward way of going." As the carriage was being prepared, Markie and Mrs. Lee went to dress.

> Cousin M hearing that it wd be an hour before the carriage was ready thought that entirely too much time to waste on personal adornment, seized that propitious time, for the cutting out of servants clothes and what was my dismay when at the end of the hour I walked into her room with my bonnet on to find that she was just about commencing her toilette – and altho' we had to procure tickets at some of the Hotels wh would involve some considerable time with the chance of not getting them, on account of our tardy application, still, there was not the least hurry thought necessary & the carriage was at the door a half hour before we were ready to get in.   At the last minute the hurry was violent.

Everyone was rushing around looking for various items of clothing that Mrs. Lee had misplaced.   Markie sat on the sofa "very composedly," mending the lining of her Uncle's cloak, which "I ought to have thought of before.   But unfortunately the love of procrastination stamps the family and I cannot except myself." Mr. Custis "preserved as usual, a look of the most patient impatience and said nothing."

They made it to Washington in just an hour and at the second hotel they tried managed to get tickets. In the end, they arrived in plenty of time to get good seats. Markie was very impressed with Mr. Everett's appearance, and with his address, which extolled Washington's virtues.[37]

The Arlington grounds included a spring that was a popular site for picnics in the summer. Markie's account of one of these is very entertaining and revealing:

> This was the day appointed for the great pic-nic at Uncle's Spring. He was of course, invited to be there, to meet the guests & never was a girl of sixteen more elated at the prospect of a Ball, than was dear Uncle with this anticipation. It is astonishing, that he should, at the age of 70 odd retain so much relish for amusement. I am sure, I never, unless it might have been at fourteen – ere a single cloud, had shaded my young career – felt half so strong an interest in scenes of festive gayety. The morning was fine & everything propitious. Uncle shaved, put on a clean shirt – which is always my special province to button just before he goes away – and even changed his coat. From these extraordinary arrangements we all knew that it was a high day with him. I reminded him to put on his cravat which else I am afraid would have been regarded as superfluous – and put on his chin myself a piece of coat-plaster to hide a gash wh had been made in shaving. An old brown cloth coat & a buff vest which I remember to have seen for many years on the premises, formed his best attire. I wonder what the fashionable modern belles thought of his costume. But, with all Uncle's eccentricity of dress he always looks the intelligent gentleman. He begged that I wd go in the garden, & take a servant to hold an umbrella over my head and gather a large basket of flowers and send down to him for the Ladies. Soon after his departure, therefore, I was in the garden gathering flowers & by the earliest opportunity sent them down. Uncle retains his feelings of gallantry for the Ladies I was both pleased & amused at his asking me to get some long wreaths of Ivy & other pretty flowers for decking the hair as on a prior occasion the Ladies had decked their hair with leaves, which he did not like so well.

The same day, President Pierce came to call. He was a fairly frequent visitor, but Markie had never been there before when he came. "When Cousin M introduced me, the President arose came forward & shook hands with me – by the bye, he has the softest hand for a man I ever felt."

> He has very mild, gentlemanly manners – not polished. His countenance bore the impress of care & was a little sad in expression. We spoke of Mr. Sumner. He said no right minded person could fail to deplore both the cause of Mr. Sumner's misfortune and its consequences – that there never had been such disgraceful conduct in Congress as during the present session....[†] The President then remarked that he had called by to look in upon the festive scene at the Spring on his way up & said what a charming place it was and how much interested he had been in looking at the Mount Vernon silver (wh by the bye, Uncle had sent to the house for this morning). His Excellency then expressed himself most happy to have been enabled to come over even for so short a visit & apologized for not having been before this spring and hoped Mrs. Pierce & himself would be able to drive over before very long & make us another visit. Mrs. Pierce was here about a fortnight since. They both look sad & in wretched health. Alas! What a trying position, must be that of the chief magistrate of the Nation. Were I to choose for myself a lot in Life how far from me it would be, to select a position in which I should be obliged to live so much in the world and for the world. My love of freedom,

---

† Charles Sumner (1811-1874) was a senator from Massachusetts, a radical Republican who fought for the end of slavery and denounced the pre-Civil War compromises such as the Kansas-Nebraska Act. In a speech he made in May 1856, he attacked one of the authors of the Act, Andrew Butler of South Carolina, in very personal terms. Two days later Preston Brooks, a congressman from South Carolina and Butler's nephew, confronted Sumner in the Senate chamber and beat him severely with a cane. Sumner was absent from the Senate for three years while he recovered from the trauma of the attack. Some have argued the critical importance of this incident in the rise of the Republican Party as a major political force, culminating in the election of Abraham Lincoln. From *www.wikipedia.org*.

revolts, at the shackles they impose! Far rather would I select the Life of a Shepherdess where I might ever live among the Hills & woody vales, or on the Banks of Streams where I might enjoy God's <u>beautiful</u> blessings, <u>always</u>.[38]

Markie had missed meeting the President two years previously, and had therefore gained a very poor opinion of him:

> I cannot help being amused at the true democracy of President Pierce. His want of courtesy is positively disgraceful to his office. What would an European Potentate say to the following fact – Some days ago, Uncle wrote a very respectful & courteous letter to His Excellency the President, saying he now had possession of the old Revolutionary flags and wished through the medium of His Excellency to present them to the archives of the government, to be preserved – and thinking after the old fashioned style, that it would be more elegant to send the letter by his own servant posted Daniel off with it. Instead of the president writing a reply he sends word verbally, that "he will decide about it & write him word." This, is certainly, <u>etiquette</u> for a <u>President</u>!

The President also sent word that he would come to consult Mr. Custis about the matter "to-morrow or next day."

> All day, have Uncle & I been sitting up. Uncle with his new brown vest on, wh is the only change he ever makes for company & me with my black velvet spencer on the tip toe of expectation. Uncle has been so preoccupied with his visit, anticipated, that he has not been enabled to settle himself to anything. The President has been canvassed & weighed & found <u>wanting</u> – at least in the manners which belong to his station.[39]

Markie's friends and relatives also came to visit her at Arlington. For a week in April of 1856, Blanche Berard (see Chapter 3) stayed at Arlington. She and Markie visited the sights of Washington, and talked and talked.

113

Blanche is very anxious for me to write a book of travels founded upon my Journal. My fondness for literary pursuits and the time and opportunity I have for them seems to indicate it as a sort of <u>vocation</u>, and yet I am at a loss to know what I can do with my pen, that will be most useful to my fellow beings and contribute most to the glory of God.

Blanche has succeeded so well with her little History that I confess myself encouraged by her example.[40]

In May, Markie broke off with one of her suitors, Mr. Janvier. We don't know why. She had first met him in 1847 and soon they became close friends. Markie had an especially fond memory of a May day when they walked from Tudor Place to Arlington and quoted poetry to each other as they admired the wildflowers. They lost sight of each other – he went off to Italy, she to England and France – but on "the 3d of November, 1855" he came to visit her at Arlington and their friendship was renewed. Markie said:

The stranger was never forgotten – and from that day, through the period of seven long years, have I daily prayed, that God's Holy Spirit might find an abiding place in his heart, and the conviction has always been strong in my mind, that we should some day meet again, even on this earth.

However, on May 20, 1856, Markie wrote that she had gone to Washington, and there had "an interview of an hour and a quarter at Col. Abert's with Mr. Janvier. I dissolved the engagement we had made to walk to Arlington to-morrow (May 21). This was the anniversary of our first visit there, in 1847."

Alas! This is a day long to be remembered for its varied emotions, its sadness, its <u>broken bond</u> of friendship. God forgive me, if I have acted wrongly – I implored his direction in all the affairs of this day & more especially, with regard to my interview with Mr. J and I humbly trust what has happened may eventuate in our good, though it is for the present, grievous to be borne.... This is not the last of one for whom I have prayed. The broken bond will be reunited – we shall be friends again.[41]

114

This is very suggestive of a young man who wanted to propose marriage, but was put off by Markie. Her reason? Hard to know. Did she feel a duty to her brother Orton, who was still in school? Had Mr. Janvier not had the religious conversion that Markie expected of those close to her? In any case, their friendship continued. Mr. Janvier came to visit on June 11. Mr. Janvier's first name is never mentioned.

Other visitors around this time included Markie's sister Columbia and her brother Laurence, between assignments in the Army.

Laurence, who was about to be promoted to First Lieutenant, had spent the last couple of years in the West, far from home, but by late 1855 had been assigned to recruiting duty in New York City. There he had a gay time, going to the theater, and even becoming engaged. This however, was short-lived, and was broken off by "Miss Scott" in April 1856. Laurence was still depending on his sister to influence his career. He wrote that he would probably have to go West again unless Markie could get him an appointment to West Point. This, however, was not to be, and by September the new First Lieutenant was at Ft. Ridgely in the Minnesota Territory, the "loneliest & most desolate of places." He asked Markie if she was drawing, painting, or "laying any one low.".[42]

On Christmas day, Lolo wrote again to Markie, a letter certainly calculated to put <u>her</u> in the same depressed frame of mind that he was suffering. Why hadn't they written to him? He was utterly depressed. "This unbearable climate – this objectless, eventless, existence – has effectually steeped me in a perfect quagmire of disgust." Everyone preached that one should depend on one's internal resources, but he had come to the conclusion that beyond certain limits, this was not possible. His was "<u>a liberally educated mind, expanding with age – only to waste itself upon the contemplation of 50 square miles of frozen – bleak – barren – desolate prairie.</u>" He went on to say: "I hope you may enjoy yours with as much zest as mine bids fair to be miserable." A good thing that she would not likely receive his letter until Christmas was well past! Laurence asked Markie if she knew Mr. French in the Ethical Department at West Point.

> If so – write to him and tell him I am sadly in want of a dose of moral philosophy and am most desirous, <u>consequently,</u> of imparting morality to others – especially the young – and tender – gushing youths at the Point.[43]

115

By the following spring he still had not heard from Markie about a reassignment for him. "Little can be done without some influence in Washington." In the end, Markie had no luck with Mr. French, and Laurence was destined to remain out west until 1860, participating in the Army's campaign against the Mormons.[44]

On the same Christmas day that Laurence wrote his depressing letter, Markie had an unfortunate accident. Her account of it reveals a lot about her character:

> For many months, we have been in great terror of meeting the Rail Road cars on our trips to Washington & Alexandria.... I had always said, since an accident caused to the carriage about six weeks since, by wh I was very much hurt, that when we saw the cars approaching I should stop the carriage and get out. What was my astonishment then, as we were driving close along side the rail-road to hear Mary exclaim with a countenance filled with horror, Oh! Here are the cars! Daniel stop, stop the carriage! The cars passing so much more rapidly than the carriage, however, I suppose made me believe, that the carriage had stopped and opening the door I sprung from it. As might have been foreseen, I was thrown to the ground, on my back, striking my head with considerable force.... I soon arose & walked toward the carriage wh, was still going on – for it appears that the coachman could not be made to hear & was entirely unconscious of my exit, notwithstanding the repeated attempts from Mary to arrest his attention.
>
> The cars had also passed, but, I felt that the people in them had seen me fall and I feared I had made an indelicate exposure of my under garments – this really distressed me more than any physical pain I was suffering & was greatly augmented, by Mary Lee's observing when I was in the carriage again "Well, I suppose this will be in the papers to-morrow – I hope they get the right name – for I wd not wish any one to think it was me." The cars stopped as soon as they could and all the people looked out of the windows & a gentleman came forward and asked the coachman if the

<u>Lady was hurt</u>. I thanked him mentally for the delicacy he showed in not looking in the carriage.

Like the mother who was going to whip the child for falling down stairs & breaking her neck my cousins filled up the time between the accident & our arriving at the church door in greatly upbraiding me for my foolishness – "You," they said, "who pride yourself on your great presence of mind."

If there is anything calculated to humble oneself in their own eyes, it was such a fall as mine – Perhaps I <u>had</u> prided myself on my presence of mind – this is perhaps one of "the things we do" that "we would not" as St. Paul says – but, now, at all events, my pride was deeply mortified & this allusion, <u>has deeply</u> wounded me to the quick. To jump from a carriage, when the carriage is in rapid motion, does seem, I acknowledge, perfect madness – it is what I have often said of others myself & I do not blame others for making the same remark, but, "<u>there is a time for all things</u>." No one knows what he wd do, unless exactly situated in a similar circumstance – this teaches me a lesson of <u>charity</u> in speaking & judging of others actions.[45]

Another incident in May of 1857, involving a lost note, also caused her great chagrin. Markie wrote a note to one of her seminarian friends concerning standing sponsor for a child who was to be baptized. She "committed it to the care of Cousin Mary, who highly disapproving of my writing notes to gentlemen, took it with great reluctance." Given the nature of the note, however, she agreed. That afternoon, the recipient of the note, Mr. Potter, arrived at Arlington and said "he had terrible news to tell me.... I have lost your note – and before I read it."

I was amazed beyond all expression and did not attempt to disguise my feelings. Of course, there was nothing in the note, that might not with propriety have been seen – but, I could not bear the thought, that it should be read by Tom, Dick & Harry – that my written sentiments should be picked up & read by a stranger. Mr. P suggested that he might have dropped it in the vestry-room in wh case, Dr. Richards wuld take charge of it. This consoled me, for a few moments, but, then

117

the possibility of its having fallen in the hands of persons less reliable, was perfectly <u>annihilating</u> to me. I tried however, for Mr. Potter's sake, to forget it or at least to talk on another topic.[46]

An account of a party at the White House that Markie attended in May of 1857 is also revealing, about Markie herself, and about social life in Washington at the time.

> On the 16th of May, I accepted an invitation to a Pic Nic to the White House. Deeming it as I do, inconsistent with the profession of a Christian to Dance, or what is the same thing, to take pleasure in attending dancing parties, I would willingly have declined the invitation.

Some Lee relatives, the Childes (Robert E. Lee's brother-in-law and niece), had recently returned from living in Europe, however, and Markie felt an obligation to accompany them. They joined some others of the party in Alexandria and proceeded to Washington by boat.

> Of course, as I refused all invitations to dance, I became a <u>Wall-Flower</u> – most of the day trying most ineffectually to entertain Edward Childe – part of the time sitting quite alone on a long form beside the white-washed wall and the rest of the day, was entertained by Mr. Marbury – who after sitting sometime beside me in the Ball Room, contrived to be seated next to me at Dinner – conversed with me some time after dinner and then, we took a walk to-gether – a lovely walk on the sandy shore – the afternoon was beautiful & we enjoyed the scenery extremely. The placid river before me & budding trees around – Mr. M sought for me a pleasant seat on the Banks of the River and taking his place at my feet we enjoyed a quiet converse which for its perfect orthodoxy might have with propriety taken place, within the walls of a Church. In fact, we spoke of the experiences of Life and religion in its application to them. Then, I was not sorry that I had come to the Pic-Nic, since I had had an opportunity even there, of doing or saying a little, that might eventually prove to the Glory of God.[47]

Shortly after this event, Markie noted in her diary that it was Orton's 18th birthday. Taking stock of her brother's character on this milestone, she noted:

> When he was younger, I was always endeavoring to implant in his heart a love for poetry and flowers – but, he never showed any great predilection for either. Of times, I have been in perfect despair as I saw with how little appreciation he listened to my teachings on these subjects – but, <u>now</u>, whenever he comes to read to me, he brings a book of poetry – is constantly quoting from the standard authors – expresses profound admiration for Shakespeare & sometimes wears a rose bud in his button hole. I ask myself, often, is this peculiar to Orton, or is it one of the phases through which, all boys have to pass – on the road from youth to manhood. I would rather think it the fruit of my early instructions. I am convinced that he is a remarkably good Boy – to use the term as it is generally used. He seems to strive to do right. He is so amiable to me and so affectionate & so refined and delicate in his feelings, though sometimes boyish in his manners & cant in his expressions.[48]

Orton had been at school in Alexandria during her stay at Arlington, first at Episcopal High School, near Alexandria, and then with Benjamin Hallowell, a Quaker who ran a school in Alexandria that Robert E. Lee had attended for a short time before going to West Point. Orton was very unhappy at Episcopal, probably with good reason. A contemporary of his at the school wrote the following account:

> In my day the boys were numbered. I was No. 59, and the teachers addressed me as such. The dormitory on the top floor was one huge room. The beds, or cots, were arranged side by side in rows about four feet apart. At six o'clock in the morning the bell rang, and the boys were given fifteen minutes to huddle into their clothes and get to the lavatory in the basement. The luckless lazy ones were deprived of their matin meal. There were not furnaces, and the wood-stove heated the room only in spots.[49]

In an interesting coincidence, the school was housed in a building that had once been the home of Orton and Markie's great-aunt, Eliza Custis Law. That building still houses the administrative offices of Episcopal High School.

Orton, like his brother Laurence, was determined to follow in his father's footsteps by joining the Army, and hoped for an appointment to West Point. This would be practically impossible for him, for there was a regulation in force that only one member of a family could be educated at West Point. Robert E. Lee had pointed this out to Markie as early as 1853[50], and in addition had said that he did not recommend the Army life to anyone. He did not, however, succeed in discouraging the Williams brothers or even his own sons from following that career.

In 1856, Markie had started the process of trying to get Orton admitted to West Point, despite the regulation. At that time, General Totten had acknowledged that Orton had "strong claims" to special consideration because of his father's heroic service in the Mexican War, but he was "obliged, in candor" to say that the rule was considered too important and of late, had "hardened." He would put Orton's name before the President, and counseled Markie to get her friends to use their influence. By early 1857, another officer wrote to Markie that "I am afraid he must abandon the idea of going to West Point" and advised that Orton try for a career in civil life and recommended the "high school near Alexandria" for further education.[51] Orton had already attended that school for a brief period, and did not return there, but for the next two years did continue his studies in Alexandria, still with the Quaker Benjamin Hallowell, and continued to pine for a military career.

Markie continued to be indefatigable in doing anything she could for her beloved younger brother. At about this period, Robert E. Lee wrote to his wife:

> Markie's employment, in making picture frames for Orton, must indeed for her be a labour of love. I have no doubt it will stimulate him too to greater exertion & cause his creations to be more worthy of their setting. He will have to shine hard, if he wishes by his success, to measure his efforts to repay, his Sister, for more than a Sister's love. His own love, I know, will lighten his labour & sustain his efforts, to compensate her for her unceasing watchfulness over him from infancy, & her days of labour & nights of anxiety for his welfare.[52]

Now, at the age of 18, Orton was even more determined to enter the Army, preferably by way of West Point. Again, it fell to Markie to write the necessary letters to various government officials. A week after Orton's birthday, she wrote a letter to the Secretary of War, J.B. Floyd. She wrote of her father's service in the Mexican War and of her brother's determination: "He has set his heart on being a soldier, it has been his day-dream from infancy, he says, it is impossible to think of any other profession and I cannot bear to picture to myself of his disappointment if he should eventually fail to succeed." "What particularly urges me in this matter," Markie wrote, "is, that he is an orphan, without the Parental guidance which his years so much need, and without the means of an education, such as his position in society might demand." Markie acknowledged that she had applied unsuccessfully under the previous administration to both President Pierce and his Secretary of War, Mr. Davis, but she hoped that the new administration would make an exception to the rule, quoting a letter she had received from General Totten of the Engineer Department in 1856: "If exceptions are ever to be made to the rule which bears against the application, this case would seem to call loudly for one."[53]

Despite all Markie's efforts, Orton was not admitted to West Point. In 1858, Orton and Markie were trying to secure him a position with the U.S. Coast Survey. They failed in this as well, but the next year Orton was part of a surveying expedition to Minnesota (part of the Great Lakes mapping project begun by his father), under Captain George G. Meade of the Army's Corps of Topographical Engineers. This experience, together with a talent for drawing, led finally to an appointment with the Coast Survey in 1860, now supervised by Commander Sydney Smith Lee, Robert E. Lee's brother.[54]

This was not what Markie had hoped for her brother, who, despite all indications to the contrary about Orton's interests, had noted in her diary, "Oh! How ardently do I wish & how devoutly pray, that my dearest Orton may one day become a Minister of Christ."[55]

As time went on, Markie began to chafe a bit at her isolated life at Arlington. Little did she know, her circumstances would soon change drastically.

My life this summer has been varied by few incidents of interest or importance. The family have been alternately arriving & departing while dear Uncle &

121

myself, have remained constant to our home. Not being subject to chills it seemed my especial duty, to be the one, to stay with Uncle & I am most glad, whenever I can be a comfort to him. Since the unhealthy season & the Broken Bridge we have had but little company comparatively – indeed, evening after evening, now passes without an arrival. Dear Lum's visit and Agnes Lee's being here, makes it more pleasant & cheerful, than when we were quite alone, but, at twilight, when my mind & hands are unoccupied with the various employments of the day, I miss the large family & I long for a little change. Uncle appears more feeble, than I have ever known him.... In the morning he goes to the farm as usual for a few hours, then comes home, & paints for some time and when he is weary, repairs to his old corner chair by the hearth in the old parlor and reads. He is fond of reading novels – and one of these is his constant companion. Every now & then, however, he becomes satiated -- says he has lost his taste for this sort of reading & takes up Lamartine's History of the Girondists.... Three or four times, since I have been to Arlington, (which has been, nearly, if not quite, four years) he has gone through this course. This history of the Girondists, he says, he has read <u>four</u> times & that it is historical & interesting from the <u>first page to the last.</u>[56]

Mr. Custis' diminishing health was brought home to Markie most vividly one day when he said to her: "Markie I will get you to answer that letter for me to-morrow. I will have to have an amanuensis now."

As many many times, as I have offered my services in this line & been refused! In this admission of physical inability, what a sad record is written. It speaks more than his tottering steps, even, of how much he is failing, for it is a point he has never before yielded.[57]

The return of the Lee family to Arlington allowed Markie a short respite and she went to visit some cousins at Chantilly, a plantation in Virginia about 22 miles from Arlington. Mr. Custis had seemed better, but while she was away developed what at first was thought to be just a cold but soon became an "extreme illness." Markie hurried back and wept in relief when she found she had arrived in time. "Uncle had asked several times if I had been sent for & when I was coming. This touching remembrance, brought back the tears and I wept in gratitude." She went in to see him: "He pressed my hand so warmly & earnestly & said my dear child, ...I have several times given up all prospect of ever seeing you again. I replied, it is a great blessing to me, dear Uncle, that I am permitted to be here – to see you once more." George Washington Parke Custis died on October 10, 1857.

As all the family gathered for the funeral, Markie consoled herself with weaving a wreath of flowers and leaves gathered by her brother Orton for the coffin in which her great-uncle was to be buried beside his wife.

> This was a beautiful autumn day. In the morning, I gathered autumn leaves, ivy wreaths and flowers to adorn the grave, of my blessed aunt. Mr. John Goldsborough kindly accompanied me in to the Garden, where we added to our collection, some beautiful morning-glories – fit emblems I thought, of mortal frailty & yet so typical of the delicacy and purity of her, for whose grave they were intended. I wonder if she saw me from her high abode – as I stooped & decked her grave with flowers? -- was the spirit of her husband already with her's in heaven? I thought, as his body will soon be beside her in the earth? They were digging the grave of my poor Uncle – Oh how my heart ached, to see that cruel act & when I had finished my office of love, I could not refrain my bitter tears. Mr. G kindly took my hand and led me away – but, we spoke not a word, save that as we wended our way along the shaded path, while the autumn leaves fell fast, I observed that "it was a beautiful time to die" and he responded to the idea.[58]

A couple of weeks later, she noted:

> My heart is sad and lone and dreary – What an aching void I feel! On no day so much as on Sunday, do I miss my beloved Uncle. He was more constantly in the parlor on that day. He was always on the portico as the carriage returned from Church – always ready to help us out. To-day, when Mrs. Fitzhugh asked us to remain a little longer after Church, Cousin Mary cd not

say – "No I thank you, Father will be waiting"! No, he waits no more for us, on this earth! Oh! How I missed him then, & remembered that he would not be at home, to welcome us again.

Last evening, Cousin Mary told me to call Ephraim to shut up the house. From the force of habit, I got up & going to the door leading into Uncle's room, I called him (just as he used always to do). Cousin M however soon brought me to myself and to a flood of tears (in a few minutes afterwards when I left the room) by remarking in a subdued tone – "Markie, Ephraim does not stay in that room now." No! it needed not that his valet should now stay in that room, to keep up the fire for his master to go to bed by. Sad reality for us! I trust it is a better change for him! God grant, that my poor and feeble prayers for his eternal good, may have mingled with those, of more exalted Christians & reached the Throne of our Heavenly Father!

I often feel that my sadness is a restraint on the rest of the family, who are so cheerful and loquacious.[59]

Markie at this time felt that she should not stay at Arlington, but was unsure what to do. At the time of her Grandmother's death "when I first felt myself homeless," she had thought about "seeking a position as Teacher in some family," but nothing had come of that idea.[60] Her cousin Britannia Kennon, now the owner of Tudor Place, was soon to be forced to rent her home for income, so Markie truly was homeless, although the Lees were quick to assure her that she would always be welcome at Arlington.

After a visit to friends in Philadelphia, Markie returned to Arlington for Christmas, and stayed well into the new year. She was back at Tudor Place for her birthday on March 28, however, where she awaited "with some interest the issue of my first manuscript." What was this publication? Sadly, we don't know.[61]

In May, Markie was staying with her Aunt Margaret Orton at her house on F Street between 21st and 22nd Streets (today's Foggy Bottom), when she had a long-awaited visit from her old friend Dr. Austin Flint.

What quiet, silent anxiety had been mine all day! Had my youthful hopes never known a disappointment, I should have looked forward with joyous rapture, incontrollable delight, unspeakable pleasure, to the arrival of my adopted Brother; but, as it was, I went about all day, looking thoughtful & subdued, occupying every moment of my time – Wondering in my heart of hearts, if the evening would bring me happiness or misery for unhappily for me, I know of no median state, where those I love are concerned.... [When he finally arrived] I could not speak, with agitation of joy, but, saying not a word, I walked out of the room & closing it, I opened the front door. It was really the Dr. We greeted each other and I hastened to usher him into the parlor.[62]

What the future would hold, Markie did not know. For the moment, she was happy.

How strange, that all things regarding me should be as they now are. With my aunt & Cousin whom I so long ago parted with in Paris – living in Washington, among old friends, to whom previous circumstances has rendered me a stranger – in the vicinity of a locality, which was my home when a child.[63]

[1] Ltr., RELee to MCW, 9 Sept. 1853, in Avery Craven, ed., *To Markie*. Cambridge: Harvard Univ. Press, 1933.
[2] Diary of MCW at Arlington House, entry for Nov. 1, 1853.
[3] Ibid., Oct. 28, 1853.
[4] Ibid.
[5] Ibid., Nov. 1, 1853.
[6] Ibid., June 5, 1856.
[7] Ibid., April 6, 1855.
[8] Ibid., April 29, 1857 and May 10, 1857.
[9] Ltr., RELee to MCW, 16 Sept. 1853, in *To Markie*.
[10] Ibid., Nov. 7, 1853.
[11] Diary, Oct. 29, 1853.
[12] Ibid., Feb. 13, 1855.
[13] Ibid., Oct. 30, 1853.
[14] Ibid., March 10, 1854.
[15] Ibid., Jan. 8, 1854.
[16] Ibid., Feb. 27, 1855.
[17] Ibid., May 1, 1857.
[18] Ibid., May 26, 1856.
[19] Ibid., April 3, 1854.
[20] Ibid., Feb. 27, 1854.
[21] Ibid., Nov. 7, 1853.
[22] Ibid., Nov. 20, 1853.
[23] MCWC, "Views on Slavery," undated, Arlington House Archives.
[24] Ibid., Oct. 30, 1853.
[25] Ibid., March 5, 1858.
[26] Ibid., Oct. 30, 1853.
[27] Reminiscences of Mrs. Annie Baker (age 77) and Mrs. Ada Thompson (age 75) as told to Arlington House staff, March 5, 1930. Arlington House Archives.
[28] Ibid., May 17, 1857.
[29] *Southern Churchman*, v. 23, no. 19 (Friday, May 15, 1857), p. 76.
[30] Ltr., MCW to MCL, June 13, 1854, TP Archives, MS-6 (3-1).
[31] MCW Arlington House Diary, Oct. 23, 1854.
[32] Ibid., Nov. 7, 1854.
[33] Ibid., Aug. 9, 1856.
[34] Ibid., Feb. 22, 1855.
[35] "Hail Columbia" was the first American national anthem. It was composed for George Washington's presidential inaugural as "President's March." It was first performed with lyrics during President John Adams' administration.
[36] Ibid., March 1, 1855.
[37] Ibid., March 28, 1856.
[38] Ibid., June 3, 1856.
[39] Ibid., April 7, 1854.
[40] Ibid., April 9, 1856.
[41] Ibid., May 20 & 21, 1856.
[42] Correspondence, LAW to MCW, 1854-56, TP Archives, MS-6.
[43] Ltr., LAW to MCW, 25 Dec. 1856, TP Archives, MS-6 (1-21).
[44] Correspondence, LAW to MCW, 1857-1859, TP Archives, MS-6.
[45] MCW Arlington House Diary, Dec. 25, 1856.
[46] Ibid., May 10, 1857.
[47] Ibid., May 19, 1857.
[48] Ibid., July 7, 1857.
[49] John White, *Chronicles of the Episcopal High School in Virginia, 1839-1989*, p. 21.

[50] Ltr., REL to MCW, 16 Sept. 1853, in *To Markie*. In fact, Lee wrote to Markie that two members of the same family were not permitted to attend *at the same time*, but by the time Orton applied, the policy had obviously been restricted further.

[51] Ltr., Gen. Totten to MCW, Nov. 27, 1856 and L. Thomas to MCW, Jan. 27, 1857, TP Archives, MS-6 (1-2).

[52] Ltr., REL to MCL, ca. 1856, Virginia Historical Society, Lee Papers (MSS1-L51c-203).

[53] Ltr. (draft), MCW to Hon. J.B. Floyd, July 14, 1857, TP Archives. MS-6 (3-1).

[54] Ltr., N.P. Tillinghast to Sec. of Navy, Nov. 10, 1858, TP Archives, MS-7 (1-2). George G. Kundahl, *Alexandria Goes to War – Beyond Robert E. Lee*. Knoxville: Univ. of Tennessee Press, 2004.

[55] MCW Arlington House Diary, April 5, 1857.

[56] Ibid., Aug. 27, 1857.

[57] Ibid., Sept. 12, 1857.

[58] Ibid., Oct. 13, 1857.

[59] Ibid., Nov. 1, 1857.

[60] Ibid., undated draft letter in folder 5.

[61] Ibid., Nov. 1857 through March 1858.

[62] Ibid., May 1858.

[63] Ibid., Dec. 31, 1857.

CHAPTER 7

THE CIVIL WAR –
FAMILY TRAGEDY

> My darling Orton….How my heart is troubled when I
> see how few religious advantages that dear child now
> possesses in the matter of religious influence. Oh! God,
> I pray thee, even through all these adverse
> circumstances, bring his heart to thee. [1]

Markie worried about Orton's lack of spirituality, especially because he was seeking a direct commission as an Army officer and might be sent far away from her. Lolo, a First Lieutenant in the Army, stationed at Camp Scott, Utah Territory, was concerned about him, too. He wrote to Markie that he did not like a letter which he had received from Orton because it reflected "his being a fast young man." He hoped that, if he went into the Army, that he would not get bad habits "from a certain class of men."

When Markie came back from Paris, she put off taking art lessons "until a more convenient season."[2] The convenient season seemed to be just over the horizon. Lum, age 32, was quite independent although she took turns living with various relatives; Kate, age 25, was married; Lolo, age 26, was in the Army; and Orton, age 20, soon would be in the army, if his wish were granted. It was time for Markie to think about her own future.

The previous September (1858), Markie took Orton with her when she visited Aunt Margaret who then lived in Philadelphia. For Markie, the highlight of their month-long visit was their afternoon spent with Mr. and Mrs. Rembrandt Peale, friends of Uncle Custis and the Lee family. "We went quite as strangers, without any introduction, but [with] my card having on it the name of Martha Custis and Arlington, we were received with great courtesy….Both were most polite & agreeable." They cheerfully discussed their various paintings. Mrs. Peale's specialty was heads and figures, but "when her eyes had become so bad," she had been "obliged to take up landscape painting." Mrs. Peale (nee Harriet Cany) was "very communicative." She said that she had been an artist 12 years before her marriage when she was 40 years old. "She was very enthusiastic about the art, and Mr. Peale & herself, both remarked during our visit, that they never allowed a day to pass without painting two or three hours."[3]

Rembrandt Peale was the second son of Charles Willson Peale, the most prominent portraitist of the Federal Period. He (the father) studied with Benjamin West in London. He was a volunteer in the American Revolution and painted portraits of prominent officers when he had time. Although he painted a number of famous figures, he is most famous for his 14 portraits of George Washington. He was the principal founder of Pennsylvania Academy of the Fine Arts where Markie hoped to study. His devotion to the cause of the arts helped to make Philadelphia a leading center of the intellectual and artistic life of the country. Rembrandt studied under his father and then spent a great deal of time in Europe studying under famous artists. He gained fame as a portrait and historical painter. By 17, he had painted his first portrait of George Washington from life. (Washington died four years later.) He claimed that he produced over 70 copies of his famous painting, and enjoyed calling himself "the only painter living who ever saw Washington."[4]

Markie's visit with the Peales strengthened her enthusiasm for pursuing an art education. The following year she returned to Philadelphia, with Orton in tow, and enrolled in the fall antique class at the Pennsylvania Academy of Fine Arts. Orton returned to Arlington, and Markie began her class that concentrated on drawing the plaster casts of ancient statues.[5]

In the mornings, she faithfully attended classes, and in the afternoons usually practiced drawing or enthusiastically read one of the many art books that covered the table in her bedroom. After six months, she wrote to Annie Lee, "I get very much disgusted with the production of my crayon, sometimes, & think I shall never do anything fit to be seen, but I work as hard as at the beginning, and my zeal for the arts has not in the least abated." She was "drawing the Head of Augustus Caesar – a fine model said to have been taken from life," and was pleased that Dr. Vinton said that he liked it very much. The Academy of Fine Arts would open an exhibition on the first of April, and "they are very busy getting Paintings for the Exhibition." She further wrote to Annie:

Church's *Heart of the Andes* and *Niagara* are now on Exhibition, drawing multitudes to see them. Mr.

[Frederic] Church,[*] himself, created a great excitement among the students the other day by making his appearance in our midst. I was so fortunate as to have a pleasant little interview of about fifteen minutes with him, much to the envy (I heard afterwards) of the rest of the students, who had not the pleasure of an introduction. He was made quite a Lion. His *Heart of the Andes* is perfection, in its way. I enjoy it often.[6]

Although Markie worked hard studying and practicing drawing, she was continually apprehensive about her siblings, especially Orton. She kept abreast of his activities through her correspondence with members of the Lee family. Unlike his brother and sisters, Orton seldom wrote to her.

Neither of Markie's brothers aspired to any career other than that of an Army officer, following the examples of their father and Robert E. Lee. Orton was unsuccessful in getting an appointment to the Army until Lee wrote a long letter of recommendation for him to the Secretary of War on February 1, 1860. Although Lee may have heard rumors about Orton's drinking and quick temper, he knew only the courteous, talkative, intelligent Orton who had spent so much time at Arlington. His letter dwelt on those qualities he could honestly endorse – the young man's heritage, his draftsmanship, mathematical ability, and knowledge of engineering and surveying, as well as an "inventive turn of mind, &...ingenuity." Lee asserted, "he possesses those acquirements & qualities necessary to a soldier & always required in the military service."[7] The following year Second Lieutenant William Orton Williams was a junior member of the Staff of General Winfield Scott, General-In-Chief of the Army.[8] General Scott's Chief of Staff was Markie's "old friend," Colonel E. D. Townsend,[9] whom Orton had greatly admired when he was a young boy.[10] An observer in Georgetown noted that Orton "wore his uniform with panache" and that he was attracted "by the sight of a dashing young cavalry officer showing off the paces of his handsome black charger."[11]

---

[*] *Niagara,* completed in 1857, and *Heart of the Andes,* in 1859, "guaranteed for Church, still a young man, the role of America's most famous painter." (Biography, Frederic Church, 1826-1900, www.artchive.com/C/church.html)

130

While Markie was still in Philadelphia, she received an invitation from Mrs. Lee to accompany her and Agnes to St. Catherine's Well, known for its curative water. Mrs. Lee, who was becoming more and more debilitated from arthritis, had visited various healing springs in Virginia without lasting benefit. Now she was willing to travel all the way to Canada, hoping at last to be free of pain.[12] Markie hoped that the "sainted waters," as Lt. Colonel Lee referred to them, would relieve her neuralgia. Before they left, she wrote a long letter to Lee, seeking his advice about her career as an artist.[13]

Markie, Mrs. Lee, Agnes, and Custis, as an escort, made the two-day trip to Niagara Falls and 12 miles more to St. Catherine's, described by Mrs. Lee as a "pretty little village....[which] looks very much as if it had fallen into Rip Van Winkle's sleep." They stayed in "a sweet little vine covered cottage" and faithfully pursued the course of treatment, beginning with a daily wineglass of a salty concoction two hours before breakfast, followed by exercise, and swimming. By the end of their stay, Mrs. Lee felt that the waters had relieved her arthritis, but they were not a cure. When they left St. Catherine's, they went to New York City, where Agnes and Markie stayed behind to visit friends, and Mrs. Lee traveled by train to Washington, D. C.[14]

Markie had made plans to study painting in New York City at The Cooper Union for the Advancement of Science and Art, established in 1859, and among the nation's oldest institutions of higher learning. Founder Peter Cooper had designed his experimental school, on which he lavished six hundred thousand dollars, to offer working men – and women – tuition-free night classes in engineering, chemistry and art. It had an underground Great Hall where on February 27, 1860, Abraham Lincoln made his famous, anti-slavery speech, *Right Makes Might*, which he claimed made him president.[15] Markie must have known about Lincoln's speech, but she did not confide her thoughts to her diary.

In January 1861, she received a letter from Robert E. Lee, on duty at Fort Mason, Texas, in response to her "kind letter of the 28th July." He was unable "to form an opinion as to the advantages of the course of study you propose to yourself. There is scarcely anything that is right that we cannot hope to accomplish by labour & perseverance.... Could your progress keep pace with my wishes, your advancement & works would equal the most renowned Masters of the Art, & the love of your friends would be exceeded by their admiration."

Lee mentioned that the letters which he received from Arlington frequently mentioned Orton and "in one of the last it was stated that he & Custis (Lee's son, George Washington Custis) were looking forward to captaincies in the Army of the Southern Republic! The subject recalls my grief at the condition of our country. God alone can save us from our folly, selfishness & short sightedness." He was fearful that calamity "is upon us."

> I am unable to realize that our people will destroy a government inaugurated by the blood & wisdom of our patriot fathers, that has given us peace & prosperity at home, power & security abroad, & under which we have acquired a colossal strength unequalled in the history of mankind. I wish to live under no other government, & there is no sacrifice I am not ready to make for the preservation of the Union save that of honour. If a disruption takes place, I shall go back in sorrow to my people & share the misery of my native state & save in her defence there will be one soldier less in the world than now. I wish for no other flag than the *Star Spangled Banner,* & no other air than *Hail Columbia.* I still hope that the wisdom & patriotism of the nation will yet save it. [16]

Although Markie continued her studies in painting and enjoyed seeing her friend, Dr. Austin Flint, she was anxious about the possibility of war. She had heard that the atmosphere was so tense in Washington, D. C. that when Custis was away, he asked Orton to stay at Arlington. On February 1, Mrs. Lee wrote that Custis had been away for three weeks and that Orton "is here at night to protect us lone feminines..."[17] On March 1, Lt. Colonel Lee returned to Arlington. He had been summoned to Washington, D. C. for discussions with General Scott, General-In-Chief of the Army [18]

Markie always made a special note of her birthday, March 28; this year she was delighted to celebrate it with "her dearest and best friend," Dr. Flint. On the same day, she learned that Robert E. Lee had been promoted to full colonel.

Two weeks later, the Confederates bombed Ft. Sumter. The nation was at war.

General Scott, who considered his fellow Virginian the best officer in the U. S. Army, offered Colonel Lee command of the Union Army, which he refused, explaining that he could not lead an invasion into the Southern States. Lee resigned from the U. S. Army on April 20. On April 22, he left Arlington, never to return, to take a position with the Confederacy.[19] He encouraged Mrs. Lee to prepare to leave Arlington, but she could not convince herself that it was necessary. One early afternoon in May, when she was sitting in her "morning room," copying an oil portrait of Rob (Robert E. Lee, Jr), Orton burst into her room, warning her that she must leave because Federal troops would soon take possession of Arlington Heights. Mrs. Lee felt that their good friend General Scott had sent Orton. There was a delay in the troop occupation of Arlington which gave Mrs. Lee and Custis time to supervise the loading of furnishings onto wagons and carriages for the ten mile journey to Ravensworth where her aunt, Mrs. A. M. Fitzhugh, lived.[20] Agnes worried because Orton had not come to say farewell. Later, she learned that on May 7, two weeks after being promoted to First Lieutenant, he told General Scott that his sympathies lay with the South. He was arrested and sent to Governor's Island because of his knowledge of Union war plans.[21] Orton had refused General Scott's offer for duty "at a distance from the scene of active operations."[22] Colonel Townsend also had tried to convince him to remain loyal to the Union. Mrs. Lee was angry because Colonel Townsend had told Orton that he would be considered a traitor if he enlisted in the Confederate army.[23]

When Markie learned of Orton's incarceration, she was "in the depth of anxiety about him."[24] She immediately visited him and helped him prepare a letter of resignation to General Scott explaining why he wished to resign, assuring him that General Lee did not advise him to take such a course, and thanking him for his "great kindness" and the opportunity to serve on his staff. "I shall cherish to my dying day, the same devoted affection for you which a son feels for an honored parent."[25] In June, when his knowledge of Union war plans was no longer considered of value to the rebel mobilization, Orton was paroled with his promise not to go to the South for a month. He had been detained in the home of the post commander where he was reported to have fallen in love with his jailer's daughter. She considered herself engaged when he left.[26] On July 8, General Lee wrote to his wife that Orton came to his headquarters at the end of his parole, but Lee did not put him on his own staff to avoid additional, erroneous publicity about Orton's intended betrayal of the Union. He sent him to General Leonidas Polk in Tennessee.[27]

133

Markie had stayed in New York so that she could be close to Orton, although she was distraught by the news that she was reading in the press and receiving from family and friends. She wrote to Agnes Lee that she wept bitterly when Helen Peter, a friend of Mary Custis Lee, told her of the Lees' last day at Arlington House. She asked what was done with her things of great value and importance to her which she had left in her bedroom closet. She reported that her brother-in-law, Harry Upshur, was on the *Constitution* which left "yesterday for New Port, R. I., ...expects to return in a week. He has received orders to the *Wabash,* does not know where she is bound....Poor Kate is at Mansion House in Brooklyn, [in a] state of sad anxiety."[28]

Studying painting at Cooper Union, which had meant so much to her, seemed unimportant compared to other events affecting her life and the lives of those she loved. In response to her inquiry, Mr. Thomas in Washington, D. C., replied on May 24: "I see no difficulty in your coming to Georgetown....Alexandria is in possession of our troops, & several regiments occupy the Heights of Arlington."[29] As soon as she could make arrangements, Markie returned to Washington, D. C. Because she no longer had a home at Tudor Place, occupied by renters, or at Arlington, occupied by Union troops, she stayed with the Abert family.[30]

Markie immediately wrote to her friend, Colonel Townsend, whom she had met when she was 17 years old while visiting the Lees at Fort Hamilton, New York. She asked for a permit from General Scott to allow her to visit Arlington. In a letter to Mrs. Lee, she reported that he quickly replied with "a full permit to visit the place & do whatever I might wish, giving directions to Lieut. Kingsbury to facilitate me in every way....I asked my friends, Mr. & Mrs. Campbell, to accompany me. We went in a hack & crossed in a ferry boat from Georgetown." At Arlington there was "a large encampment... and tents and soldiers along the roadside & interspersed everywhere. I was blinded with tears & choked with sorrow as I tried to gaze on scenes once so familiar. Now, strangely distorted." The sentinel directed their carriage to halt at the house of Selina Gray, a slave and Mrs. Lee's personal maid, whom she left in charge of Arlington. Selina "led the way to the house, through the tents & soldiers. The poor House looked so desolate....Oh! Who in their wildest dreams could have conjured all this last summer? It was but one year ago that we were all there, so happy & so peaceful." Markie packed her trunk with as many of her things as she could, but had to leave many. She found Annie's letters and took them, too. Selina told Markie that she had not seen Puss, the family cat, since the Lees left. When Markie opened "the garret door, however, I heard a mournful mewing and calling Puss, he timidly came up & rubbed his little head against my dress in the most affectionate way." She picked him up and covered him with kisses and pitied him, "but I suppose his instincts teach him not to leave his garret home."[31]

Markie told Mrs. Lee about her conversation with the slaves and reported that, "All asked after you, all with interest." As Mrs. Lee had instructed Ephraim, he sold the produce of the garden and got with it "tea, sugar, etc. & divided it among the other servants (slaves)." He said that he never let the family be demeaned. She ended her letter saying, "Dear, dear Cousin Mary, how can I express to you all the deep sympathy I feel for you. Give my warmest love to all my cousins & tell them how much I love them and how I long to hear from them."[32]

Anna Maria Thornton recorded in her diary that Markie had visited her and intended to leave at the end of July to be with Kate and her four children in Germantown, but first had to go to Annapolis to collect her sister's things there.[33] Kate's husband had been an instructor at the Naval Academy from 1859 to 1861.[34] In a letter to Blanche a month later, Markie referred to her time in Washington as sad weeks. "It made my heart bleed to see the changes there – and to go to my beautiful home (Arlington) – to enter that old familiar gate through a sentinel guard – to approach the dear old house through an encampment of soldiers – to pass through an armed band up to my very door & show a permit ere I could enter...."[35]

It was, indeed, a sad time for Markie.

> My country, my home & my friends, all so warmly loved & so <u>dearly cherished</u> are torn from me & my breast is mutilated by conflicting feelings & interests....My Brother Laurence is, you know, aid to Gen. McClellan; Harry (Kate's husband) on board the *Wabash* in Comr. Stringham's fleet, blockading the Southern ports – many dear army friends in Washington & elsewhere arrayed against the South, while in the Confederate Army, is my dear Brother Orton, aid to Gen. Polk....It is needless to say, my sympathies are, in this great contest, <u>with the South,</u> but I have no home there now, and so I feel it my duty to remain near poor Kate, who with her little family of

135

four children, the last only a month old, are now boarding in Germantown."

Markie hoped all of those at West Point understood that Orton did not break his arrest or do anything dishonorable.[36]

Markie probably did not know that another friend, who would play a most important part in her future, was also "arrayed against the South." Her "earliest admirer," Seaman Samuel P. Carter, had been transferred to the Union Army and this month was promoted to Brevet Brigadier General.[37]

Markie told Blanche that her normal condition was a wearied body, sick at heart, and that she "had lost all zeal, even for my drawing, which once was a theme of so much enthusiasm."[38] However, when sister Kate's situation improved, relieving Markie of her duties, she once again enrolled in a drawing class at the Pennsylvania Academy of Fine Arts in Philadelphia. She sometimes recorded in her diary that she had a day of suffering with neuralgia, especially when she read in the newspapers about the South losing a battle. On February 13, 1862, she wrote, "Bad news in the papers of the reverses of our armies at Roanoke. I went to the Academy after reading the paper, but suffered so much that I had to return." Nevertheless, she was serious about her drawing - attended classes and practiced at the Academy and at home. Occasionally, "Painted in my room all day." In March, she "Arranged with Mr. Bensell to take my first lessons in oil painting at his studio next Tuesday. Am enchanted at the thought." She looked forward to these classes as well as her drawing classes at the Academy.

On March 17, Markie received "a letter of farewell from dear Lolo....My heart is sad." The next day, Major Laurence A. Williams arrived in Alexandria to take command of the Sixth Cavalry Regiment, which became known as the "The Fighting Sixth." On March 27, the regiment embarked on transports to Fort Monroe. When Virginia seceded from the Union, President Lincoln quickly had Fort Monroe on Old Point Comfort reinforced so that it would not fall to Confederate forces. It was held by Union forces throughout the Civil War, and several sea and land expeditions were launched from there. Union control was extended to include the coasts of both North Carolina and Virginia.[39]

At Fort Monroe, the Sixth Cavalry began its participation in the Peninsula Campaign, General George B. McClellan's plan to capture Richmond and end the war a year after it began. That day Markie's diary read, "Had a sad & heavy heart all day, thinking of my dear Brothers & friends, probably on the Battle field. God defend & bless them & give Victory to the just cause." She revealed which cause that she thought was just when she added, "At the Academy the Ladies were all making flags except one." Ten days later, she wrote: "Painted at the Academy all day. It was a trying morning. The students (Ladies) sat for their Photographs surrounded by [their] Star Spangled Banners & I absented myself from the group. It is my birthday."[40]

After reading the newspapers, which usually depressed her, she tried to shut out the war by concentrating on her private painting lessons with Mr. Bensell in the morning and attending drawing and painting classes at the Academy the rest of the day. Occasionally she stayed after the other students had left and became so engrossed in her lesson that she missed dinner. One evening she "Intended to have gone to Church but inadvertently remained long past the hour which mortified me very much." When she wasn't involved in her art work, she kept her mind off the war in other ways. She attended church often, went to lectures, made calls, entertained friends, and visited with sister Kate and Aunt Margaret Orton. After she had spent a day visiting Aunt Margaret and Uncle Orton, both Unionists, she wrote, "Uncle Orton refrained from talking politics which was a comfort." She regularly wrote that she spent part of the weekday with "Willie," who sometimes accompanied her to her classes; and she received "Mr. Etting" in the evenings. He accompanied her when she visited Kate.

On April 10, Markie suffered too much all day to go out because she was anxious about Orton and was grieving over "the terrible news of the Battle of Pittsburg Landing, but cannot believe it." Better known as the Battle of Shiloh, this was one of the most important battles of the Civil War. It took its name from Shiloh Church, southwest of Pittsburg Landing in Tennessee, where most of the action took place. The Union Armies turned back the Confederacy's supreme bid to regain the initiative in the Mississippi Valley, a crucial region for the South. The battered Confederate Armies were forced to retreat from the bloodiest battle in the history of the United States, up to that time, but which became commonplace during the next three years. It launched the country onto the floodtide of total war.[41] Markie did not yet know that Orton was safe and had distinguished himself at Shiloh, being twice mentioned in general orders and promoted to Chief of Artillery. She would have been devastated had she known that prior to the battle, when he was inspecting the troops under his command, he "drew his saber and thrust it" into the body of a soldier, killing him, because he refused to salute a second time.[42]

During the rainy month of April, Markie often felt "intense anxiety about my dear Brothers & friends." On May 1, "A rainy, cold, gloomy day" she "felt extremely sad." Brother Lolo was also disconsolate about rain. Frequent rains impeded operations during April; even heavier rains bogged down the armies during May.[43] Lolo had led the Sixth Cavalry Regiment within six miles of Yorktown, but rain precluded offensive operations. On May 1, when it was about two miles from Williamsburg, the Sixth Cavalry was ordered to advance and charge. As the head of the column reached a strip of swampy woods, the central battlefield of the next day, General Cooke ordered Major Williams to attack the enemy's left. His report read:

> I was ordered to make a detour through the woods and take a battery on the enemy's extreme left flank. I accordingly proceeded with the Sixth Cavalry through the woods indicated, and after going about half a mile at a trot, debouched upon an open but undulating ground in front of the enemy's line of fortifications. The ground was very heavy, and between the woods and the fieldworks there was a deep ravine only passable by file.... Four of the squadrons and a portion of the fifth had already passed the ravine (it was belly deep to the horses in mud), when two squadrons of rebel cavalry rushed from the barracks in rear of the fort, and endeavored to cut off Captain Sanders' company. Captain Sanders wheeled his company about, charged and repelled the enemy with great gallantry. I cannot speak too highly of the officers and men on this occasion. Though every one felt that few would survive if the guns of the fort were turned upon us, not one showed the slightest concern. Captain Sanders showed great prudence and bravery in the timely manner in which he met the enemy, though taken at a disadvantage by superior numbers.[44]

By May 12, the regiment reached White House Landing on the Pamunkey River, not far from Williamsburg. Nearby, Mrs. Lee, Annie and Mildred were still in residence at the White House, home of son Rooney (W. H. Fitzhugh Lee). Since the first of April, General Lee had been encouraging Mrs. Lee to move. He wrote to her, "No one can say

138

what place will be perfectly safe or even quiet, but I think a locality within the route of an invading army will be least so." Mrs. Lee wanted to remain on the property to protect it. It was where Grandmother Martha Dandridge Custis and George Washington were introduced by mutual friends and where she accepted his proposal three weeks later. Here, on January 6, 1759, they were married – she wearing a deep yellow brocade overdress trimmed with silver lace at the neck and sleeves and opened in front to show a petticoat of white silk interwoven with silver. She wore pearls in her dark hair, and her shoes were purple satin trimmed in silver. The groom, who resigned his commission a few days earlier, wore a suit rather than a uniform.

Mrs. Lee thought that their presence might dissuade Federal troops from desecrating Rooney's home as they had done at Arlington. Finally, on May 12, General Lee prevailed. With advance enemy troops only a few miles away, Mrs. Lee and the girls abandoned the White House property. Before she drove away in a carriage, Mrs. Lee tacked a defiant note to the front door of the old Custis home that Rooney had inherited:

> Northern soldiers who profess to reverence Washington, forbear to desecrate the home of his first married life, the property of his wife, now owned by her descendants.
> A Grand-daughter of Mrs. Washington.

She and her daughters moved not far away to a house called Criss Cross, and watched enemy troops come into the area a few days later.[45]

On May 15, pickets reported Major Williams for alleged communication with the enemy (Mrs. Lee), and he was promptly arrested. On the 17th he wrote a letter to Headquarters telling of his arrest and saying, "I respectfully request that a Board of Examination be appointed by the General Commanding to investigate the circumstances." On the same day, he was released by an order from Headquarters of the Army of the Potomac and resumed command of his regiment.[46]

It was almost a week before Markie read in the newspaper an "account of the arrest of my dear brother Laurence." She immediately wrote letters to General McClellan and Colonel Townsend. Later that day, she received a letter from Lolo, saying that he had arrived at the White House, now General McClellan's headquarters. He sent flowers that "Cousin Mary left in water to ameliorate the ferocity of the vandals; she had just departed. All Lees are near Richmond. Orton is with the General in Richmond."[47] Because he didn't mention his arrest, Markie continued to be anxious about his situation. The next day, she received a letter from Colonel Townsend, "which relieved my anxiety about Lo." The day was made even brighter by a visit from her dear friend, Blanche Berard, with whom she could honestly discuss her opinions, anxieties, sorrows and joys.

On May 20, Mrs. Lee wrote to Martha Kennon, Britannia's daughter, that "the White House is now in their possession....I was much comforted to hear Lolo was in command at the White House believing that he would endeavour to protect it." The following day, not knowing that she was the "enemy" with whom Lolo was accused of communicating, she wrote that a friend "reported that Lolo had been arrested for his supposed sympathy with the South," and that "25 thousand men were at the White House, quartered in our fields." On May 23, she added that "we have had crowds of Yankee troops here....they have behaved well & a guard is around us. I heard from one of the officers who came to see me that Lolo had gone on with the Army to Richmond & was not arrested as I had heard."[48] Mrs. Lee had seen more of the enemy than her husband who was sitting at a desk in Richmond, making plans.[49]

On May 24, Markie received a letter from General McClellan, which was later published in the newspapers:

> My dear Miss Williams: Your note of the 21st has just reached me. The moment your Brother's arrest was made known to me, I examined the subject and at once released him from arrest. He is now commanding his regiment at the head of the advanced guard, displaying daily a degree of gallantry & skill, which gratifies me extremely. You have every reason to be proud of your Brother. He has fully justified the interest I have taken in him. It may interest you to know that Mrs. General Lee is within our lines – at the place of Mrs. Sayre's near Old Church – Miss Mary & Mrs. Fitzhugh Lee are with her. They are well & will of course be kindly taken care of. Very truly & respectfully, Your friend, Geo. B. McClellan[50]

When Markie's painting lessons with Mr. Bensell ended, she commenced portrait painting instructions at Mr. Rothermels' studio. Her drawing lessons were coming to an end, too. On June 9, she wrote, "Went to the dear Academy for the last time." She continued her portrait painting until it was time to travel to Georgetown. On June 16, "With a sad heart packed my trunks to leave the familiar scenes of the past year & the kind friends whom I have made. Mr. Etting escorted me to the cars & [I] journeyed to Washington under Capt. Steadman's escort."

Markie would find that Washington was a much different city. Antebellum Washington was a thoroughly Southern town. For the Southern political and social elites, the war spelled abrupt disaster. Suddenly most of Washington's old Southern elite was gone. Into the vacuum rushed a host of newcomers. Soldiers were everywhere. Washington quickly became a city of barracks and hospitals. Volunteers who had come to save the Union were overrunning the city. In 1860, the population of the district was 75,000. By the end of 1861, it was 199,000.[51]

Markie thought that "Washington looked never so unattractive. The spacious [Pennsylvania] Avenue dotted here & there with dust begrimed soldiers, & Georgetown is like a deserted village." After moving into her "grandmother's old room" and walking about the grounds, she "began to enjoy the beauties of the trees & scenery" and found it a pleasure to be at Tudor Place with Lum and Aunt Brit "after so long an absence."

Until this year, Britannia Kennon had not lived at Tudor Place since 1858 when she rented it to the Pendleton family. The war broke out while she and her daughter, Martha, were in Philadelphia, and "we packed our trunks and went to Staunton, Va." They moved several times, eventually arriving in Norfolk. "Fearing that the Government might take 'Tudor' for a hospital, we decided to return home....We took the Confederate boat at Norfolk and were met in mid-water by the Federal 'flag of truce' boat where we were transferred." When they arrived in Baltimore, they "went immediately to Brother's"[*] where Britannia left daughter Martha "and came to 'Tudor,' arriving at home on January 1st 1862." After she "took possession of the dear old place again," still being concerned that the government might confiscate Tudor for a hospital, she "concluded to take boarders....nearly all of them were 'Yankees.'"[52]

---

[*] George Washington Peter, Lynwood, Ellicott City, Maryland.

141

On June 26th, Markie was "delighted to get a letter from dear Lolo," but she was anxious about him because of the battle at White House Landing. She would have been more distressed had she known that he was quite ill, with a high fever, but in the saddle, fighting to repulse Cousin Robert Lee's attack on Federal forces.[53] Also in the battle was Lolo's childhood friend and cousin, Rooney Lee, a favorite officer of the audacious General J. E. B. Stuart. He had recently accompanied Stuart around McClellan's army to get information that Lee needed to plan this counter offensive close to Richmond.[54] President Lincoln warned McClellan, who was reluctant to pursue the enemy, "By delay the enemy will relatively gain upon us." McClellan did not act. When he was within five miles of Richmond, he stopped, giving General Lee the opportunity to plan his all-out effort to destroy the Army of the Potomac. General Joseph Johnston wrote to General Lee, "No one but McClellan could have hesitated to attack."[55]

In an attempt to cut off McClellan from his base at White House Landing, General Lee crossed the Chickahominy River and attacked Union forces at Mechanicsville, the first major battle of what became known as the Seven Days Battles (June 25-July 2, 1862). The muddy terrain along the Chickahominy swamps and in much of the rest of the area was a handicap for both sides.[56]

Despite having won what he described as a "complete victory" at Mechanicsville, McClellan did not go on the offensive. Believing that his northern supply line was threatened, McClellan shifted his base and supplies to the James River on the south side of the Peninsula, giving up his plan to capture Richmond. Although McClellan suffered only one tactical defeat in the Seven Days' Battles, he constantly retreated, thus giving General Lee a strategic victory by saving Richmond, with all that meant for morale in the respective armies and on the home front.[57] General McClellan retreated with his huge army to Harrison's Landing on the James, secure within a fortified perimeter, supplied by water, and supported by naval guns. McClellan was safe....23 miles from Richmond. A month later, he moved his troops close to Washington, D. C.[58]

After the Battle of Mechanicsville, a doctor declared prostrated Lolo unfit for duty and ordered him to proceed by steamer to Old Point Comfort, near Norfolk, Virginia, with other sick and wounded, but the hospitals there were overcrowded, too. He was sent to Washington, D. C. where a physician reported that he had "returned from the Chickahominy Swamps with Typhoid Fever and Dysentery."[59]

According to The Civil War Society's *Encyclopedia of the Civil War*, while the average soldier believed the bullet was his most nefarious foe, disease was the biggest killer of the Civil War. Bacteria and viruses spread through the camps like wildfire. About half of the deaths from disease during the Civil War were caused by intestinal disorders, mainly typhoid fever, diarrhea, and dysentery, all of which tormented Lolo. A soldier wrote home, "We would rather die in battle than on a bed of fever." John William De Forest wrote, "They cannot be kept in their wretched bunks, but stagger about, jabbering and muttering insanities, till they lie down and die....We can distinctly hear the screams and howls of patients in their crazy fits."[60]

On June 30, Markie, not knowing Lolo's fate, was indisposed all day because of the "greatest anxiety about my beloved brother & relatives engaged in the fearful Battle going on at the White House." The next day she believed that "I have thus far reason to thank God for his blessing in the preservation of my dear Lolo, but still tremble for him & for others. Ah me! Ah me!" Nevertheless, she "Went to Washington to inquire after dear Lolo," and to her "inexpressible surprise," saw him in the street. He had returned "with typhoid fever & looked feeble & thin. I was distressed & happy in the same moment....but anxious as I am, I sincerely hope he will not be strong enough to return to this detestable war." Lolo remained on sick leave in Washington, D. C. until he requested to be returned to duty. General Scott ordered him on limited duty in New York City where he lived with Dr. Lewis W. Sayre who treated him at Bellevue Hospital[61] At the end of July Markie "Rec'd a letter from dear Mrs. Sayre kindest & best of friends – I am thankful to hear that dear Lolo is still with her & improved in health. I bless God for the good friends who strew my sad path way."

Markie had enjoyed Lum's company, but it was time for them to part once again. During the Civil War Lum lived with various relatives. Prior to the previous May, when she came to Tudor Place to visit Aunt Brit, she had spent a year with her cousins at *Audley*, a mile and a half from Berryville, Virginia, where Aunt Lewis (Nellie Custis Lewis) lived with the family of her son, Lorenzo, the last few years of her life.[62] Now Lum was going to visit Kate who had written from Philadelphia four months ago:

> Harry is at Port Royal still & sends you much love, he joins me in begging you will come immediately to my house here & make it your home. You would be a great

143

comfort to us all, darling, & I am so glad at last to have a shelter to offer you. Come by the earliest opportunity & be sure of a warm welcome from your attached Sister, Kate
P. S. Love to all our loved relations & thanks to each for their kindness to you.[63]

Markie wrote in her diary that when she "went over to the depot in Washington with dear Lum to see her off" she rode "in the Washington city rail cars (horse cars) for the first time. They come as far as the State Department now." The Washington and Georgetown Railroad Company, the first horse-drawn car line, was chartered on May 17, 1862, to build three horse car lines using the same track gauge as the Baltimore and Ohio Railroad. The first streetcars (horse cars) were installed on Pennsylvania Avenue from Georgetown to the Washington Navy Yard. The system was so successful that the lines were extended and new lines were built.[64] "The first car that ran up the Avenue (Pennsylvania) was crowded almost to suffocation, and an extra horse had to be put on before it could proceed around the curve at the Treasury....The service did not at once give perfect satisfaction." The cars were crowded and "Weary business men were aggrieved at being ejected from their seats....to make room" for women wearing crinolines that "occupied a disproportionate amount of space."[65] Nevertheless, the citizens were relieved to have this convenient transportation and something other than the war to discuss.

Markie had a ceaseless uneasiness about the war. After restive sleep, she met the day with apprehension and sought ways to find peace of mind. She kept herself busy to avoid thinking about the war, but she missed her art classes, although she did paint or sketch almost every day. She played the piano, sometimes practicing half the day, and encouraged visitors to sing with her. She sewed and worked on a tapestry, made calls and attended church services. She always had a book handy, especially the Bible, and in the past several months had read *Life of John Randolph*, *Life of Faust*, *Les Misérables*, and *Theologia Germanica*. She was delighted to receive mail; "Few things now give me as much pleasure as letters." She was especially pleased to hear from Dr. Flint, but occasionally even "my dearest & best friend" wrote "in a sad mood." He was treating wounded and sick soldiers in New York City hospitals.[66] She and Britannia often received guests, especially Mr. Tillinghast, their pastor, at Tudor Place in "the temple," a lovely circular portico (featuring sash windows) that protruded into the house, creating a fascinating interplay of exterior and interior spaces.[67] Sometimes she wrote that Mr.

Tillinghast "sat with me alone." She regularly commented on the beautiful moon-lit nights that she enjoyed in the temple. She faithfully continued to read the newspapers although they made her "Feel sad & dispirited – Oh! When will this direful war & all its horrors end." When she wrote that "we won," meaning the Confederates, she still was despondent "because of the terrible loss of life."

After the horse car lines were completed, Markie went to Washington more often to visit the Aberts. "I rode all the way from Georgetown. What a blessing & a comfort." After the Second Battle of Bull Run (August 28-30, 1862) when she "passed the day with the Aberts, who were in a state of great anxiety," she "saw long processions of wagons & ambulances going to the Battle field." The next day, she wrote, "Ah! What sad, sad days we are passing. Although the victory has been ours, it has been dearly won & I am heart sick at the suffering." The following day, "The scene on the avenue [Pennsylvania] was heart sickening. Long lines of omnibuses & ambulances bringing the wounded & prisoners." Two days later she and Britannia went to Washington and found "The avenue was filled with regiments of soldiers & army wagons going to & fro." For the next two nights "Regiments [were] passing through all day & night." When she went to church, "The town [was] a scene of the greatest confusion. The streets filled with army wagons & soldiers....Two poor war worn soldiers were going away from the Church. I invited them in."

From Centreville to Washington, the roads and bridges were choked with ambulances and carriages bringing the wounded and dying. For over a week, the wounded came back to Washington by train or boat and in vehicles of every description. Washington was so crowded that it was almost as difficult to move about in the back streets as on Pennsylvania Avenue. People walked the streets looking for food. The bakers, unprepared for the demand, could not supply enough bread.[68]

Before the war began, Washington was a relatively rural town with very few medical facilities. The Washington Infirmary (E Street Infirmary) was the only hospital in the District, and it was destroyed by fire on November 3, 1861. The military quickly began converting public buildings into hospitals. The Patent Office had been used as a hospital for over a year. Nevertheless, as the wounded arrived, there was still not enough room in the hospitals, so they were taken to City Hall where they were provided with cots and blankets.[69]

145

Following the early defeat of the Army of the Potomac in 1861 and 1862, Washington became a vast hospital complex with more than 10,000 wounded troops. The government established 25 military hospitals in the city and in neighboring counties, but they overflowed and makeshift hospitals were opened in public places. At the peak of the Civil War, it was claimed that the Washington area included as many as 85 hospitals. One of the largest Civil War Hospitals was the Armory Square located where the present National Air and Space Museum stands. The 1,000-bed hospital had overflow tents which spread out across the Washington Mall. In Washington, as well as in Georgetown and Alexandria, sick and wounded men lay in hotels, warehouses, private houses, schools, lodges of fraternal orders, churches and seminaries. Georgetown College was turned into a hospital; so was the H Street mansion of the rebel sympathizer, Mr. W. W. Corcoran. Miss Lydia English's Female Seminary became "Seminary Hospital" from June 30, 1861, to June 24, 1865.[70] This was the school which Markie and her sisters attended and where Dr. Armistead Peter (son-in-law of Britannia Kennon) volunteered his services during the war.

Feeling that she was not doing anything worthwhile for others, Markie "formed a [Sunday School] class of little boys. It seemed like old times to be teaching my own class." She also agreed to teach at the Parish School during the week. In October while she was teaching, "Aunt B. sent for me at 12 o'clock to come home to see dear Lolo who had arrived. He stayed but an hour or two, poor fellow, & it was sad to part with him." He had reported to the U. S. Army Headquarters for an examination and now returned to New York City where he was assigned to limited duty (mustering and disbursing duty)[71] and continued to be under the care of Dr. Sayre.

October 23 was "A memorable day, in so much as I received a letter from dear Cousin Robert Lee. It seemed to come as a recompense for all I have suffered in the past few days:"

I only rec'd yesterday [October 1, 1862], dearest Markie, your affectionate note of the 8th Aug. I view with affection your mementoes of A [Arlington] and read with tearful eyes the account of your visit. I have to dismiss from my thoughts of the past, and now have but little of pleasure to dwell upon. I am very grateful for your remembrance and affection. I know how little I deserve your kind feelings....Your Cousin M [Mrs.

146

Lee] will be very glad to hear of you. She often speaks of you, and thinks of you constantly. She is now in R [Richmond] with C [son, Custis], who is highly esteemed by his Commanders, is with Genl Bragg....The boys are all well and as you know, in the Army....I did not get the letter you spoke of. We shall have to resign ourselves to non-intercourse until peace is once more restored to this distracted land. I feel assured of your sympathy and affection, and you must believe you have mine.[72]

Less than three weeks later General Lee's daughter, Annie, died of typhoid fever. In November, when Markie learned of her death, she immediately wrote to Mrs. Lee and a little later to Agnes:

Our precious Annie! I cannot at all realize that I shall never see her again....I long to see you all & since I have heard of this deep affliction, have felt that I must go to you & try to comfort you – but this cannot be....[It] was a great shock to me, for I had but a week or two previous, received a letter from Cousin M [Mrs. Lee], enclosing one from Annie to her....My heart is with you all, dearest Agnes - Believe that you have the love & sympathy of your attached, sympathetic friend, Cousin Markie[73]

On Thanksgiving Day, Markie was "deeply sensible for the blessings of the past years as well as for those I now enjoy & [I] desire to be truly thankful." On Christmas Day her complete diary entry was: "Went to church in the morning & visited an afflicted friend in the afternoon." However, Orton was continually in her thoughts. Although she often wrote to him, she had not heard from him "for more than a year." She had asked Agnes Lee to "tell me if you hear from my dear, dear Brother & how & where he is. Tell me everything you know about him....I wonder sometimes if he ever thinks of or cares for me....Give much love to him."[74]

Agnes and Orton had been friends since childhood. In 1853, when Agnes began her first diary, she had difficulty knowing what to record: "The everyday life of a little school girl of twelve years is not startling." She did note that "Orton - for he is too big to be called Bunny now - walked in while I was practicing." He was 14 years old. Two years later, Orton visited Agnes when Brevet Colonel Lee was Superintendent

147

at West Point. In April, she wrote: "Friday night I had a farewell talk of about three hours with Bunny – wasn't that 'charment'?"[75] Markie remembered "darling Agnes & Orton, sitting around the nursery fender, telling fairy tales." When they "had grown up, it was always, 'Where are Agnes & Orton?'" Often they were horseback riding, "Agnes with her 'glowing face and streaming hair' and Orton with 'his admiring glances' at Agnes."[76]

Now that Orton was in the Confederate Army, Agnes, too, did not often hear from him. She wrote to him from "White House, Dec. 1, 1861,"

> I have been hoping, dear Orton, ever since I sent mylast long letter written the 29th of Sept. from Clydale, to have a response in due time. But 'hope told a flattering tale' this time sure enough. I have been tempted to believe you have   forgotten your old Virginia friends generally, me in particular, but ashamed of this skepticism in regard to 'our brave defenders' I am going to do what I rarely ever do – write again....I wish indeed that you would come....Remember to take care of yourself....I pray daily dear O His blessing may be upon you, & how I wish your own voice may ascend as often for yourself. Your friend, Agnes L.[77]

A year later, Orton surprised Agnes by appearing during Christmastime at Hickory Hill[*] where the Lees were residing. He was a colonel in the cavalry, handsomer than ever, tall, blond, erect, scrupulously groomed, wearing "kepi, hussar jacket, duck trousers, Wellington boots" and a rattling saber in his belt. The Wickham children at Hickory Hill found this dashing officer wonderfully "handsome and charming." They admired the gifts that Orton had brought for Agnes, "a pair of ladies' riding gauntlets and a riding whip." They watched each day as Agnes and Orton went on long horseback rides in the woods. Much to their disappointment, the end of the visit was not a happy one. After Agnes and Orton had a long session in the parlor, Orton came out, bade the family goodbye and rode away alone.[78] He had not received the answer he anticipated.

---

[*]Hickory Hill, near Ashland,Virginia, belonged to General Lee's uncle, William Wickham.

Perhaps Agnes refused his proposal of marriage because he had a reputation for drinking and fearlessness, hard to distinguish from recklessness, which her father and brothers would have known. They would have heard, too, that he had killed a soldier who refused to salute him a second time. As required by the investigation, Orton submitted a report which concluded with the statement: "For his ignorance, I pitied him; for his insolence, I forgave him; for his insubordination, I slew him." The investigation was superseded by the Confederate's withdrawal from Columbus, Kentucky, to Corinth, Mississippi. The investigation was dropped,[79] but Orton was transferred to the staff of Major General Bragg, Second Corps Commander in the Army of the Mississippi. At the Battle of Shiloh, Orton distinguished himself by scouting for the general. Another officer wrote, "I saw Orton continually….He was a fearless and daring officer, and Gen. Bragg appeared to rely more on him than any member of his staff in the execution of important orders."[80] Nevertheless, the officers and men, having heard of his slaying of one of his own men, refused to serve under him. While the army regrouped after Shiloh, Orton initiated legal action to change his name to "Lawrence William Orton." He served as commander of General Bragg's headquarters escort during the summer and fall of 1862 and was promoted to colonel.[81] During his busy year of 1862, Orton found time to publish a book on military tactics, which received wide recognition; a number of general officers wanted to see it adopted by the entire army.[82]

Markie first knew about Orton's name change in early 1863 when she received his letter of December 18, 1862, which ended with, "Your Affectionate Brother (I have changed my name), Lawrence William Orton." Markie later commented, "As his Brother's name was Laurence, this was unaccountable. I wrote a letter of remonstrance, but do not know whether my letter ever reached its destination."[83]

Laurence (Lolo) was still under the care of Dr. Lewis A. Sayre and on limited duty in New York City. Nevertheless, he had been ordered to join his regiment in the field. Dr. Sayre wrote a letter to the Secretary of War saying that Major L. W. Williams had been under his charge since the "seven days fight on the Peninsula." He had returned from the Chickahominy Swamps with Typhoid Dysentery, and Dr. Sayre deemed it his duty to state that he considered him "totally unfit for that duty."

He is entirely prostrated physically, from the effects of Typhoid fever and the labors of that campaign. Upon a slight exertion, he has had lately several times quite serious hemorrhages, which totally unfit him for active service in the field in command of his regiment. The anxiety of Maj. Williams as an Army Officer, to be employed upon some service is natural and proper. That which he is now engaged he can perform without detriment to his health, in my opinion, but believing as I do, that he is utterly unfit for active service, I cannot as his physician give my consent to his undertaking the same.[84]

Dr. Sayre was concerned because Lolo "repeatedly went to David's Island and Staten Island to inspect troops when he was not in physical condition to do so and in direct violation of my advice. On one of these visits to Staten Island he was seized with a hemorrhage from the bowels which threatened to prove fatal." Dr. Sayre's advice was ignored. A few days after this attack Lolo received orders to report immediately for duty. Notwithstanding the advice of Dr. Sayre and Dr. Edgar, an Army doctor, not to do so because it would threaten his life, Major Williams did go to Washington and reported for duty, but to his great surprise, found he had been dismissed from the Army.[85]

Lolo immediately applied to be reinstated in the Army, but without success. General McClellan had won most of the battles of the Peninsula Campaign, but lost the campaign. For his part in the Peninsula Campaign, Lolo lost his health and his career, but he did not blame General McClellan. Dr. Sayre believed that on one of his visits to the New York Club, Lolo "made some bitter enemies by his manly defense of General McClellan from charges (treason, cowardice and other crimes) which he knew to be false." As a result, he "had been misrepresented to Secretary of War Stanton," causing Stanton to dismiss Lolo from the army.[86] Stanton certainly would have been irritated to learn that Lolo, or any officer, had defended General McClellan. He had a fanatical hatred of McClellan. It was well known that Secretary Stanton and General McClellan despised each other. While Secretary Stanton carried on a personal campaign against McClellan, he wrote letters to him that were fulsome with love and loyalty. They did not fool McClellan. In the general's eyes, Stanton was "the vilest man...the most unmitigated scoundrel," and "the most depraved hypocrite and villain."[87]

Dr. Sayre was concerned about Major William's overall physical condition, but his wife, Eliza, concentrated on Lolo's heart. During his long, worrisome recuperation, because of Mrs. Sayre, a joy-filled event happened: Lolo met Sallie. Mrs. Sayre was a friend of Sallie Law, the daughter of George Law, one of the wealthiest and most influential men in New York.[88] Lolo presented Sallie with a gold brooch with a wreath made of his hair and the initials, "LW, March 17, 1863," engraved on the reverse side.* Today, nineteenth-century hair jewelry is invariably associated with mourning. While it was worn for that purpose, hair jewelry was also made to mark happier circumstances, such as an engagement.[89]

Orton was also thinking about marriage, although he had not mentioned the news to Markie. After his visit with Agnes, he went to Richmond where he was given orders to report to General Bragg at Shelbyville, Tennessee.[90] In April, 1863, he was assigned command of a cavalry regiment in the second brigade. At his request, his cousin, Lt. Walter (Gip) Peter, was transferred to serve as his adjutant. During this time, Orton met a young, attractive woman who represented herself as the widow of Colonel Hamilton of South Carolina. On the rebound from his rejection by Agnes, Orton imagined himself in love and proposed marriage. This time, his proposal was accepted.[91] Soon they were separated because again Orton's past had caught up with him, and he was not well received by the cavalry regiment, causing disruption among the troops. Learning of the dissension, General Bragg rescinded Orton's assignment order, leaving the two cousins in limbo. Orton was "mortified by this state of affairs," and set out to make his mark on the war in the West. Orton Williams and Walter Peter were about to become legendary names in the history of the Civil War.[92]

At Fort Granger, on a bluff above Franklin, Tennessee, on June 8, 1863, about dark, two men rode up to a union headquarters.[93] They wore Federal uniforms and caps covered with white flannel havelocks with flaps hanging down the back of their necks for protection from the sun - cap covers usually worn by soldiers in the French foreign legion.[94] They dismounted and walked forward to meet Colonel John P. Baird, Commandant of the post. The taller of the two introduced himself as Colonel Auton of the Army of the Potomac, and his companion as Major Dunlop, his assistant in the inspection of Western troops, for which they had been sent directly from Washington. A soldier, who was watching, wrote, "The elder of the two – he was as fine looking a man as I have ever seen, about six feet high." Colonel Baird was impressed with Colonel Auton, for "there was something engaging about this handsome, dignified young officer, with his easy grace of bearing; a note of brilliance to his conversation, which was withal frank and quiet; an indefinable air of distinction and individuality in all that he said and did."

---

* This brooch is in the Tudor Place collection.

151

Dr. Wilson Hobbs, Surgeon of the 58th Indiana Infantry, wrote for *Harper's Weekly*, "he was one of the most intellectual and accomplished men I have ever known. I have never known anyone who excelled him as a talker." Although Major Dunlop said little, Colonel Baird liked his frank and handsome face. He was described as "a generous, warmhearted, gallant man, six feet in height, straight as an arrow, a splendid horseman, and every inch a soldier."[95]

Each stranger presented four documents that verified his identity. One was signed by E. D. Townsend, assistant adjutant general. A letter signed by Brigadier General James A. Garfield, future president of the United States, further confirmed their orders and identity. Once Colonel Baird was satisfied with their papers, he invited the officers to spend the night, but Colonel Auton insisted that they must continue on to Nashville. The commander gave them passes and fifty dollars, which Auton had asked to borrow, although Colonel Van Vleck, who had silently observed all that went on, had told the commander that he suspected the men were not whom they represented themselves to be.[96] Before they rode off into the night, Auton had one more request: he asked for and pocketed his host's cigars.[97]

After the strangers departed, Baird began to have doubts about their authenticity, especially when he learned that fellow officers shared Van Vleck's opinion.[98] Baird sent Colonel Louis D. Watkins to apprehend them. When he caught up with them, Auton "courteously consented to return to the fort." When they reached Watkins' tent, they willingly went in to await Colonel Baird. After waiting longer than he anticipated, Auton looked out the door and was surprised to see guards posted around the tent. He asked, "What does this mean, Colonel, this guard?" Watkins replied that he and Major Dunlop were prisoners, but if they were who they represented they were, they would be delayed only a short time.[99] When Baird arrived, he examined their papers more carefully and they seemed to be in order, but he telegraphed queries to the officers who had supposedly signed them. The replies from those officers indicated that they knew nothing of Colonel Auton or Major Dunlop. General Garfield replied, "There are no such men in this army, nor in any army, so far as we know. Why do you ask?" At this point, Baird undertook a closer inspection of the suspects. Major Dunlop consented reluctantly to a search; Colonel Auton protested, placing his hand upon his hilt, but submitted to the search in light of the overwhelming numbers against them. Etched on Major Dunlop's sword was his identification, "Lt. W. G. Peter, C.S.A." Each man had his real name and Confederate rank in the band of his headgear.[100] Colonel

Williams was carrying a thousand dollars in Confederate money,[101] about $20,000 at today's value.[102] The captives confessed their deception, but denied being spies or having any intention of obtaining military intelligence. Baird reported his findings to General Garfield, and received the general's directions: "The two men are no doubt spies. Call a drum-head court martial tonight, and if they are found to be spies, hang them before morning without fail. No such men have been accredited from these headquarters."[103]

A drumhead court martial was held at 3 A. M. "Charges: being spies."[104] Because Lt. Peter had not known the purpose of their mission or why they had entered Federal lines, Colonel Williams spoke for the pair. He testified freely, saying that he was pursuing a goal which had to remain secret. The trial lasted barely an hour. After sunrise the two men were told the verdict: death. After the chaplain had administered the sacrament, the men asked permission to write a few letters and were given pen and paper. To Markie, Orton wrote:

> My dear Sister,
> Do not believe that I am a spy – With my dying breath
> I deny the charge. I hope you will not grieve too much
> for me – I believe in "Jesus Christ who came into the
> world to save sinners." – Although I die a horrid death
> I will meet my fate with the fortitude becoming the son
> of a man whose last words to his children were – "Tell
> them I fell at the head of the column." I remain, with
> love to my sisters, Brother & relatives.
> > Your devoted Brother
> > Lawrence W. Orton

He also wrote a note of farewell to the young woman to whom he was engaged. In part it read:

> When this reaches you I will be no more. Had I
> succeeded I would have been able to marry you in
> Europe in a month. The fate of war has decided against
> us. I have been condemned as a spy – you know that I
> am not....

Gip Peter wrote to his family, expressing his love, and saying they had been found guilty of being spies. "We are innocent."[105]

At daybreak, a scaffold was built on a wild cherry tree, which still stands. At 9:00 A. M., the garrison was assembled around the gallows and two poplar coffins.[106] The condemned officers took their place on the platform of a cart. They embraced and the cart moved out from under them at 9:20 in the morning of June 9. The corpses, in Federal uniforms, were cut down and placed in the coffins. Orton was buried wearing a gold chain and locket containing the portrait and braid of hair of his intended wife. Her image was also placed in his vest pocket. The caskets were buried in the same grave.[107*] Colonel Baird wrote:

> The officers I executed this morning, in my opinion, were not ordinary spies and had some mission more important than finding out my situation....after they confessed, [they] insisted they were not spies in the ordinary sense....Said they were going to Canada and something about Europe; not clear. Though they admitted the justice of the sentence and died like soldiers, they would not disclose their true object. Their conduct was very singular, indeed; I can make nothing of it.[108]

Newspaper reports of the hanging of spies at Fort Granger appeared the following day. The headline of *The New York Times* was, "Two Prominent Rebel Officers Arrested as Spies and Hung." It reported that Colonel Lawrence Williams Orton, was formerly Lawrence Williams, causing Lolo additional grief.

Armistead Peter, Jr. reported that Aunt Brit learned of Orton's death at the dinner hour and "had to go to the table and sit through the meal with all those Union officers and say nothing." To prevent Tudor Place from being used as a hospital, Britannia Kennon had "taken in boarders and nearly all of them were 'Yankies.'"[109]

Markie wrote to Blanche that she thought that she could "not live through such a sorrow."

---

* In 1864, Gip's brother, Dr. Armistead Peter, had both bodies brought back to Georgetown and buried at Oak Hill Cemetery. Their spurs are on display in the southwest bedroom at Tudor Place. (TP Archives, Family History.)

I have never faltered in my faith, but oh Blanche what a fate for one so young, so noble, so brave, so loving & beloved by all who knew him!....The whole thing is a mystery to me – I cannot comprehend it. I believe the facts will be found to be different from what was stated in the paper, if they ever come to light. Oh! That I could hear a statement from some private source....I have but one earthly consolation that is that he laid down his life in a cause which I consider so righteous & true.

Markie added that a friend had received a letter from Orton saying that he had married the widow of Colonel Hamilton of South Carolina. She longed to go to the young bride to love and comfort her, but she did not know the bride's first name or any of the circumstances. She had received "no letters from the South for a long time."[110]

Lolo and Sallie were busy with plans for their June 16th wedding when they read the news of Orton's death. Although Sarah Law was the daughter of George Law, one of the great tycoons of the nineteenth century, they decided not to have an elaborate wedding in New York City. Instead, Laurence Abert Williams and Sarah Virginia Law were married quietly by Reverend Dr. Vermilyea on Tuesday, June 16, 1863, at Linden Hill, on Staten Island, a summer house that Mr. Law had purchased from Commodore Vanderbilt.[111]

Markie did not attend the wedding, but met Sallie when Lolo and Sallie visited Aunt Margaret. She wrote to her cousin, Dr. Armistead Peter, that "Sallie is a kind hearted & very sensible woman and I think will make him a better wife perhaps than if she had more personal attractions. She is very affectionate & anxious to make herself agreeable to his (Lolo's) friends. In appearance though plain, she is rather stylish & lady like in manner." Maggie Peter described her as cheerful and that she "always had some fun in reserve."[112] Lolo was described by his physician as reserved and unassuming, one of the gentlest and refined of men, but of a striking and commanding presence. Unlike brother Orton, Lolo never faltered in his loyalty to the Union. He could not understand how a Union soldier of honor and high character could draw his sword for the Confederacy.[113]

Although Markie had said that she thought that she could not live through the sorrow of Orton's death, she had a defiant spirit when she felt that one of her siblings had been unjustly accused. She hoped to

155

dispel any thought of Orton's having committed a dishonorable act. She wrote to Blanche:

> Do you remember reading the chaplain's letter in wh
> he says Orton acknowledged himself to be a spy? You
> know I told you that I knew that precious child so well,
> that I felt certain that he had never spoken to the
> chaplain on any other subject than his spiritual welfare.
> I wanted no proof of this myself but I wrote to the
> chaplain again, that I might prove it to others. I said in
> my letter – 'Did my brother acknowledge to you that
> he was a spy? Or did you hear him make this
> acknowledgment to anyone else?'

The Chaplain replied that he did not hear Orton say that he was a spy. When his sentence was announced in the Chaplain's presence, Orton claimed to be innocent of the charge. The Chaplain did not interrogate the prisoners and they did not make other allusions in his presence.

Markie wrote, "I shall continue to make every possible inquiry by letter." She felt that "if I only had certain data I could define his motives."[114]

In reply to her letter to Ft. Granger, asking for more details about the circumstances surrounding her brother's death, Colonel Van Vleck, who suspected Orton and Gip of being spies as soon as he saw them and served on the court that convicted them, wrote a long reply, part of which read:

> Your brother died with the courage of a true hero. He
> stepped upon the scaffold with as much composure as
> though he had gone to address the multitude. There
> was no faltering in his step, no tremor in his nerves. He
> thanked the officers for their kind treatment, and said
> that he had no complaint to make; that one of the cruel
> fates of war had befallen him, and he would submit to
> it like a man. On the scaffold the unfortunate men
> embraced each other, and Lieutenant Peter sobbed and
> said: 'Oh Colonel, have we come to this!' Your brother
> at once checked him by saying, 'Let us die like men.'
> And they did die like men, with the heartfelt sympathy
> of every man who saw them die....the object of his

mission....to this day is a most mysterious secret to us all.[115]

A hundred years later, Margaret Sanborn, the author of the article, "The Ordeal of Orton Williams," wrote that Orton was "in all probability" on a diplomatic mission. She claimed that there is evidence in the official Confederate Correspondence that Orton had previously worked as an agent or scout for Secretary of War Judah P. Benjamin. Three weeks after Orton and his cousin were hanged, Benjamin, who by this time, had become Secretary of State, wrote a letter to a Lieutenant J. L. Capston saying that, in accordance with his proposal, the Army had detailed Capston for special service under his (Benjamin's) orders. He wrote in part:

> The duty which is proposed to entrust to you is that of a private and confidential agent of this government, for the purpose of proceeding to Ireland, and there using all legitimate means to enlighten the population as to the true nature and character of the contest now waged by our enemy to obtain recruits for their army....Throw yourself as much as possible into close communication with the people where the agents of our enemies are at work....Lay all these matters fully before the people who are now called on to join these ferocious persecutors in the destruction of this nation.

Sanborn claimed, "It is possible that Orton Williams may have been Lieutenant Capston's predecessor."[116]

On June 27, Markie received Orton's farewell letter to her. Immediately she wrote to Blanche, saying that "God in his mercy has given me the greatest consolation my broken heart could have – a record of his (Orton's) last thoughts – a testimony of his innocence." The letter had come in Lieutenant Peter's valise which he had sent to friends. Markie asked Blanche to "show my precious Brother's letter to all my friends & dear Papa's friends at West Point. It is a perfect transcript of his mind & heart. You cannot think how it has comforted me, stricken & crushed as I still am....My heart is now filled but with one sentiment & that is gratitude for this letter."[117]

In memory of Orton, Markie wore a gold, oval brooch surrounded with pearls, and Orton's blond hair worked into a cross, resting atop a field of Markie's brown hair. A hairwork and gold anchor, symbolizing hope, is suspended from the brooch, engraved "Orton and Martha" on the back. This brooch is in the Tudor Place collection.[118]

Orton is remembered in another way. In Alexandria, on May 24, 1889, Governor Fitzhugh Lee, a nephew of General Robert E. Lee, delivered the dedicatory address at the unveiling of the Solitary Confederate Sentinel, a bronze statue, located at the intersection of Washington (Alexandria's main throughway) and Prince Streets. It is in memory of the Confederate dead of Alexandria who lost their lives in the "War Between the States." The senior officer, of the one hundred names inscribed on the base of the standing figure, is "Col. Wm. Orton Williams, C.S.A."[119]

Markie, who found solace because Orton had "laid down his life in a cause which I consider so righteous & true," did not explain why she thought spying would have been a dishonorable act.

Two of the men whom she most admired depended upon spies: General Robert E. Lee and General George Washington. According to Harnett T. Kane who wrote, *Spies for the Blue and Gray,* Robert E. Lee, more than perhaps any other Southern general, used spies. He also counted on secret agents to supply him with every available Northern newspaper. The *Philadelphia Inquirer* provided information of a withdrawal by McClellan; as a result, Lee shifted his troops. Lee himself had an agent insert a fake story in Confederate papers, hoping a Union general would believe it. Confederate General Braxton Bragg received a *New York Times* clipping which explained precisely how the Unionists would fool him into a shift of position. Bragg stayed put.[120]

Alexander Rose in *"Washington Spies – The Story of America's First Spy Ring,"* refers to General George Washington as the first spy master. In the summer of 1778, General Washington desperately needed to know where the British would strike. He unleashed his secret weapon: an unlikely ring of spies in New York charged with discovering the enemy's battle plans and military strategy.[121]

The rest of 1863 was full of anxiety for Markie. "All bright spots on earth for me, seem to be vanishing now." Rooney (Fitzhugh) Lee, who was seriously wounded at the Battle of Brandy Station in early June, had been captured in his sickroom at Hickory Hill. She could not believe that the reports about the Battle of Gettysburg were true. When she read that Union prisoners were to be executed in retaliation for Orton's death, she wrote to General Lee, begging him to intercede to save their lives. Lee wrote to his wife and asked that she reply to Markie, telling her that she had been misinformed. No prisoners would be executed in retaliation for Orton's death.[122]

After "being very much an invalid," herself, Markie was "unexpectedly called to Germantown to care for sister Kate" who "has been in bed with rheumatism for three weeks, not able to turn without assistance, & her five little almost babies – the youngest three months old, servants entirely incompetent & Mr. Upshur [Kate's husband] has just arrived quite an invalid. I have undertaken all my duties quite naturally but it is so new to me that I feel quite worn out."[123] When Kate recovered enough to take care of herself, as well as her children, she began making plans to join her husband at Fort Monroe on Old Point Comfort, Virginia. Her husband was assigned to the steam frigate *Minnesota* of the North Atlantic Blockading Squadron.[124] When Kate left in the fall of 1863, Markie moved to Philadelphia to live with Aunt Margaret.

Markie continued her search for information about Orton. She, Lolo and brother-in-law Harry visited Orton's fiancée. They discovered that the woman was not the widow of Colonel Hamilton from South Carolina, as she had claimed, but his wife. At the end of December, Markie wrote to Agnes Lee in response to her inquiry, "I was horrified to hear that her husband died after my poor brother. This would seem to be something without extenuation & make her words to me and to Orton most false." Lolo and Harry spent more time with her and thought her very strange, "although they believe in her love for Orton. Lo now thinks she is deranged – Poor girl she has my deep pity – I wish I could do something for her…I am much grieved at what I have heard & do not see how I could ever again have any communication with her….I can easily imagine the interest you feel in all connected with him. You were children together….I have never been to Georgetown or Washington since my great grief – I feel as if I never ever could go again – Every place there is associated with him – especially dear Arlington."[125]

Two weeks later "dear Arlington" was sold to the highest bidder, the United States Government, because of delinquent taxes. Mrs. Lee had tried to pay the taxes through the mail or by having an intermediary pay them for her, but she was told that she must appear in person. In May, 1864, The Secretary of War designated the Arlington estate a national cemetery.[126]

159

For Markie, during the Spring of 1864, the war was eclipsed by her concern for Kate who was seriously ill, especially because she was at Old Point Comfort which seemed so far away. "For days and weeks my anxiety was so great that I was incapable" of even writing a letter. In April, "Finally I was summoned to her and remained through a long and painful illness until death. When it came [it] seemed like an angel of mercy sent to relieve her of her severe sufferings. Soon after, I returned to the North (Philadelphia) with her poor little children." Katherine Alicia Williams Upshur died on August 22, 1864.[127]

Markie said that until a year later, she was so absorbed in the care of her charges and her domestic duties that she lived a life "out of this world."[128] She had very little time for anything else, even for reading the newspapers. But she could not have missed the victory celebrations or the huge, bold headlines announcing Union victories at Richmond and Appomattox. Celebrations were held throughout the North from villages to big cities.

In Washington, D. C., when a telegraph operator received a message beginning, "From Richmond," without reading the rest of it, he ran to the window, bawling, "Richmond has fallen!" Newspapers confirmed the victory, "Glory!!! Hail Columbia!!! Hallelujah!!! There was a deafening salute of eight hundred guns; church bells were clanging; and bands mysteriously turned out blaring the national airs. When Lee surrendered at Appomattox, again the capital was in an uproar of salutes, bells, music, cheers and speeches.[129]

In upstate New York, thirteen-year old Caroline Cowles recorded in her diary the impact on a typical small town when learning of Lee's surrender at Appomattox. "We were quietly eating our breakfast this morning about 7 o'clock, when our church bells began ringing...." She called to a passerby who said, "The war is over. We have Lee's surrender." She went downtown where "Every man has a bell or horn, and every girl a flag and a little bell....I am going downtown again now, with my flag in one hand and bell in the other and make all the noise I can."[130]

The bold, half-page headline in the April 10, 1865, *The New York Times* read: "HANG OUT YOUR BANNERS – UNION VICTORY! PEACE!

In Philadelphia, where Markie resided, when the papers announced, "Richmond is ours," a joyous celebration followed. Six days later, when   Lee surrendered at Appomattox, the city went wild. Steam whistles, church bells, fireworks, a salute of 200 guns.[131]

Markie had written three years ago, "Oh! When will this direful war & all its horrors end?" Finally, the "direful war" had ended, but not with the outcome that would encourage her to join the celebrations. She was quietly taking care of her sister's children whose father had fought on the side of the victors.

[1] MCW Diary, 1857, Arlington House Archives.
[2] MCW Diary, 1853, Arlington House Archives.
[3] MCW Diary, 1858, Arlington House Archives.
[4] Daniel M. Mendelowitz, *A History of American Art*, New York, Holt, Rinehart and Winston, Inc. 1970; http://en.wikipedia.org/wiki/Charles_Willson_Peale.
[5] Ltr., Archivist, Pennsylvania Academy of the Fine Arts, to Archivist, TP, Feb. 23, 1994, TP Archives.
[6] Ltr., MCW to Annie Lee, Mar 11, 1860, LOC.
[7] Mary P. Coulling, *The Lee Girls*, Winston-Salem, John F. Blair, 1987.
[8] George G. Kundahl, *Alexandria Goes To War – Beyond Robert E. Lee*, Knoxville, University of Tennessee Press, 2004.
[9] Edited Appleton's Encyclopedia (http://famousamericans.net/edwarddavistownsend).
[10] Avery Craven, ed., *To Markie, The Letters of Robert E. Lee to Martha Custis Williams*, Cambridge, MA: Harvard University Press, 1933.
[11] Kundahl, *Alexandria Goes To War – Beyond Robert E. Lee*.
[12] John Perry, *Lady of Arlington – The Life of Mrs. Robert E. Lee*, Sisters, Oregon, Mulmomah Publishers, Inc., 2001.
[13] Craven, *To Markie..*
[14] John Perry, *Lady of Arlington*.
[15] Harold Holzer, *Lincoln At Cooper Union-The Speech That Made Lincoln President*, NY: Simon & Schuster, 2004.
[16] Craven, *To Markie.*
[17] Ltr., MACL to Helen Bratt, February 1, 1861, Lee Family Papers, Washington and Lee University Library.
[18] Emory M. Thomas, *Robert E. Lee – A Biography*, New York: W. W. Norton & Co., Inc., 1995.
[19] James M. McPherson, *Battle Cry of Freedom – The Civil War Era*, New York: Ballantine Books, 1988.
[20] Murray H. Nelligan, *Arlington House – The Story of the Robert E. Lee Memorial*, Burke, VA., Chatelaine Press, 2001.
[21] George G. Kundahl, *Alexandria Goes To War – Beyond Robert E. Lee*.
[22] Ltr., Orton Williams to General Scott, May 14, 1861, TP Archives, MS-6 (3-20).
[23] Kundahl, *Alexandria Goes To War*.
[24] Ltr., MCW to BB, September 15, 1861, MOC.
[25] Ltr., Orton Williams to General Scott, May 14, 1861, TP Archives, MS (3-20).
[26] Kundahl, *Alexandria Goes To War*.
[27] Coulling, *Lee Girls*.
[28] Ltr., MCW to Agnes Lee, May 8, 1861. VHS.
[29] Ltr., L. Thomas to MCW, May 24, 1861, TP Archives, MS-6 (1-3).
[30] Diary, Anna Maria Thornton, LOC.
[31] Ltr., MCW to MACL, July 13, 1861, VHS.
[32] Ibid.
[33] Diary, Anna Maria Thornton, LOC.
[34] John Henry Upshur, Rear Admiral, U. S. Navy (http://www.arlingtoncemetery.net./jhupshur.htm.)
[35] Ltr., MCW to BB, September 3, 1861, MOC.
[36] Ibid..
[37] Ltr., Beverly Lyall, Archives Technician, U. S. Naval Academy, to Judy Carter, January 13, 1995.
[38] Ltr, MCW to BB, September 3, 1861, MOC .
[39] Fort Monroe: Facts and details, Encyclopedia Topic (www.absoluteastronomy.com/f/fort_monroe).

[40] Unless otherwise noted, information in the following text comes from MCW Diary, 1862. TP Archives.

[41] James M. McPherson, *Battle Cry of Freedom*.

[42] Margaret Sanborn, *The Ordeal of Orton Williams*, V. 29 #4, TUSMA, Winter 1970.

[43] McPherson, *Battle Cry of Freedom*.

[44] W. H. Carter, *From Yorktown To Santiago*, Austin, State House Press, 1989.

[45] Thomas, *Robert E. Lee: A Biography*; Coulling, *The Lee Girls.*.

[46] W. H. Carter, *From Yorktown To Santiago*.

[47] Ltr., LAW to MCW, May 17, 1862, TP Archives MS-6 (1-23).

[48] Ltr., MACL to Martha Kennon, May 20, 1863, VHS.

[49] Thomas, *Robert E. Lee*.

[50] Ltr., George B. McClellan to MCW, May 24, 1862, TP Archives MS-6 (4-12).

[51] Kathryn Allamong Jacob, *Capital Elites – High Society in Washinton, D. C. after the Civil War,* Smithsonian Institution Press, Washington, DC, 1995; Constance McLaughlin Green, *Washington, Villace and Capital, 1800-1878,* Princeton University Press, 1962.

[52] *Family Papers Collected by Armistead Peter, Jr., (Reminiscences of Britannia Kennon)*, TP Archives, MS- (69-23).

[53] Ltr., LAW to Adjutant General of the Army, January 18, 1875, TP Archives MS-12.

[54] Mary Bandy Daughtry, *Gray Cavalier-The Life and Wars of General W.H.F. "Rooney" Lee*, Cambridge, Massachusetts Da Capo Press, , 2002.

[55] McPherson, Battle *Cry of Freedom - The Civil War Era*.

[56] Virginius Dabney, *Virginia – The New Dominion,* Garden City, NY, Doubleday & Co., Inc., 1971.

[57] McPherson, Battle *Cry of Freedom - The Civil War Era*.

[58] Thomas, *Robert E. Lee – A Biography*.

[59] Ltr., Dr. Lewis A. Sayre to Secretary of War, February 22, 1872, TP Archives MS-6 (3-25);

Ltr., LAW to Adjutant General of the Army, January 18, 1875, TP Archives MS-12.

[60] Bell Irvin Wiley, *The Life of Billy Yank – The Common Soldier of the Union,* Baton Rouge, State University Press, 1987; *Civil War Medical Care, Battle Wounds, and Disease, (*www.civilwarhome.com/civilwarmedicine.htm)

[61] Carter, *From Yorktown to Santiago with The Sixth Cavalry;* Ltr. Dr. Lewis A. Sayre to Secretary of War, February 22, 1872, TP Archives MS-6 (3-25).

[62] John W. Wayland, *The Washingtons and Their Homes,* Virginia Book Co, , Berryville, Va. 1973

[63] Ltr., Kate Upshur to Lum Upshur, March 23, 1862, TP Archives, MS-6.

[64] Washington and Georgetown Railroad Co. (http://www.answers.com)

[65] Margaret Leech, *Reveille in Washington – 1860-1865,* Harper & Row, New York, 1941

[66] *New York Times*, July 9, 1862.

[67] *Saloon*, Docent Handbook, TP Archives.

[68] Margaret Leech, *Reveille in Washington 1860-1865,* Harper & Row, New York, 1941; *Civil War – Wounded Ciy* (Exploredc.org); *Historic Medical Sites in the Washington, DC Area* (www.nlm.nih.gov*)*.

[69] Ibid.

[70] Ibid.

[71] Ltr., E. D. Townsend, Adjutant General, to Honorable Philip Cook, Of Committee on Military Affairs, House of Representatives, Washington, D. C., March 24, 1876. TP Archives.

[72] Ltr., REL to MCW, October 1, 1862. VHS.

[73] Ltr., MCW to Annie Lee, November 18, 1862, LOC.

[74] Ibid.

[75] Mary Custis Lee deButts, ed., *Growing Up in the 1850s – The Journal of Agnes Lee,* The University of North Carolina Press, 1984.

[76] Ltr., MCW to Agnes Lee, December 1863, VHS

[77] Coulling, *The Lee Girls.*

[78] Ibid.

[79] Margaret Sanborn, *The Ordeal of Orton Williams.*

[80] Kundahl, *Alexandria Goes to War.*

[81] Ibid.

[82] Margaret Sanborn, *The Ordeal of Orton Williams.*

[83] Ibid.

[84] Ltr., Dr Lewis A. Sayre to Secretary of War, January 01, 1863, TP Archives MS-12 (1-4).

[85] Ltr., Dr. Lewis A. Sayre to Secretary of War, February 22, 1872, TP Archives MS-6 (3-25).

[86] Ltr., Dr. Lewis A. Sayre to Secretary of War, January 01, 1863, TP Archives MS-12 (1-4).

[87] Margaret Leech, *Reveille in Washington – 1860-1865.*

[88] Ltr., Mrs. Lewis A. Sayre to Sarah Law Williams, September 5, 1864, TP Archives MS-11 (1-1).

[89] Irene Guggenheim Navarro," Hairwork of the Nineteenth Century," *Antiques Magazine,* March 11, 2001.

[90] Margaret Sanborn, *The Ordeal of Orton Williams.*

[91] Kundahl, *Alexandria Goes To War.*

[92] Ibid.

[93] Ibid.

[94] John White, *Chronicles – Of the Episcopal High School in Virginia, 1839-1989,* Dublin, NH, William L. Bauhan, Publisher, 1989.

[95] Margaret Sanborn, *The Ordeal of Orton Williams.*

[96] Ibid.

[97] Kundahl, *Alexandria Goes To War.*

[98] Ibid.

[99] Margaret Sanborn, *The Ordeal of Orton Williams.*

[100] Kundahl, *Alexandria Goes To War.*

[101] John Perry, *Lady of Arlington – The Life of Mrs. Robert E. Lee.*

[102] *The Inflation Calendar* (www.westegg.com/infltion/infl.cgi).

[103] Kundahl, *Alexandria Goes To War.*

[104] John White, *Chronicles – Of the Episcopal High School in Virginia, 1839-1989.*

[105] Margaret Sanborn, *The Ordeal of Orton Williams.*

[106] Kundahl, *Alexandria Goes To War.*

[107] John White, *Chronicles – Of the Episcopal High School in Virginia.*

[108] Kundahl, *Alexandria Goes To War.*

[109] *Family Papers Collected by Armistead Peter, Jr., (Reminiscences of Britannia Kennon),* TP Archives, MS- (69-23).

[110] Ltr., MCW to BB, c. June 20, 1863, MOC.

[111] Ltr., L. J. Porter to LAW, June 15, 1863, TP Archives M-12 (1-1); The New York Society Library, New York.

[112] Ltr., MCW to Dr. Armistead Peter, November 16, 1863, TP Archives M-13 (1-1); Ltr., Maggie Peter to AP, Jr., June 27, 1899. TP Archives, MS 14 (2-7).

[113] *Northampton (Massachusetts) Courier,* June 22, 1879.

[114] Ltr., MCW to BB, undated, c. June 26, 1863, MOC.

[115] Margaret Sanborn, *The Ordeal of Orton Williams.*

[116] Ibid.

[117] Ltr., MW to BB, June 29, 1863, MOC.

[118] Irene Guggenheim Navarro, "Hairwork of the Nineteenth Century."

[119] Kundahl, *Alexandria Goes To War;* brochure, *The Confederate Statue,* Office of Historic Alexandria, Virginia.

[120] Harnett T. Kane, *Spies for the Blue and Gray,* Garden City, N. Y., Hanover House, 1954.

[121] Alexander Rose, *Washington's Spies – The Story of America's First Spy Ring,* New York, Random House, Inc., 2006.

[122] Ltr., REL to MACL, August 8, 1863, VHS.

[123] Ltr., MW to BB, April 5, 1863, MOC.

[124] John Henry Upshur, Rear Admiral, U. S. Navy (http://www.arlingtoncemetery.net./jhupshur.htm).

[125] Ltr., MW to Agnes Lee, December 29, 1863, LOC.

[126] Douglas Southall Freeman, *R. E. Lee – A Biography,* New York, Charles Scribner's Sons, 1936.

[127] Ltr., MCW to Mr. Benson Lossing, July 13, 1866, TP Archives.

[128] Ibid.

[129] Margaret Leech, *Reveille In Washington – 1860-1865,* New York, Harper & Row, Publishers, 1941.

[130] *The War Ends – A Small Town's Reaction, 1865,* EyeWitness to History, (www.eyewitnesstohistory.com).

[131] Carl G. Karsch, *The Civil War Years,* (www.ushistory.org/carpentershall/history/civilwar.htm - *Bk).*

CHAPTER 8

POST-WAR RESPONSIBILITIES (1865-76)

Four years ago, on March 27, 1861, Markie's diary read, "Had a sad & heavy heart all day, thinking of my dear Brothers & friends, probably on the Battle field. God defend & bless them & give Victory to the just cause." Now victory had been achieved, but Markie was having a difficult time believing that her prayer to "give Victory to the just cause" had been answered.

Two weeks after General Lee's surrender, she wrote to him expressing her distress over the outcome of the war and her concern for the Lee family. Lee thanked her for "your constant kindness & sympathy....but you must not be too much distressed. We must be resigned to necessity, & commit ourselves in adversity to the will of a merciful God as cheerfully as in prosperity....I am thankful that we are all well & have such abundant causes for gratitude to the Giver of all good."[1]

In reply, Markie suggested going to Europe. Lee again tried to console her, telling her that she must not be so sorrowful. "We all have much to be thankful for, & you who can do so much good, & make yourself useful to others, have great cause for joy. I can do but little but am resigned to what is ordered by our Merciful God, who will I know do all that is good for us." Although visiting Europe would be a great gratification, "there is much to detain me here, & at present at least it is my duty to remain. I shall avoid no prosecution the Govt thinks proper to institute. I am aware of having done nothing wrong & cannot flee." [2]

General Lee, along with others, had been indicted for treason by the United States District Court at Norfolk. An appeal to General Grant, on the basis of the terms of surrender, brought quick action by Grant. After he threatened to resign if President Andrew Johnson abrogated what Grant believed was his pledged word at Appomattox, he wrote to Lee that he need not worry about standing trial for treason.[3] Lee was convinced that when he applied to the federal government for a pardon, he was dramatizing the importance for all parties to adhere to the conditions and spirit of the surrender. General Grant wrote to President Johnson urging that Lee be pardoned, but hatred and retribution dominated Congress.[4] No action was taken until 110 years later. On

August 5, 1975, at Arlington House, President Ford signed legislation restoring posthumously the long overdue, full rights of citizenship for General Robert E. Lee.[5]

As far as we know, for several years after the war, Markie did not keep a diary or write many letters except to the Lee family. What Markie was doing and thinking from the time that Lee surrendered until his death is mostly revealed in the letters that Robert E. Lee wrote in response to her letters. She did not keep copies of her own letters, but fortunately, she kept his letters.

Although Lee patiently comforted Markie and other friends about the misfortunes of war, he was anxious about his own future. He had no idea where he and his family might live. On Christmas eve in 1861, the lonesome General Lee wrote to his wife that he wished that he could buy Stratford, where he was born, the only setting other than Arlington "that would inspire me with feelings of pleasure and local love."[6] However, neither was within his reach. Help was offered from many quarters, including places to live and opportunities for employment, usually at the price of advertising his name. He often told his wife that he would prefer to live on a quiet, small farm, but on October 2, 1865, he became the President of Washington College (now Washington and Lee University) in Lexington, Virginia, which none of the family had ever seen.[7]

Markie was in Philadelphia and quite exhausted from her despair over the outcome of the war and the care of her four charges, but she always found time to be in contact with the Lees. After she put the two boys, Custis, age 14, and George, age 10, in a boarding school, she took time to re-read *Imitation of Christ*[*] by Thomas`a Kempis and to send it to Lee. In late December he thanked her, but said that he preferred to read the Bible. He apologized for not answering her September letter sooner, but he "had so much writing to do; & my occupations are so continuous, that I am compelled to defer replying to those with whom I would prefer to communicate."[8]

His "occupations" during the past three months included getting the President's house ready for his family. He had been living in a hotel where he took meals with son Custis who had accepted a teaching position at the Virginia Military Institute. Lee kept reminding his wife to

---

[*] Second to the Bible, it is the most widely read book of spiritual devotion.

be patient as he was "trying to find lumber, carpenters, and plasterers" who could renovate the house provided for the president of Washington College.[9]

Early in the morning of December 2, 1865, General Lee welcomed his wife, daughters and Rob who traveled by private boat. When they arrived at their new home, they found very little furniture. The one piece of furniture in the parlor was a Steif piano presented by the manufacturer. The carpets and curtains, rescued from Arlington by Britannia Kennon, were in place although the carpets, made for more spacious rooms, were tucked in around the walls.[10] With utensils and campstools from General Lee's Army camp chest, they ate a hot breakfast, courtesy of the mathematics teacher's wife. Upstairs, Mrs. Lee found a pleasant surprise: Her rooms were beautifully furnished, a gift from Baltimore friends.[11]

In February of 1866, Lee was summoned to Washington, D. C., to appear before the Joint Committee on Reconstruction. After his appearance before the committee, he visited Cousin Britannia at Tudor Place. He had hoped that Markie would be there, too, but she was in Philadelphia. He wrote to her that he felt reticent about calling upon some of his friends in Washington. "I am considered now such a monster that I hesitate to darken with my shadow the doors of those I love lest I should bring upon them misfortune.... I did not approach Arlington nearer than the railway which leads to the city. I know very well how things are there." He suggested that she and her nieces visit the family in Lexington. "You must feel no hesitation in visiting us here, on account of the size of your party....Our house is small, quite small, but the whole of it is open to you. By prudent distribution, I think all can be accommodated." He enclosed "a sheet of autographs as you desire" and some photographs. "You must send on any, & as many, as you choose, for my signature, & do not think it will weary me to do anything I can for you."[12]

Markie now felt free to travel with nieces Kate, age five, and Gertrude, age four. In August they spent a few weeks with her cousin, at Audley, near Berryville, Virginia.[13] Next, they visited the Lee family in Lexington and then returned to Tudor Place. Markie intended to help Britannia arrange for transport of the Lee's belongings that Mrs. Lee had been trying to get released from Arlington House, the Patent Office and an Alexandria warehouse.[14] Unfortunately, it was the following year before Mrs. Lee received her furniture and other household items. At the end of the year, Markie took the children to Brooklyn, New York, to visit their father, Commander Upshur.[15]

Just before Christmas, Lee wrote to Markie that if he were an artist like her, he would draw a true picture of Traveller, representing "his fine proportions, muscular figure, deep chest, short back, strong haunches, flat legs, & black mane & tail....Such a picture would inspire a poet....He might even imagine his thoughts through the long night-Marches & days of battle through which he has passed." He then reminisced about the war, and briefly described each of the battles in which he and Traveller had participated, "& in 1865[he] bore me to the final day at Appomattox Ct House....You can, I am sure from what I have said, paint his portrait."[16] At this time, Markie was busy caring for Kate's children and probably didn't have time to devote to painting. In any event, there is no record of a portrait of Traveller painted by Markie.

Markie continued her peripatetic lifestyle with the children, visiting the Lee's several times. In the summer of 1867 she was in the "beautiful town of Orange," New York, where Dr. Flint visited her and the four children on weekends. She was pleased to hear from Lee, but was concerned about his health, when he wrote that he had become quite ill at Old Sweet Springs. "It seems to me if all the sickness I ever had in all my life was put together, it would not equal the attack I experienced." He hoped that "your sweet little nieces are well & happy....& our earnest wish is that the boys may grow steadily in wisdom and goodness." He added that Washington College, which had only a handful of students when he became president, now had 400 students."[17]

On New Year's Day in 1868, Lee wrote to Markie hoping that "the New Year may bring you every happiness, & that all Heavenly blessings may be showered upon your head!....I am glad to inform you that your Cousin Mary's general health was I think improved by her visit to the W.[hite] Sulphur Springs last summer....better able to take exercise than when you saw her." He referred to the wedding of Fitzhugh (no longer called Rooney) saying, "I am glad you liked my new daughter." He was pleased with "your thoughtful present of the picture of the latter (Fitzhugh's wife, Mary Tabb Bolling), for which I thank you every time I look at it....How are you progressing with Travellers portrait Markie?...I am perfectly satisfied with what you have done for his rider."[18]

Commander Upshur, the children's father, married Agnes Kearney in 1868.[19] Evidently, it was left to Markie to make the decision about where the children would live. In April, Lee wrote to Markie in New London, "I am very glad that you have secured so comfortable a house & hope that both you & the children may feel the benefit of it. Fresh air & exercise is of the greatest advantage." He also cautioned her, "You must not say you will never marry....I am sure that no one would make a better wife than you, Markie, & you ought therefore to be willing to give the world the benefit of your example and conduct."[20]

In another letter, also addressed to her at New London, Connecticut, he wrote, "I am much concerned Markie to hear of your perplexities." Concerning "Mr. Henry Ward Beecher of whom you asked, I have been informed by some of the Trustees that he has given his bond for $1000. to the College & I was gratified at his kind remarks of the Institution." Markie had become interested in the women's suffrage movement and sought Lee's opinion about women's rights. In reply, he wrote: "I am disposed to grant not only every right but every privilege to women, that they may do even more good in the world than they now do." But, he did not want them "to engage in the rough & tumble of life. Do not therefore imitate Mrs. Lucy Stone, even though you approve her course."[21] Lucy Stone was well known in the 19th century for her work in demanding women's rights, including suffrage. She was also an abolitionist.

Lee wrote to Markie twice in February, 1869, perturbed about her health, but again teased her about the portrait of Traveller that she had promised to paint.[22] In his second letter, he expressed more apprehension about her health. She had asked for his advice about the "disposition" of the children. Lee replied that he was concerned because "your health is still feeble, & that the cares & anxieties of your life consequently weigh heavily upon you. I can well understand of what deep interest to you is the future of your sweet nieces & nephews." Although he said that he could suggest nothing to her, he wrote:

> The disposition of them must be a subject of most earnest consideration, & its decision depends entirely upon what may seem for their good. You seem to have gone over the whole ground & to have taken a proper view of the question from every point....It is a matter that you will have to determine yourself. No one can help you. I beg that you will fully weigh the last consideration in your letter: the delicacy of your health; the heavy care; & whether it would not be to their advantage to relinquish them, especially the boys, to

their father. It is a grievous question & you must decide it with all the lights before you, if you do not live with their father....I think you will decide rightly & will therefore leave you to your own reflections.[23]

In April, Lee went to Baltimore for a meeting concerning the one enterprise to which he gave his support while he was President of Washington College: the Valley Railroad Company - not for his own financial benefit, but because he thought the undertaking would help the college and the town of Lexington. When he left Baltimore on May 1, he traveled to Washington, D. C., at the suggestion of the White House, and called on President Grant. Because no full account of the interview by an eye-witness or participant exists, the nature of their conversation can only be surmised. After leaving the White House, he went to Tudor Place to visit Britannia Kennon. He stayed for two or three nights and slept his last night in Washington, D. C., in the southwest bedroom of Tudor Place.[24]

Lee's letter of July 20, 1869 to Markie in Brooklyn, New York, revealed that the children were no longer living with her. Lee "borrowed a little space" in his wife's letter to Markie, "to say how glad I am that you are coming to see us....Your first duty to yourself & friends is to recover your health." He wrote that "I shall have to stop for I am using your cousin Mary's room as well as pen & paper." The room was so dark that he couldn't see because "Mary is taking her siesta."[25]

After visiting Lexington, Markie spent the summer with Mrs. Lee at Rockbridge Baths whose waters she had enjoyed three seasons earlier. General Lee, Agnes, and Mildred went to White Sulphur Springs in West Virginia whose waters Lee thought were more beneficial to him. The girls were delighted with the social life, dances day and night, and the young people gathered on the lawn to play the newest rage, croquet.[26] Lee suffered a severe cold in October which affected him all winter. Horseback riding or rapid walking caused pain and difficulty in his breathing. He was often tired and depressed. In March he wrote to Mildred that "The doctors and others think I had better go to the South in the hope of relieving the effects of the cold, under which I have been labouring all the winter....I have consented to go, and will take Agnes....I wish also to visit my dear Annie's grave before I die." Annie died in 1862 and was buried at Warrenton Springs, North Carolina.[27]

While her husband was away, Mrs. Lee planned her own vacation. She and Markie made a leisurely trip from Lexington to

Richmond by canal boat; from there, by the new train to the rail stop in New Kent County where they traveled to the White House by carriage. They enjoyed visits from family members, and on May 13, General Lee and Agnes, having come back from their trip, joined them. Mrs. Lee wrote to Mildred that Robbie, Fitzhugh's son, was riding on "the General's knee." He now says, "Markie," "Agnes" and many other words. Mrs. Lee confided to her brother-in-law Carter, "Robert is not well." Later in the summer, he went to Hot Springs for relief.[28]

Lee wrote to Markie on August 27, "I have been benefited I think upon the whole by my visit, feel better, have less pain & if I could, would remain a week longer." He closed his letter with, "Good bye, most truly, R. E. Lee."[29] Recently he had closed other letters by saying, "Good bye," which was strange for him. Usually, he used affectionate terms and sent love from the family, for example, "All unite in much love & I am most truly & affectionately, your Cousin, R. E. Lee."

A month later, September 28, he fell gravely ill. On October 12, 1870, General Robert E. Lee died, at age 63, in his home in Lexington, Virginia.[30]

Mrs. Lee immediately wrote to Markie, who was living in Philadelphia, about her husband's death. She suggested that Markie not try to travel to Lexington as "the Bridges were all down & the roads in such a dreadful condition" that she could not get there. Markie wrote to Agnes on the day of Lee's funeral, "I am in a distant country as it were – in a strange boarding house, pacing my little room weeping alone & mourning without one responsive heart…I think so much of you all – your dear, dear Mother – this is the overwhelming sorrow of her life – and she is so helpless – My heart bleeds for her." She expressed her regret for not being with the family, but "I felt that I was not needed or wanted."[31] Obviously, Markie had hurt feelings, but Mrs. Lee was right in claiming that Markie would not be able to reach Lexington. For several days, very heavy rains, followed by floods, interrupted access in and out of Lexington. [32]Although out of town friends and relatives were not able to attend General Lee's funeral, the entire town of Lexington mourned their hero with respect and dignity.[33]

In the summer of 1872, Markie joined Mrs. Lee at Warm Springs where she was continuing her project to raise money for Grace Episcopal Church which was planning a new church building as a memorial to General Lee. Donations had not reached the anticipated amount, so Mrs. Lee turned her artistic talents to raising funds for the church. For some time, she had been coloring and selling photographs of paintings of George and Martha Washington, General Lee, and herself. She took her pictures and her paints with her to Warm Springs where she sold the photos to friends and visitors as fast as she could produce them. The two artists returned to Lexington with nearly $1,000 ($20,000 at today's value) for the church building fund.[34]

After a short stay in Lexington, Markie went to New London, Connecticut, to see Katie and Gertie who soon would be leaving for Wiesbaden, Germany, where their father was to be stationed. Markie and Lum had begun receiving cheerful letters from Katie and Gertie as soon as they became comfortable in their new surroundings. Katie wrote to "My dear Aunt Lummie" and closed with "Your loving Godchild," usually thanking her for gifts sent to her and Gertie. Apparently, they took turns writing to their aunts or, perhaps, each wrote to her own Godmother. Katie wrote to Lum that they had received a very interesting book, *The Wonderful Cats*, from Aunt Markie and that Gertie was going to write her a thank-you letter.

On September 24, 1872, Katie wrote to "Darling Aunt Lum" that she was so glad that "Darling Aunt Markie" was visiting them. "Gertie is going to sleep with her to night and I am going to sleep with her another night. We have enjoyed Aunt Markie's visit very much and we are sorry she is going away so soon." Aunt Markie had surprised her nieces by "marching" them to the bookstore where she bought journals for them to use in their new adventure. "We are first going to Liverpool then to either London or Paris, but we are going to live in Wiesbaden." When Markie returned home, each of the girls sent her a lock of hair.[35]

The following summer, Markie and Mrs. Lee went to Hot Springs. When they returned to Lexington, they were shocked to find Agnes seriously ill. When her death was near, Agnes commented, "How strange that I should die between Father & Annie. He died on the 12th Annie on the 20th." She told Mildred how she wanted her personal effects distributed. To Markie, she gave her Bible. "You know Orton gave it to me." Mildred wrote, "We were all collected in that still room, looking wistfully at the slight form on the bed, & listening to her breathing. Dear Jinnie Ritchie was putting hot irons to her feet – Cousin Markie doing all she knew how….Day was just about dawning in the East [on October 15] when her pure, her heroic spirit took its flight."[36]

Mrs. Lee never recovered from her grief over the death of Agnes. Her physical and mental state deteriorated; she thought that she was in her beloved Arlington with her "little children." Mildred described her last weeks as "cruel tortures." Mary Randolph Custis Lee, at age 66, died in her sleep on November 5, 1873.[37]

After Mrs. Lee's funeral, Markie returned to Tudor Place where she found letters from Lolo's wife Sallie. On November 26 she wrote to Sallie, responding to her letter of sympathy, commenting on Mrs. Lee's cheerfulness and resignation to her infirmities as well as her industry. With her painting of pictures and crocheting of little doll clothes, which she had no trouble selling, she had contributed more than any other church member to the building fund for the church building being built in memory of General Lee. Mrs. Lee had dressed a little doll which she gave to Markie to deliver to Nannie, Sallie and Lolo's daughter.

"She always took an interest in Lolo and in you & the children." Markie was glad to hear that Sallie and Lolo were in good health, and closed her letter with, "Much love to you, Lolo & the children – Your attached Sister, Markie."[38]

To read this letter one would think that Lolo and Sallie, with their children, were living together as one happy family. In fact, they had a troubled marriage. Only two of their four children had survived, Lolo had not fully recovered from the effects of typhoid fever, and he had been unsuccessful in getting employment. Although their living conditions appeared luxurious, they were not ideal. They lived most of the year with her parents at the Plaza Hotel on Fifth Avenue, in New York City. They spent summers and autumns in Batavia, New York, property which Lolo referred to as belonging to him.[39] It is where their son George was born. Because Lolo was never financially able to purchase the Batavia property, it is likely that it was part of his father's estate. Batavia, the administrative center for the Holland Land Company, is close to Buffalo, where William G. Williams had been stationed. Construction of railroads began while Captain Williams was living in Buffalo.[40] Occasionally, they spent time at Content Farm, Cambridge, New York, which belonged to Sallie's father, but she used it most often and eventually owned it.

In New York, they lived in the Law section of the Plaza Hotel as did their two children, her two sisters, brother-in-law and two brothers. The next census shows the same pattern with only the father and the brother-in-law employed, except for the mother who was "keeping house" with the assistance of only thirteen servants.[41]

Lolo desperately wanted to be "independent of Mr. L[aw]," Sallie's wealthy, domineering father, but his efforts to be reinstated in the Army had failed as had his attempts to get employment in the business community. In letters to Markie, he continually wrote enthusiastically about positions he anticipated getting, but he was always disappointed. His health was precarious and his education and experience were military related, but he had been dismissed from the Army.

The death of their third child, at age three months, in August, 1870, and Sallie's pregnancy, less than a year later, had been a difficult time for her. Lolo avowed that "whatever may be her pitiable infirmity," he was happy living with her, but she was not happy with him.[42]

Within two months of Anna's birth, January 22, 1872, Lolo was living in a rented room, having been "ruthlessly torn from my wife and family, & suddenly & without warning thrown upon the world, penniless, forsaken, and homeless & all through the insane jealousy of the woman, whom I married, who is the mother of my children, and with whom I had lived happily up to the very moment of the Catastrophe." Their separation was caused by Sallie's accusing Lolo of having an affair, based on an anonymous letter, which he believed that she had written. From his dreary room, he had written a long letter to her, doing "all that I can to allay a perfectly causeless jealousy."[43] Sallie evidently expected that her accusation would remain between her and Lolo, but when her father learned about the situation, he forced Lolo out of their living quarters at the Plaza Hotel. George Law was a formidable man - self-educated, self-made millionaire, six foot tall, weighing over 300 pounds. *The New York Times* claimed that when he left his father's farm at age 18 he had only $40 in his pocket, but that he was a millionaire by age 33 when he ended his career as a bridge contractor. He turned his attention to finances, railroads and canals. When he disposed of his interests in various companies, he then made additional fortunes throughout his life.[44]

Another reason for Lolo having been evicted may have been his drinking which Sallie wrote about to Markie before they were separated. A year later, Lolo admitted to Markie, who had become their arbiter and intermediary, that he had tried to drown his sorrow in drink "driven by a daily accusation of the most calamitous, heart rendering and sickening circumstances. But thank God! I am relieved from these causes of disquietude," He insisted that he never had been "habituated to the use of stimulants" and that now it disgusted him.[45]

Six months after Lolo's eviction, Sallie invited him to the christening of Anna, whom they called "Nannie," to be held in Cambridge on July 7, 1872. Sallie's family must not have been invited because Lolo looked forward to attending the ceremony and planned "to stay in Cambridge for health and economy."[46] A few days later he wrote to Markie that he did not go to Cambridge because he was ill.[47] Sallie had encouraged him to study art in the studio of a great artist which he thought "would be an agreeable occupation."[48] He had "commenced painting instructions, beginning every morning at nine." In addition, he had tried, without success, to get employment – as a foreign correspondent, an artist, and Superintendent of Mt. Vernon.[49] In November, he wrote to Markie that "Sallie has made a sensible and kind proposition: to give up trying for employment now – bring my mind to calm over winter, then in spring try for army or art."[50] On December 28, he reported that Christmas had been gloomy because he had been confined to his room suffering from rheumatism and pneumonia. However, he was happy that Sallie had brought Georgie to his studio in the morning and spent the day with him. He was delighted that Lum was pleased with the painting he had sent her.[51]

The style of living, in which Sallie found herself, provoked her, also, "to the use of stimulants" to overcome her depression. Because Markie was very fond of Sallie, Lolo hesitated to write to her about Sallie's drinking, especially because "she begged me not to." He may have thought that Markie would be able to help Sallie overcome her addiction. He explained that he did not "write this to you in any spirit of anger, but one of true and sincere pity – for she has, with her warm heart and maternal instincts, a great deal to make her unhappy, treated as she is, at times, by her family – she seems to be rendered perfectly desperate...." During the past month, she had been drinking to excess. He was embarrassed because she had been drunk on the street – "think of the dreadful exposure – what a horrible, mortifying, fearful thing to have a wife and mother commit herself to such a disgrace." On Sunday afternoon, when she was on the street with Georgie on her way to visit Lolo, "the poor little fellow was so frightened at the manner in which she was staggering," that when he saw his father, he said, "Papa take my hand, won't you – I'm afraid Mamma will fall down." [52] He did not explain how Markie might have helped Sallie to overcome her addiction. In any event, they both stopped their excessive "use of stimulants," and a sober Sallie made daily visits to a sober Lolo.

In June, 1873, they began what became their annual summer visits to Content Farm in Cambridge. He wrote Markie that he was painting daily and would send Markie a palette [like his]. "Sallie and the children are well." In August he wrote that he had "diarrhea and a cough all of the time....also suffering from sciatica." He planned to leave Cambridge soon.[53]

Later, he wrote from New York,

> S[allie] and the children are well – she brings them to the Studio daily – and they are most interesting children – the little girl is growing to be very pretty and is extraordinarily bright and engaging – I was very much amused yesterday at a request of L. père, who asked Sallie if she would not bring her around to see me. The père seems to have also mollified as for the lst time since our separation he has commenced to give S money – as that is the test of his emotions, S esteemed it a great concession.[54]

In almost every letter that Lolo wrote to Markie, he mentioned money, either requesting or receiving it. She was sending him far more than his share of the income from their father's estate and the trust fund set up by their Grandmother Peter. When he became determined to make himself financially independent, but his effort to get employment in the business community had failed, he seriously considered going to "Washington and get back into the Army," although he "detested the idea."[55] He wrote this to Markie as if he had forgotten that he had tried and failed to "get back into the Army" immediately after he was summarily dismissed at the request of Secretary of War Stanton.

In Markie's effort to help Lolo, it appears that she first learned that he had not received a medical discharge, but had been dismissed without cause; that is, he did not receive an honorable discharge that would have made him eligible to be reinstated and placed on the retired list. Had she known at the time of his dismissal, or anytime since then, she surely would have tried to get the situation rectified because Lolo had been erroneously accused of being AWOL. Now that she did know, she immediately began an effort to restore honor to the name of Major Laurence A. Williams. The first person she turned to was Edward Townsend, now Adjutant General of the Army.[56] After an appointment with General Townsend in October, 1871, Lolo took no further action; in fact, he asked Markie not yet to contact General McClellan, as she had suggested.[57] In defense of Lolo, at this time he had a serious family problem that consumed his attention, he was not well, and he did not receive General Townsend's letter written to him after their meeting.

Finally, Markie took charge; again she contacted General Townsend who wrote to her on December 16, 1874:

> My dear Miss Martha, In examining the papers in your brother's case, I find the enclosed letter sent to him but never received. This settles the matter of absence without leave. I send also the Order of dismissal....I think if you can come down pretty soon ,you may be able to see the President [Grant] this morning.
> Yours sincerely, E. D. Townsend.[58]

The attachment was the letter that he had written to Lolo after their meeting. He had corrected Lolo's regimental returns "as the period embraced is covered by medical certificates filed by you, during the said period, in this office."[59] Now the Congress must pass a bill as a substitute for the original bill ordering his summary dismissal.

When the bill to have Lolo reinstated and placed on the retired list passed the House of Representatives, General Townsend wrote on January 13, 1875, "My dear Miss Martha, I see your Bill passed the House."[60] Because it was a simple matter of correcting an administrative error, their hopes were high that it would be passed by the Senate. However, it was defeated because of derogatory statements made by General W. W. Belknap, the Secretary of War.[61]

To prepare information for a new bill, the Chairman of the Committee on Military Affairs of the House of Representatives requested Major Laurence A. Williams' military history, circumstances of his removal, copies of papers touching on questions of his reinstatement, and an explanation as to why he "waited until now" for relief. General Townsend requested Lolo to get statements from officers who participated in the fight at Mechanicsville and knew about his illness. General McClellan and Dr. Lewis A. Sayre wrote directly to General Belknap, explaining why his statements to the Senate were untrue.[62] Markie did not see President Grant, but she wrote to everyone whom she thought might help, including the President and General Belknap.

As General Townsend was preparing the requested information for the Committee on Military Affairs, General Belknap, who had influenced the Senate to defeat Lolo's bill, was impeached by unanimous vote of the House of Representatives for allegedly having received money in return for post tradership appointments. He resigned on March 2, 1876.[63]

On March 24, General Townsend took a package of information, with a forwarding letter from Major Laurence A. Williams, to the Committee on Military Affairs of both the House of Representatives and the Senate as well as to Secretary of War Alfonso Taft. The Report of the Committee on Military Affairs, to accompany bill H. R. 3371, stated: "The committee, believing that injustice was done this officer by his summary dismissal recommended this bill as a substitute for the original bill, and ask that it do pass."

On her copy of the Calendar for Friday, June 23, 1876, Committee of the Whole House, 44th Congress, Markie wrote, "Calendar containing the Bill of dear Brother's which was passed to my great joy and delight. MCW." However, again there were delays in the Senate, partially caused by the Secretary of War position being held by three different men in 1876.

At this time, Markie was living in Baltimore at Mrs. Gwinn's boarding house to be near sister Lum, but General Townsend kept her apprised of Congressional developments. Indeed, he had been a faithful friend to "My dear Miss Martha" for over 30 years, even during the war when he was a Union officer and she was loyal to the South. He had a busy, impressive career. In 1861, he became Chief of Staff for General Winfield Scott and the principal executive officer of the War Department. He was perhaps brought into more intimate personal contact with President Lincoln and Secretary Stanton than any other military official.[64] He served as Adjutant General of the Army and represented the United States Army during the lengthy funeral proceedings for President Lincoln.[65] The idea of a medal for valor originated with Townsend and is known as the Medal of Honor.[66] Of the several books that he wrote, *Anecdotes of the Civil War in the United States* was the most popular and was used extensively by authors who wrote about the Civil War.[67]

Markie hoped that General Townsend would soon give her good news about "Lolo's bill," and in the meantime was enjoying her friendship with Madame Betsy Patterson Bonaparte who also lived at Mrs. Gwinn's boarding house.[68]

Alas, the year 1876 ended without Lolo being reinstated and placed on the retired list.

179

[1] Avery Craven, ed., *To Markie, The Letters of Robert E. Lee to Martha Custis Williams,* Cambridge, MA: Harvard Univ. Press, 1933.

[2] Ibid.

[3] Emory M. Thomas, *Robert E. Lee – A Biography,* New York, W. W. Norton and Co., 1995.

[4] Paul C. Nagel, *The Lees of Virginia – Seven Generations of an American Family*, New York, Oxford University Press, 1990.

[5] Gail Jarvis, *Robert E. Lee.* (LewRockwell.com).

[6] Ltr, REL, Dec. 25, 1861, to MACL, (www.stratford.org).

[7] Captain Robert E. Lee, *Recollections and Letters of General Robert E. Lee,* Garden City, New York, Garden City Publishing Co., Inc., Copyright, 1904, 1924, by Doubleday, Page & Co.

[8] Craven, *To Markie.*

[9] Nagel, *The Lees of Virginia;* John Perry, *Lady of Arlington – The Life of Mrs. Robert E. Lee,* Sisters, Oregon, Multnomah Publishers, Inc., 2001.

[10] Douglas Southall Freeman, *R. E. Lee – A Biography,* Volume IV, NY, Charles Scribner's Sons, 1942.

[11] Perry, *Lady of Arlington.*

[12] Thomas, *Robert E. Lee;* Craven, *To Markie.*

[13] Ltr., MCW to Benson Lossing, August 13, 1866, TP Archives, MS-6 (3-21)

[14] Ltr., MACL to My dear sir, September 12, 1866, W&L.

[15] Craven, *To Markie.*

[16] Ibid.

[17] Ibid.

[18] Ibid.

[19] John H. Upshur (www// Ancestry.com).

[20] Craven, *To Markie.*

[21] Ltr., REL to MCW, February 9, 1868, MA 1045 (1), The Pierpont Morgan Library.

[22] Ltr., REL to MCW, February 5, 1869, MA 1045 (1), The Pierpont Morgan Library.

[23] Craven, *To Markie.*

[24] Freeman, *R. E. Lee, Vol. IV, Chapter 22; Family Papers collected by Armistead Peter, Jr., (Reminiscences of Britannia Kennon),* TP Archives, MS-14 (69-21).

[25] Craven, *To Markie.*

[26] Captain Robert E. Lee, *Recollections and Letters of General Robert E. Lee.*

[27] Ibid.

[28] Perry, *Lady of Arlington.*

[29] Craven, *To Markie.*

[30] Mary Bandy Daughtry, *Gray Cavalier – The Life and Wars of General W. H. F. "Rooney" Lee,* Cambridge, Mass., Da Capo Press, 2002.

[31] Ltr., MCW to Agnes Lee, October 15, 1870, Lee Papers, LOC.

[32] Thomas, *Robert E. Lee.*

[33] Mary Bandy Daughtry, *Gray Cavalier.*

[34] Perry, *Lady of Arlington.*

[35] Correspondence, 1870-72, in the Upshur-Brown papers, a family collection in Richmond, VA.

[36] Mary Custis Lee deButts, ed., *Growing Up in the 1850s – The Journal of Agnes Lee,* Chapel Hill and London, The University of North Carolina Press, 1884.

[37] Mary Bandy Daughtry, *Gray Cavalier.*

[38] Ltr., MCW to SLW, November 26, 1873, TP Archives, MS-6.

[39] Ltr., LAW to MCW, June 18, 1872, TP Archives MS-6 (1-27).

[40] History of Batavia, New York (www.batavianewyork.com).

[41] United States Census – 1880.

[42] Ltr., LAW to MCW, March 27, 1873, TP Archives, MS-6 (1-26).
[43] Ibid.
[44] *New York Times,* November 19, 1881.
[45] Ltr., LAW to MCW, March 27, 1873, TP Archives, MS-6 (1-26).
[46] Ltr., LAW to MCW, July 2, 1872, TP Archives, MS-6 (1-27).
[47] Ltr., LAW to MCW, July 7, 1872, TP Archives, MS-6 (1-27)
[48] Ltr., LAW to MCW, June 3, 1872, TP Archives, MS-6 (1-27).
[49] Ltr., LAW to MCW, June 18, 20 and 24, 1872, TP Archives, MS-6 (1-27)
[50] Ltr., LAW to MCW, November 29, 1872, TP Archives, MS-6 (1-28).
[51] Ltr., LAW to MCW, December 28, 1872, TP Archives, MS-6 (2-1).
[52] Ltr., LAW to MCW, February 10, 1873, TP Archives, MS-6 (2-2).
[53] Ltr., LAW to MCW, August 11, 1873, TP Archives, MS-6 (1-30)
[54] Ltr., LAW to MCW, Sunday, 1873, TP Archives, MS-6 (1-30).
[55] Ltr., LAW to MCW, June 10, 1872, TP Archives, MS-6 (1-27).
[56] Ltr., E. D. Townsend to LAW, October 30, 1871, TP Archives, MS-12 (1-2)
[57] Ltr., LAW to MCW, October 26, 1872, TP Archives, MS-6 (1-27).
[58] Ltr., E. D. Townsend to MCW, December 16, 1874, TP Archives, MS-12 (1-16).
[59] Ibid.
[60] Ltr., E. D. Townsend to MCW, January 13, 1875, TP Archives, MS-6 (3-7).
[61] Ltr., Lewis A. Sayre, MD, to General W. W. Belknap, February 22, 1875, TP Archives, MS-6 (3-25).
[62] Ibid; Ltr., George B. McClellan, to W. W. Belknap, Secretary of War, January 29, 1876.TP Archives MS-6 (3-25).
[63] Biography, William W. Belknap. (http://en.wikipedia.org/wiki/William_W._Belknap).
[64] Biography, Edward Davis Townsend, Appleton's Encyclopedia (http://famousamericans.net)..
[65] Ibid.
[66] *Medal of Honor.* (http://www.medalofhonor.com).
[67] Biography, Edward Davis Townsend. Appleton's Encyclopedia (http://famousamericans.net).
[68] MCW Journals, 1875-1877, The Pierpont Morgan Library, MA 1045(1).

CHAPTER 9

MARRIED LIFE AND BEYOND (1877-99)

During the summer of 1877, Markie left Madame Bonaparte in Baltimore and once again returned to Tudor Place. In September, she wrote to Blanche Berard:

> If you have heard no rumors of me lately you will be surprised to hear the news [that] I am going to communicate. I am going to be married on the 3rd of October (God willing) to my old friend & earliest admirer, Capt. S P Carter of the U S Navy – You remember when we first met at West Point so many years ago – [1]

Among Markie's keepsakes is a dried flower bouquet with a note, "From the Cemetery at West Point – given me during a walk with my friend Mr. S. P. Carter, U. S. Navy – Sep 18 1850 in remembrance of another day six years ago [1844]."[2] This day in 1844 was when they first met through their friendship with Blanche Berard. Markie was seventeen years old; Midshipman Carter, twenty-five. When they met again in 1850, they "were warm friends & correspondents" for a couple of years and then "we parted – a little more than a year after, he married . . . ."[3] At the time that they parted, Markie, having lost both of her parents, was deeply concerned for the welfare of her four younger siblings.

Samuel Perry Carter was born in Elizabethton, Carter County, Tennessee, on August 6, 1819, to Alfred Moore Carter and Evalina Belmont Perry Carter. There is a mystery as to why and when Samuel changed his middle name to Powhatan. His siblings claimed it was because they called him "Big Chief." Others in the family said it was because he was the sixth great-grandson of Indian Chief Powhatan. His grandmother, Elizabeth Maclin, proudly proclaimed that through her mother's family, she was descended from Indian Princess Pocahontas.[4]

Carter County was named for Samuel's grandfather, Landon Carter, and Elizabethton, for his grandmother, Elizabeth Maclin Carter.[5] He attended Washington College in Tennessee and New Jersey College (now Princeton University) before being appointed a midshipman in the U. S. Navy. He was in the U. S. Naval Academy Class of 1846, the first class to graduate at the new Naval Academy. He was promoted to passed midshipman, assigned to duty on the *Ohio,* and almost immediately was called to the colors at the outbreak of the War with Mexico, in the course of which he received his baptism of fire in the taking of Vera Cruz. He served on the *U.S.S. San Jacinto* of the Asiatic squadron, and on the *Seminole* of the Brazil Squadron, and was twice on the staff of the Naval Academy.[6]

Upon the urgent request of President Lincoln, Lt. Carter reported to the Secretary of War on July 11, 1861. He was transferred to the Army and ordered to special duty in East Tennessee to organize and train volunteer forces. Later, as a Brigadier General, he took command of the Federal forces in East Tennessee and distinguished himself for gallantry in a number of engagements.[7] He was called the daring "sailor on horseback" for leading the Yankee cavalry in the raid from Kentucky into East Tennessee. In *Carter's Raid – An Episode of the Civil War in East Tennessee,* author William Garrett Piston relates an exciting story of "the first long-distance raid staged by the Union cavalry" of a significant and often overlooked turning point in the Civil War.[8] The "Sailor on Horseback" was acclaimed a hero, the first Federal officer to make use of cavalry on a wide-scale raid. Carter was showered with congratulatory messages from his superior officers and was recommended for promotion to major general. Chief of Staff Henry W. Halleck in Washington called the expedition "without parallel in the history of war." The people in the North who had been accustomed to hearing of the bold, spectacular raids of John Hunt Morgan, Nathan Bedford Forrest and J.E.B. Stuart, were heartened to learn that not all the daring was on the Confederate side.[9] After commanding the left wing of the Union forcers in the Battle of Kingston, North Carolina, Carter was promoted to Brevet Major General.[10]

Upon being honorably mustered out of the Army in 1866, he returned to Navy sea duty as Commanding Officer of the steamer *Monocacy,* Asiatic Squadron. He had been promoted to the rank of Commander while serving as a Brevet Major General.

From 1870 to 1873 he was the thirteenth Commandant of the United States Naval Academy and was promoted to Captain in October of 1870. He was Commander, *Alaska* from 1873 to 1875 when he was appointed a member of the Light-House Board and commissioned a Commodore in 1878. He retired in August 1881 and was honored by promotion, on May 16, 1882, to the rank of Rear Admiral on the retired list. He is the only officer in the history of the United States to hold flag rank in both the Army and Navy.[11]

Carter was remembered by fellow officers as "tall, handsome and dignified, graceful in carriage and very affable...of sincere piety and undoubted courage."[12] Lt. Colonel G. C. Kniffin remembered that his winning address was coupled with dignity and self-restraint....The habit of command sat easily upon him, and the control which he speedily acquired over his men increased in veneration....[He was a] Christian, whose courage was unquestioned and whose piety was so sincere."[13] Joseph W. Wilshire, Captain, 45th O.V.I., told about General Burnside and General Carter riding side by side into conquered Knoxville and being received by an overjoyed community. "Gen. Carter was a most devout and sincere Christian, who did not hide his light under a bushel, but let it shine forth at all times, both through spirit and song....General Carter was indeed a fine character, a courteous, Christian gentleman, courageous and fearless at all times, a strict disciplinarian, yet just and compassionate even to evil doers, and to the unfortunate or those in distress, as tender and sympathetic as a woman....We never sat down at mess, or even partook of a hasty snack...with the General present, that we did not await the uncovered and bowed head of our Chief followed by an earnest supplication of grace."[14]

Captain Carter's first wife, Caroline (Carrie) C. Potts, died May 24, 1875, in Tyrol, Austria,[15] while he was commanding the steam sloop *Alaska* on the European Station.[16] She was buried in Oak Hill Cemetery in Georgetown beside her seventeen year old son, Alfred P. Carter, who died in 1869. The inscription on her monument reads, "Beloved wife of S.P. Carter....Lovely in mind and person, a faithful devoted wife & mother, a warm friend; a Sincere Christian, a true noble woman."[17]

In the summer of 1877, Captain Carter came back to Markie after a separation of twenty-five years to prove "his depth & sincerity of his early attachment." He told her that he had never recovered from that evening in 1844 when they first met.[18] After Captain Carter and Markie became engaged, he told his future brother-in-law, Abel B. Upshur, husband of Markie's sister, Columbia, that he had written his first wife's family to tell them that he was going to marry his first love. "You didn't tell them that, Carter!" exclaimed an astonished Upshur. Carter replied, "I did, isn't it the truth?"[19]

A day before their wedding, Markie and Captain Carter applied for their marriage license[20] and signed a prenuptial agreement in Markie's favor:

> Whereas the said Martha Custis Williams is possessed of and has in expectancy certain property real and personal hereinafter named And whereas marriage is agreed upon and intended upon to be shortly had and solemnized by and between said S. P. Carter and M. C. Williams And whereas it was agreed upon by and between the said S. P. Carter and M. C. Williams that, the said M.C. Williams should not withstanding her intended marriage, have, hold, enjoy and possess, all the said property hereinafter described with all and ever the right, title, interest and profits of & in and only of, the same, free and separate from all claims and demand of the said S. P. Carter arising from the consummation of the marriage aforesaid....[21]

Captain Samuel Powhatan Carter and Martha Custis Williams were married, with only the immediate family present, on a Wednesday evening, October 3, 1877, by the Reverend Alexander Shiras[*] at Tudor Place,[22] where her parents' wedding also took place and where she was born fifty years before. Their wedding announcement,[23] sent to family and friends, read:

> *Capt. S. P. Carter, U.S.N.*
> *Miss Martha Custis Williams*
> *Married*
> *Wednesday October 3rd 1877*
> *Tudor Place*

Thus began the happiest period of Markie's life, which was reflected in her diary and correspondence, and even in the accounts section of her diary. She referred to her husband, not by his first name, but sometimes by his rank or Powhatan and most often by endearing terms such as "my darling" or "my dear husband." She listed in receipts,

---

[*] The Reverend Shiras, previously a rector of St. John's Church (1844-1848), preached refraining from entertainments and public amusements. His teaching had a life-long influence on Markie. (Lombard, Frances B., *The Changing Face of St. John's: 200 Years in Georgetown, Washington, DC:* St. John's Episcopal Church, 1998)

"Received from my dear husband & put by to be invested in bond, $18.50." Among items purchased on October 2, 1878, was, "Gold studs for my darling." The next day, on his return from a business trip, they met in Baltimore. "This is the anniversary of our marriage. My darling returned from Philadelphia & we were overjoyed to meet again even after so short an absence. We walked down town & talked of a year ago – went to Minifro Art Store & Capt C. gave me a small traveling paint box & we went to Cook for a scarf pin for an anniversary present."[24] The following morning, they visited Madame Bonaparte. "Although not ten o'clock she received Capt. Carter & myself in her room – most kindly & graciously telling me how much she continued to miss me but adding facetiously that she gave her consent to my marriage." Captain Carter told her that Markie was such a treasure to him that he hoped she would be reconciled.

Captain Carter claimed that his meeting of Markie at West Point was "the dearest event" of his life. Markie wrote to Blanche, "If the warmest & most devoted of hearts can make me happy, I shall be so."[25] Events in the early part of their marriage certainly tested these sentiments. Because they began married life at a time when housing was at a premium in Washington, D. C., they were not able to find suitable accommodations. During the first eighteen months of their marriage, they moved five times and, while on a lighthouse inspection trip, put their belongings in storage. Both suffered extended illnesses during their first winter, which was unusually severe;[26] and Lolo, who depended on Markie to care for him, was continually in poor health. All the while, they were striving to get acquainted with each other's family and friends. Markie especially wanted to get to know Captain Carter's fourteen-year-old son, Sam, hoping that he would love her. She was pleased that when he came home from Lawrenceville Academy in New Jersey, like his father, he often sat beside her as she painted, putting out paints on her palette.

In spite of obstacles, because of their "warmest and most devoted of hearts," their marriage was destined to be an especially happy one for these two devoted friends and lovers.

On March 28, 1878, the first year of their marriage, Markie wrote,

> My Birth Day! What different feelings from those with
> which I wrote in my journal this day last year – Then I
> was so sick physically & so heart sick. How little I

dreamed that this year I should be comparatively well & happy. How I thank God for such undeserved blessings – All day I have been sitting with my dear husband enjoying his society, his dear warm love.

The day after her birthday, she wrote, "My darling gave me a heliotrope yesterday & lamented that his sickness had prevented his getting me a birthday present – I miss nothing with such warm devotion as his." In a later entry, she wrote that they walked down the avenue (Pennsylvania) and "my dear husband stopped with me at Galts and got me a beautiful pr of classical shape earrings for my birth day present."

Concerning her journal entry on her birthday the previous year, she actually made no entries from March 23 until April 1, when she wrote, "Quite an invalid & confined to room for a few days."[27] She did not say in either entry why she was "physically sick and heartsick." The previous January, she had written that Madame Bonaparte "like myself has had a sad and unfortunate life."[28] However, on the following New Year's Eve, she recorded, "Thank God for all of His blessings of the past year." To Blanche, she wrote:

We sometimes say – why could we not have been together all our lives....It was not so ordained....It is not often that such happiness comes to those of our age. At no age could I have been more beloved – more petted and indeed more entirely *lived* for, than I am now.[29]

In July 1878, Markie was busy preparing to accompany her husband on a lighthouse inspection tour. "Spent today in packing books & pictures assisted by my husband. It has been an excessively hot day." They were preparing to put their possessions in storage and leave Miss Gibson's, 1532 I (Eye) Street, where they had been living. Markie noted that they went to the Treasury Department to draw interest due on her "Georgetown Corporation which I now draw for the first time from the Treasury in Washington as the two City governments (Washington City and Georgetown), are merged into one." The day that they left, "my darling and I went down town...taking my box of business papers which we left at Riggs Bank....Then, we went to the Safety Deposit where we took a box at $10 per year for six months, for our certificates & registered Bonds."

On July 8, Lolo left for New York to visit Sallie and the children in Cambridge where he had been spending his summers.[30] Markie was anxious about him because he was "feeble and thin." She had written that, "My poor Brother's condition keeps me perpetually worried." Throughout the year he had numerous illnesses, including violent spells of coughing, hemorrhaging, and severe colds. When he arrived home from riding and could hardly breathe, Captain Carter went for a doctor, but Markie "put mustard plasters over his lungs immediately." Although Markie was treated by traditional physicians, she preferred homeopathic doctors. She was fascinated with homeopathic medicines which she sometimes prepared not only for herself, but also for her husband and Lolo.

In the afternoon of July 9, Captain Carter, Markie and Sam, Jr. "took the cars for New York," arriving at 10 o'clock and going to the Taylor Hotel. The next day they "took the sound boat 'Bristol' of the Old Colony line for New Bedford where we proposed joining the U. S. Vessel 'Verbina' with Capt Ames of the Navy on Board. Capt Carter is now on tour of Light House Inspection & Sam & I with him." Markie almost immediately became seasick, "but recovered & went to the Gay Head Light House at Martha's Vineyard." The inspection tour continued as they traveled up the coast to Portland, Maine, as well as during their return to Staten Island on September 16. Except for the times when she was seasick, Markie thoroughly enjoyed this new experience, the beautiful scenery, the view of the ocean which "was grand," and the people whom she met, especially old friends. When Captain Carter spent the day away from her, inspecting as many as eight lighthouses, he brought her flowers as was his custom at home.

On their return to Washington, they stayed at The Ebbit House, at 14th and Eye Street, perhaps with Markie's encouragement. She thought that Ebbit's coffee sodas were "the nicest thing in the world." She usually walked to Ebbit's a couple times a week for coffee sodas, sometimes saying that "after indulgence of a glass of coffee soda" she was relieved from neuralgia. Occasionally, when Markie and her husband went for a walk, she encouraged him to go with her for coffee sodas. When she paid for her soda, she faithfully entered in the accounts section of her diary: "Coffee Soda - .05" or sometimes "2 Coffee Sodas - .10."

Markie had expected Lolo to return to Washington, D. C., to follow up on his reinstatement, but he wrote to her at the end of October saying that he was staying in a facility in Northampton, Massachusetts, under the care of a physician. He was "comfortable, & contented &

188

better." He requested that Markie send his "trunk, saddle box & box of books....Capt. C. & myself went immediately to the Freight Depot and gave orders that they should be sent to-morrow....Was relieved in a great measure of my anxiety about poor Lolo."

The Carters did not stay long at Ebbit's. Captain Carter made arrangements "for us to come to Miss Margaret Washington's [1412 G Street] to board for a few weeks, until we could find satisfactory quarters for winter." After spending a great deal of time looking for accommodations, on November 30 they moved to Mrs. Pond's, 1536 I Street, where at first they were not entirely pleased with "a chamber on the 3d. story and a parlor on the first."

In the meantime, they decided to build their own home. To design their house, they chose Adolf Cluss, a German born architect, who dominated Washington's architectural scene from the mid-1860's to his retirement in 1890. As a city planner and engineer, he helped to shape the appearance of the city's streets and houses. Though public buildings seemed to interest him most, he also entered the booming housing market during Washington's rapid growth after the Civil War. He designed elaborate row houses for the new wealthy class of the city, as well as Washington's first apartment building. The Smithsonian Arts and Industries Building is the only one, of three buildings that he designed, which survives on the south side of the Mall. Cluss's clients included federal and city governments and wealthy capitalists. He became a friend of President Grant and other political and military leaders.[31]

After selecting a lot, the one that Markie preferred, and having numerous meetings with Mr. Cluss, Markie wrote on November 6, 1878,

> Went this morning to see Mr. Cluss (Architect) about
> 10 o'clock & the contract was signed for the building
> of our house on Connecticut Avenue, by Capt. Carter,
> Adolf Cluss & Mr. Naylor the builder. My dear
> husband & self walked up to the lot about 3 o'clock &
> at half past 3 the ground was broken & the excavation
> commenced for the building. We both dedicated our
> new home to God in our prayers.

Dupont Circle, the area in which their house was being built, was originally known as Pacific Circle. It began to be developed in the 1870's, spearheaded by the Board of Public Works under the leadership of Alexander Shepherd. The Circle's name was changed to Dupont as a memorial to Rear Admiral Samuel Francis duPont in honor of his Civil War Service. The Dupont Circle area became an affluent and vibrant neighborhood.[32] The Carters' house was built on Connecticut Avenue adjacent to Phillip's Row in the same block as the British Legation.

During their daily walks, the Carters regularly visited their lot and on November 25, were delighted to see the foundation being built. A few days later on their way to the site, as they were about to pass Commodore Schufelt's house, "he rushed out & said to my husband, 'Carter, I want to congratulate you – you were made Commodore to-day & I want to be the first person to tell you & to congratulate you....We were all glad at the office.' " By December 6, they found that "they had already gotten up to the first floor."

In the spring of 1879, the Carters moved into their beautiful residence at 1316 Connecticut Avenue, a fashionable part of the city,[33] with the furniture that they had been shopping for during most of their married life. Using the floor plan of their house, along with an inventory of their furnishings and Markie's correspondence, it is possible to reasonably ascertain how the Carters furnished their home.[34] The inviting parlor, with a dressed bay window, faced Connecticut Avenue. In one end of this long room was a grouping of tables and several pieces of upholstered furniture, one being a chair especially designated for the comfort of the Commodore.[35] The library part of this room, also with upholstered furniture, had bookcases, an extension table and two "fancy" chairs (Sheraton chairs of light construction with painted or japanned decoration). The dining room, with three dressed windows, was well furnished for entertaining: dining room table with matching chairs, butler's table, sideboard, China, crystal, the extensive Carter family sterling silver, and a quantity of Japanese and Chinese china that Commodore Carter had collected.[36] The entrance to the pantry was at the west end of the dining room over the kitchen and another pantry. At the other end of the dining room was the entrance to the parlor. On the second floor was the master bedroom, with a dressed, bay window, and furnished with a nine-piece set of furniture. There were also additional bedrooms and bathrooms for guests and for son Sam. On the third floor were two bedrooms and a bathroom, perhaps for the servants.

Missing in the furniture arrangement is a piano; Markie had played the piano since she was a small child. As soon as she went to live with her grandmother, her father shipped her piano to Tudor Place. She often mentioned singing, for example, when she was aboard ship, she sang for the passengers; she wrote to Annie Lee from New York that she had learned new songs which she would teach to her. Admiral Carter also enjoyed singing; his comrades mentioned that his Christianity shown forth in both spirit and song. Perhaps they did have a piano, but it belonged to Markie and would not have appeared in the inventory of Admiral Carter's estate.

Soon there was another member of the family: Markie's "little Dog," which is the way she referred to him. In August 1883 she wrote, "I am still grieving over my lost 'little Dog' which Anna, the cook, says she knows is at the "Lo-gation" (the British Legation) because she hears him & no body could be deceived in his sweet little voice." Markie felt that "not knowing for a certainty" she couldn't confront Sir Lionel Sackville-West, the British Minister.[37]

Markie's new style of living required that she add to her wardrobe. Because Washington was a disappointment as a place to buy fashionable clothing,[38] her husband encouraged her to shop in Baltimore. Apparently, it was not in Markie's nature to discuss her appearance; she tended to focus beyond herself. She didn't even describe her wedding dress. Although she cared about her appearance, her vanity was not in herself, but in her ancestors, especially Grandmama Martha (Dandridge) Custis and her second husband, George Washington.

The few insights we have as to her choice of clothing are a portrait of her hanging at Arlington House; a diary entry in 1857; a few photographs; and a letter to her from Robert E. Lee.

The portrait, which was painted by her father when she was a teenager, shows her in an off-the-shoulder, drab dress with red apron and a soft brimmed hat trimmed in red. In her diary entry for May 1, 1857, at Arlington, she described how Uncle Custis, Mrs. Lee and she were dressed to receive Lord and Lady Napier. She had been preoccupied arranging flowers and books and "had no time to think of our expected visitors..."

> However the hour of 4 o'clock drawing near, I hastened up stairs to prepare – put on my black robe (dress) flounced with purple, a rose de chene bow, attached [to]my collar with a Lava breast-pin & some lovely double flowering cherry clustering with my curls.

In black and white photographs of her as an adult, she is attractively groomed with an upswept hairstyle and drop earrings. She usually wore flowers in her hair or fastened to her dress.[39]

In Robert E. Lee's letter, he wrote that Mrs. Lee had ordered Markie's bonnet and would bring it to her.

> She also desires me to tell you that your last letter arrived too late, as your bonnet was finished & in the House & will not change its beautiful drab complexion for the spotless satin of your taste, nor can she prevail upon the drooping plume to give place to the bursting rose buds. I am afraid Markie that your present *associations* have put these *bridal* notions in your head, as no young ladies in N. York display such colours in broadway until they can shew the papers to entitle them to hoist them. Drab or some grave *couleur* are the only colours worn by the young. Yours is of drab lined with a delicate couleur de rose & weeping willow plume of a cherubina air. You will look charming in it Markie & be entirely to [Lieutenant] Neddy Townsend's [and] Bunny's taste.[40]

In the spring of 1878, a year prior to moving into their new home, Markie began shopping seriously for clothes. On April 22, she and her "dear husband" went shopping and bought her a bonnet at Mrs. Palmer's. The next day, Captain Carter took her "to the cars" to go to Baltimore to shop for clothes and furniture. At the depot, she was met by sister Lum and her husband, "Mr. Upshur," with a large bunch of dandelions, one of her favorite flowers. The next day she purchased several dresses "which I hope my dear one will like – Missed him dreadfully this evening and everyone (much to my mortification) noticed my home-sickness." On the third day, Markie looked at furniture "for our new home." In the evening, her sister brother-in-law accompanied her to see Madame Bonaparte who "seemed very much pleased to see me." On her fourth day of shopping, unexpectedly, "My dear husband came up to Baltimore this morning to my infinite delight....He spied me in Needles store & meeting me at the door gave me a kiss to my great surprise." They spent the day looking at furniture, and in the evening dined with Lum & her husband at "Russell's."

A month later, Markie was back in Baltimore where she "went to Mrs. Wickings to be measured for a black gabardine dress & to Fugles to be fitted for a cream colored & dark green bunting." When she returned home, she and Captain Carter "walked down to J & I St. on an errand about my linen dress." The next day, she, niece Katie and Captain Carter went to Miss Crampshire's, the dress-maker. He carried "my muslin dress in a package – a thing he said he never did before in his life, for anyone." In September when they were in New York, Markie and her husband again went shopping and bought Markie a leghorn hat at Macy's and a silk mantle, trimmed in lace, at Mr. Coffey's "for which I reproved myself." Eventually, she became more comfortable in purchasing clothing, casually writing, "Went to Mrs. Summer Milliner & bought a blue felt bonnet to match my walking suit." And, "Bought at Perry's a maroon brocade silk $39." Her record of expenses at the back of her diary show that she purchased a number of accessories such as, black illusion veil, lace collars & cuffs, gilt pins, gilt tipped feather, two red fans, Spanish lace scarf, and white flowered fan.

Shortly after the Carters moved into their new home, Markie joined her husband on another lighthouse inspection tour. She wrote to Blanche from the "U. S. Lt. House Steamer *Alice*, Mississippi [River], Minneiska, Minnesota" saying that they had been up the Mississippi River from St. Louis to as far as St. Paul and were now returning, "a most charming trip....We went to the Falls of St. Anthony & the lovely little Falls of Minnehaha and to Fort Snelling." Because it was Sunday, Commodore Carter was not working.

> The boat is just under a high hill & the surrounding scenery is most beautiful....We have enjoyed the trip so much. Everything is so novel on these waters – entirely different from the Atlantic coast....How strange it seems, dear Blanche, that the young passed midshipman, who wandered with me about the sentimental walks of West Point in the days of my youth, should now as a Commodore & as my husband stand with me under the Falls of Minnehaha....We sometimes say – why could we not have been together all our lives....We must accept the happiness God has given us now & be thankful, for it is not often that such happiness comes to those of my age.[41]

This year also brought grief. Madame Bonaparte died on April 4, 1879. Markie received a letter from Ellen Bonaparte (Mrs. Charles Bonaparte) acknowledging Markie's letter of condolence, "Mr.

Bonaparte is just now overwhelmed with cares....He begs me to tell you how grateful he is for the sympathy you always showed Madame Bonaparte in her lifetime, and for your thoughts of him in the past trying days." [42]

Less than three months later, Markie once again faced the death of a sibling. On June 22, 1879, her brother, Major Laurence Williams (Lolo), died of pneumonia at Northampton, Massachusetts, where he had been under the care of a physician for the past nine months. Sallie, who was in Cambridge, received a letter from Lolo on Tuesday, June 17, in which he said that his health had improved. On the following Saturday she received a telegram informing her of his serious condition. She started for Northampton immediately, in the company of her physician, and arrived in Northampton on Sunday morning. When she walked into Lolo's room, he recognized her, but then lost consciousness. His obituary stated:[43]

> His remains were taken to Cambridge Monday, arriving on the 7 P. M. train. Funeral services were held at St. Luke's immediately....the rector read the service, and the choir of the church furnished the music. A large number of the village people attended the funeral and testified their sympathy with the bereaved family. The remains were buried in Woodlands Cemetery....He spent his last few summers in Cambridge, and his gentlemanly bearing and genial manner made him many friends among the people, who sincerely regret his loss. During the last few years of his life he devoted much attention to literature and art. He was a brilliant conversationalist, thoroughly posted on all public matters, and was, in short, a cultured, genial gentleman.[44]

Lolo died without being placed on the list of retired officers of the U. S. Army. The previous January, four years after the first bill was passed by the House (but not by the Senate because of a statement by the Secretary of War) Senator Voorhees, "by unanimous consent, obtained leave to bring in the following bill," which was "referred to the Committee on Military Affairs."

Be it enacted by the Senate and House of Representatives of the United States of America in Congress assembled, that the President of the United States be, and he is hereby authorized to restore to the Army, and place on the list of retired officers of the Army, the name of Laurence A. Williams, late major of the Sixth Regiment United States Cavalry, with his appropriate rank, namely: that of colonel; the same being that which he would have attained had he not been unjustly deprived of his commission....

It seemed that at last Lolo was going to receive justice, but it was not to be. Again, a Secretary of War snatched victory from him. Instead of the bill being passed by the Congress, Secretary of War George W. McCrary was authorized to convene a "court of inquiry of officers of the Army to examine the evidence relative to his (Major Williams) dismissal from the Army."

However, no further action was taken.[45] A simple, administrative error in 1863 affected the rest of Major Laurence A. Williams' life and succeeded in denying the honor due him.

Of the five Williams children, only Markie and Lum were left. Markie sought comfort in her painting.

While Captain Carter was at work, Markie usually painted and received visitors – old friends, relatives and new acquaintances whom she had met because of her husband's position, such as Mrs. Professor Newcomb, Mrs. Senator Bailey, or Mrs. Admiral John Rogers. She made a one sentence diary entry six months after her marriage, "Mrs. Mickleham, granddaughter of Thomas Jefferson came to see me." Although she made no further comment, she must have recalled that Grandmother Martha Custis Peter detested Thomas Jefferson because she felt that he did not properly respect George Washington.[46]

At a time when telephoning and emailing were not available, visiting was an important part of social life in Washington, D. C. *The Washington Post,* on January 18, 1885, under the heading "Society At The Capital," reported social events at the White House, mentioning that walking costumes were worn at the first public reception. Among items in the Cabinet News was, "Miss Tillie Frelinghuysen was able to come down stairs...and presided over the tea table"; heading news about Senators and Representatives was, "Mrs. Speaker Carlisle finds it impossible to pay all her calls during the present session of Congress." Under "General Society," it was reported that "Mrs. Elizabeth Cady Stanton and Miss Susan B. Anthony will receive with Mrs. June H. Spofford, at the Riggs House tomorrow from 2 to 5 o'clock." Newspapers announced the days that women would receive visitors and those who would not receive on a specific day. *The Washington Post* reported on January 1, 1885, "On next Monday, and every Monday thereafter, Mrs. McMichael will receive her acquaintances after 3 o'clock." Among those listed as "Ladies Who Will Not Receive," on New Year's Day was Mrs. Admiral Carter.

A lady must know the social etiquette of visiting and leaving calling cards. This she could learn from a recognized authority: Madeline Vinton Dahlgren, the widow of Admiral John Adolph Dahlgren, the famous naval officer and inventor of the Dahlgren gun. Mrs. Dahlgren's *Etiquette of Social Life in Washington* went into five editions (1873-1881) with a final edition titled, *The Social-Official Etiquette of the United States* (1894).[47] Calling cards were a necessary part of the visiting ritual. Calls were made on "At Home" days during the hours engraved on the visiting cards. *A turned-down* corner indicated that the card had been delivered in person, rather than by a servant. Some women used cards printed in French; most used English or French abbreviations.* Whichever one of the corners was *turned up* explained the reason for the visit. Visits were short, lasting from twenty to thirty minutes. If another caller arrived during a visit, the first caller left within a few minutes. Ceremonial visits were made a day or two after a dinner party or a ball, when it was appropriate to leave a card without expecting to be received. Gentlemen also did visiting, but it was more important for the ladies who held society together. When a gentleman did the calling, it was usually the lady of the house who received the caller.[48]

It was not unusual for the Carters to visit or receive a number of guests after a busy day.

> Went, accompanied by my dear husband, to see Mrs.
> Randolph Tucker, my old schoolmate & friend.
> Afterwards, we visited the Penny Soup house on 9th
> street – New and valuable institutions for the poor. We

---

* p.f.-congratulations (pour féliciter); p.r.-thank you (pour remercier); p.c.-mourning expression (pour condoléance); p.f.N.A. Happy New Year (pour feliciter Nouvel An); p.p.c.-to take leave (pour prendre congé); p.p.-wish to be introduced to someone (pour présenter).

were surrounded by a crowd of poor black boys among whom I distributed all my package of tickets. We received eight visitors today.

The Carters and Aunt Brit often visited each other, and Britannia also sought Captain Carter's help with business matters. Occasionally, Markie with her nieces visited Britannia.

> Had a visit from Katie & Gertie in the morning....We went over to Tudor Place & spent the day there. Aunt Brit showed us the contents of her cabinets – the old China that belonged to Grandmama Washington before she was married to the General. [It] was very elegant & also Grandmother's spangled turban.

The day before Easter, Markie made another visit. "We (Katie Upshur) and I went over to Georgetown and called to see poor old Stacia our servant from Tudor Place." Stacia, formerly a slave at Tudor Place, had known Markie since she was born, likely being present at her birth. She fondly remembered Stacia for taking care of her and her siblings, especially for her attentiveness to Orton. Grandmother Peter wrote to Markie, while she was in Buffalo for her father's funeral, that Stacia had moved her bedstead along side of Orton's bed, attending to him night and day.[49]

In her diary for August 9, 1856, over 20 years before, Markie wrote that she "spent a few days at the Aberts – then, a few more days at Tudor, where I witnessed the departure of dear Aunt Brit, Bev & Miss Wight for the Springs. Britannia, who inherited Stacia when her mother died in 1854, left Stacia in charge of Tudor Place. After Markie returned to Arlington, she wrote:

> Poor Stacia's hospitality and kindness was very touching; she told me in the kindest manner, that any time that I wanted to come over to Town and did not like to dine or stay all night with any of my friends, she hoped I would come to Tudor Place. She would heartily share with me what she had and my room was always there & ready to serve me, and if I feared sleeping in the room alone, she would bring her bed & put it on the floor in my room – that anything in the world that she could do for me she was ready & would be pleased to do it.[50]

197

During the time that Britannia rented Tudor Place to the Pendleton family, 1858 to 1861, Stacia lived in "her abode" in Georgetown. On March 28, 1859, Markie wrote in her diary:

> I went to dear old Georgetown to see poor Stacia, to whom I had long promised a visit. The getting to her abode, was quite a pilgrimage, but I was fully repaid by her hospitable greeting – over & over again, did   she assure me, that she was 'so glad to see me.' How strong the tie that binds one to an old family servant – one who has known you from babyhood & witnessed for all the years of your life, the numerous vicissitudes of the family circle. It seemed to me a sacred duty to go see Stacia and therefore I selected my birth-day for its fulfillment.[51]

Markie and Britannia maintained lifelong friendships with Stacia. Britannia's household records reveal that she often made gifts of money to freed Stacia as late as 1892.[52]

The Carters' social life included attending dinner parties and receptions. In their first year of marriage, Markie wrote that she "accompanied Capt Carter to the President's house to call on President & Mrs. Hayes. It was the first time since our marriage that we had been out together at a large gathering....The President has a milk bland look, weak face. Mrs. H is very pleasing. We met Mr. Bancroft the historian." George Bancroft (1800-1891) was a diplomat, statesman, and historian whose comprehensive 10-volume work, *A History of the U. S (1834-1885)* is considered a classic.

Later, she wrote:

> Had an invitation from Admiral & Mrs. Rogers to take dinner with them. We drove out to the observatory & had a very pleasant evening. Commander Picking & Commander Dewey of the Light House Board were there. Professor Eastman of the observatory also. I was taken in to dinner by the Admiral &e &e Capt. Carter took Mrs. Eastman.

After moving out of rented rooms into their new home, the Carters were able to entertain properly. Markie wrote to Blanche apologizing for not remembering her birthday, saying that she and her husband had been continually entertaining company for the past four months.[53]

Their busy life also included regularly going to auctions and art galleries, attending concerts, frequently taking walks (especially to the Capitol to listen to congressmen discuss issues that interested them), serving in the community, attending church as well as participating in church activities, and attending lectures, usually twice a week. After a lecture about Alexander Hamilton by Dr. John Lord, Markie told him that "My Aunt Mrs. Lewis, (Eleanor Custis Lewis) said that Hamilton did not write Gen W[ashington]'s farewell address – that she sewed the pages of it herself & keeps as a relic the candlestick by which it was written."

This diary entry typifies their busy life:

> We went to market this morning & on our return in the Cars with a flower we met General Townsend, Adjutant General – my old friend – was glad to see him – This morning I went to church & after church went to speak to Dr. Paret – met dear little Katie & walked with her part of the way home. Joined my dear one at the auction room. Then we went to the art gallery together. Made visits later.

Markie's husband encouraged her painting, sometimes sitting by her hours at a time, and often buying her gifts to use in painting. "Painted all day long on my panel [of the Eastern Shore] – My dear husband sitting near me and often coming over to look at my performance." Another day, "[My dear husband] got for me a beautiful scarlet poinsettia - one of the most singular & exquisite flowers which I am to paint on a black vase." On a rainy day, "Remained in the house all day - painted my poinsettia on my black vase - My dear husband sat beside me for a long time painting for me another black vase which I am to paint flowers on." She sometimes wrote in her diary something mundane while at the same time expressing their affection for each other: "Spent the morning suffering with a headache & darning stockings & in petting my husband & being petted by him." She enjoyed these times and their evenings alone which she wrote about as spending the evening in sweet communion; reading and talking sweetly to each other; having an enjoyable time alone. Although they often read religious books and

199

prayed together, she was still concerned about their attending separate churches.

Markie, being deeply religious and faithful to the Episcopal Church, was distressed because her husband was not a member of her church. She wrote to Blanche Berard prior to their marriage, "He is not a member of my own church which is a shadow in the picture, but he is a truly religious man & essentially our views agree – We are very sympathetic & congenial in most things...."[54]

Captain Carter was probably familiar with the Civil War history of their respective churches. He chose to become a member of The New York Avenue Presbyterian Church where President Lincoln had regularly worshiped with the congregation and was attended at his death by their pastor, The Reverend Phineas Gurley. Like President Lincoln, Captain Carter was a pew holder. Pew rents were the principal source of financial support for churches during the nineteenth century.[55]

Markie was a member of an Episcopal church, the Church of the Epiphany, 1317 G Street, N.W., founded in 1842, and located in a residential neighborhood of strong Southern sympathies. Senator Jefferson Davis was an Epiphany member. Epiphany's rector, The Reverend Charles Hall, who balanced his Southern sympathies with loyalty to the Union, was so persuasive about his loyalty that Secretary of War Edwin M. Stanton began attending services at Epiphany, using the former pew of Jefferson Davis.[56] However, when Bishop William R. Whittingham, a forceful and unwavering Unionist, issued a prayer of thanksgiving for Union success to be read to congregations, The Reverend Hall reluctantly read the prayer, but told the Bishop that he should not publish controversial prayers. Three other rectors refused to read the prayer to their congregations. Promptly thereafter, the government took over their three churches for military hospitals. When their parishioners arrived for services, they found soldiers and workmen busy with saws and hammers.[57] Epiphany, like other churches, at times put planks on top of the pews to make a platform for beds for wounded soldiers. It is the only, original, pre-Civil War, downtown church building to survive to this day.[58]

Markie's papers do not tell us if she and her husband ever discussed the Civil War in which he fought in Tennessee for the North while she supported the South, Robert E. Lee, and her Confederate brother, Orton, who was hanged as a spy in Tennessee.

Markie wrote week after week that her dear husband accompanied her to the door of her own dear church, and then went to his own church and called for her as usual after church. In the early years of their marriage, she sometimes added, "Oh! What would I not give if we were united in our church relations" or that it was a "real grief" to her to have him go off to another church instead of staying with her. "I pray most earnestly that my dear one may be brought over to my church but I do not talk of it to him." One of her most heartfelt diary entries was:

> A sad day as all my Sundays are, now – for the feeling is ever present that on that day I am separated from my dear husband. We love the same God & we feel the same deep interest in the cause of religion & we possess alike I trust faith & hope in our blessed Savior but we no further worship at the same altar – God grant that he may one day be with me in my own dear church.

Apparently, it never occurred to Markie that she could leave her own church to worship with her husband at his church. They did occasionally attend church together, especially at evening services: "Went to church at the Epiphany – My dear one went with me to the door.... At night he went with me to my own church which gave me pleasure." Although they were spiritually compatible, prayed together, and often read the Bible and other religious books to each other, they continued their memberships in their separate churches during their entire marriage.

After he retired, Admiral Carter became devoted to building a new Presbyterian church: The Church of the Covenant. Urban growth, following the Civil War, had caused attendance at The New York Avenue Church to outgrow its capacity, making it necessary to turn away worshipers. Admiral Carter was among the Elders of the church who met and formed the nucleus of the Covenant Presbyterian Church. He was on the committee to solicit subscriptions and purchase a lot.

The Church of the Covenant was officially organized on October 13, 1885, and its 57 members approved the purchase of a strategic site at the intersection of N Street, 18th Street, and Connecticut Avenue, in the heart of a fast-growing residential area and very near the Carter's house. The response to the program to solicit funds was beyond expectations. A considerable amount of the subscriptions was made by newcomers of the neighborhood. "That portion of the city is improving much more rapidly than any other and it is being filled up with the best class of residences."[59] The first service of the Church of the Covenant was held on September 25, 1889, in its beautiful, Romanesque stone church with a bell tower, Tiffany windows, a gas-lit chandelier copied from one at the Church of Saint Sophia in Constantinople, and a pulpit as well as a communion table of wood from the Holy Land.[60]

Admiral Carter kept his membership at The New York Avenue Presbyterian Church, but became an associate member of the Church of the Covenant where he served as an Elder and on the Board of Trustees.[61] *The Evening Star* announced on March 23, 1889, "President Benjamin Harrison has selected as his place of worship the Church of the Covenant, the new Presbyterian Church recently erected at the Corner of Connecticut Avenue and 18th Street." Among the pew holders listed were President Harrison, Alexander Graham Bell and Admiral S. P. Carter. President Harrison had also served in the Civil War and risen to the rank of Brevet Brigadier General.

The Church of the Covenant flourished with strong lay leadership and a succession of pastors whose reputations extended throughout the nation. In 1930 The First Presbyterian Church elected to merge with the strong Church of the Covenant which then became "The National Presbyterian Church." Over the years, the once fine residential location on Connecticut Avenue became the site of many office buildings, and the leaders of the church chose to move to a spacious site on Nebraska Avenue, farther from the center of the city. The congregation first worshiped in its new home on September 7, 1969, eighty years to the month after the first service was held in the Church of the Covenant[62] to which Admiral Carter devoted the last years of his life. The new church saved the Church of the Covenant's Tiffany stained glass windows, pulpit, communion table, communion sacrament vessels, and the great chandelier from the sanctuary.[63]

In addition to his church activities, Admiral Carter faithfully gave his service to the United States Naval Academy, District affairs, and the Military Order of the Loyal Legion of the United States. Among newspaper articles concerning his service was one in *The New York Times* which reported on June 1, 1881, that Admiral Carter was on the Board of Visitors of the Naval Academy that, prior to its inspection of departments, received a salute from the *Santee* and reviewed the battalion of cadets.[64] *The Washington Post* reported in District affairs that Admiral Carter was on the committee to welcome President-elect Grover Cleveland when he arrived in Washington and "received a large number of distinguished guests."[65] *The Military Order of the Loyal Legion of the United States*,[66] was a patriotic society for the fellowship and welfare of former Union officers. The organizers served as an honor guard for President Lincoln's funeral cortege, and met after the funeral to establish a permanent organization, patterned after the Society of Cincinnati organized after the Revolutionary War.[67] The Order also participated in Admiral Carter's funeral.

Markie was active in her church, especially caring for the sick, and in community activities. She was a member of the Blue Anchor Society - the District auxiliary of the Women's National Relief Association, The Horticultural Society, and the Women's National Indian Association. Among articles that appeared in newspapers concerning these organization were:

The Washington Post reported on November 7, 1882, that the Women's National Relief Association had sent boxes, containing warm clothing, food, wine, and other necessities, to a life saving station and that they were used for thirty-five shipwrecked persons who might have perished without this aid. Among those in the Blue Anchor Society listed as "active workers in collecting articles suitable for packing in the boxes" was Mrs. Admiral Carter. The name of the District auxiliary, Blue Anchor Society, was inspired by the badge of the association which consisted of a blue anchor on white background. The Blue Anchor Society, "is formed of the wives of some of the most prominent citizens and naval officers in the city." In 1884, Mrs. Admiral Carter was elected secretary of the society.[68]

At the 1884 annual meeting of The Horticultural Society, the members heard a report entitled, "The Beauties of the Washington Territory."* Officers, predominately men, were elected, but among the members of the Executive Committee was Mrs. Admiral Carter.[69]

At the 1888 annual meeting of the Washington branch of the Women's National Indian Association, held at Ebbitt House, the president of the Association made an address about its mission work with the Omahas. Among the officers elected, was Vice President Mrs.

---

* in 1870, 150 influential citizens successfully petitioned Congress to establish a Washington, DC territorial government. It went bankrupt in 1873 and was dissolved. (Kathryn Allamong Jacob, *Capital Elites: High Society in Washington, DC after the Civil War,* Smithsonian Institution Press, Washington DC, 1995.)

Admiral Carter.[70] The Association was founded by a group of American women united against the encroachment of white settlers on land set aside for Native Americans. Its aims were for Christianization and assimilation of American Indians. It maintained missions, produced several publications and influenced national policy.[71]

Markie and her husband continued to enjoy traveling, especially to resorts, after he was no longer required to travel on business. When rail transportation made vacation sites more accessible, resorts became increasingly popular. One of these resorts was the Bedford Alum and Iron Springs which *The Washington Post* reported as situated twelve miles from Lynchburg, Virginia, and four miles from Lawyer's station, on the Danville division of the Midland railroad, where a comfortable conveyance awaited the arrival of each train to bring passengers to the hotel. "The hotel is spacious and comfortable...beautiful shade trees, a handsome fountain and a summerhouse for the accommodations of the band which discourses sweet music at intervals during the day." The promenade to the spring "is charming beyond description....The society is composed of the best people from the North and South." Among the "prominent guests" listed on August 10, 1880, were Commodore Carter and wife."[72]

After they vacationed in Yellow Sulphur Springs, which had been a popular Virginia resort since 1790, Markie wrote to Blanche that it was a place "where I do not think I shall ever go again," without saying why she was unhappy with her experience. She was delighted with another resort: *Cloudland Hotel,* built on top of the Roan Mountains in North Carolina, which she described as "a place long to be remembered for its wonderful grandeur & superb atmosphere & the perils of getting there." General J. H. Wilder had constructed a wagon road from the Roan Mountains Railroad Station before he built *Cloudland Hotel* in 1878.[73] "We were literally above the clouds for ten days & such lovely Azaleas & other flowers up there. It is quite a resort for botanists."[74] In the summer of 1881, the Carters were vacationing at the Arlington Colony in Ontario, Canada, when Markie wrote to niece Gertrude Upshur that it was unlikely that she would be present when Gertrude married William H. Hunt because her family of three expected to be in Saratoga Springs. She sent Gertrude $50.00 because "I am in a small provincial, Canadian town & so cannot find" a suitable present. She added, "I cannot wish anything better for you, than that your husband should be as good & loving & devoted as mine."[75] The following February, the Carters were present at the wedding of Gertrude's sister, Kate, who married Frank T. Moorhead at Grace Protestant Episcopal Church in Brooklyn. After the ceremony, Admiral and Mrs. Carter attended a wedding breakfast, "served to a few relatives and friends," at the residence of the bride's father, Commodore John H. Upshur, Commandant of the Brooklyn Navy Yard.[76]

Along with the joys of life for Markie at this time, came sorrows. Niece Kate's first child, Martha Custis Williams Moorhead, died when she was eighteen months old.[77] Markie's remaining sibling, Lum (Columbia Upshur), a year younger than Markie, also died.[78] Because death was all too familiar to Markie, she worried about her husband's health as early as 1884 when she wrote that he was "far from well."[79] Nevertheless, they continued their active lives and vacationed regularly in Saratoga Springs until September 1889 when they vacationed in Richfield Springs, New York,[80] known for its medicinal spring waters "remarkably potent in the treatment of many forms of disease."[81] After an eventful life in the military and his community, Admiral Carter began to seek rest and comfort at home. In a December 29, 1889, article in *The Washington Post* concerning the score of retired admirals enjoying active lives in Washington, it noted that Admiral Carter was leading a rather retired life at his beautiful home near Dupont Circle. Although he was well enough in February 1891 to travel to New York City, a few weeks later, he was seriously ill with Typhlitis. He died of "perforation of the intestine" on May 26, 1891.[82] A little while before the Admiral died, with his arms around Markie, he expressed his love to her and his concern about leaving her alone. "Ah, my poor Markie – how I pity you – It is so hard for a woman to get on alone in the world."[83] *The New York Times* and *The Washington Post* in their May 27th obituaries carried detailed accounts of Admiral Carter's remarkable career.

On Thursday, May 28, 1891, the day of Admiral Samuel Powhatan Carter's funeral, it was dismal and raining. The private service, held at the residence, was "attended by a large number of distinguished invited guests, including a committee of the Loyal Legion." A second service was held at the Church of the Covenant. As the funeral cortege moved toward the church, eight sailors walked at either side of the hearse; and then bore on their shoulders, down the main aisle, the black casket, wrapped in the flag of the United States. The Reverend Dr. T. S. Hamlin, pastor of the Church, who conducted the service, said that Admiral Carter was pre-eminently a patriot, that ten years before the war, he told a friend, "I am thoroughly loyal to my native State, but if she should array herself against the National Union I shall stand up for my Union against my State." Among expressions of sympathy and admiration read was a telegram to Markie from General George W.

205

Morgan, a comrade of Admiral Carter, "I am grieved by the cause of your bereavement....He bore the proud titles of rear admiral and brevet major general, and shed luster on both."[84]

In a drenching rain, Markie said her final farewell to her dear husband at Oak Hill Cemetery where Admiral Carter's body was interred in the Carter family burial plot. A tall, marble monument was erected at his gravesite, with CARTER engraved on the base and above it: Samuel Powhatan Carter, Rear Admiral, U. S. Navy, and Brevet Major General, U. S. Army Volunteers, Born August 6, 1819, Died May 26, 1891.[85] A large Tennessee Historical Marker, commemorating the life of Samuel Powhatan Carter, was placed in front of the house where he was born in Elizabethton, Carter County, Tennessee.[86]

Apparently, Markie and Admiral Carter had never discussed the need for wills. When he died, she and Sam having "made diligent search and inquiry in such places and among such persons as would be likely to disclose one, if such existed," found no will. "That he left him a surviving widow, Martha Custis Williams Carter, and as his heir-at-law and next of kin Samuel Powhatan Carter, his son, your petitioners, both residing at 1316 Connecticut Avenue, Washington, D. C."[87]

The estimated value of his estate was $10,000, approximately $200,000 at today's value.[88] This did not include the value of their home that real estate records show remained in the name of Samuel P. Carter (the name used by father and son) until Sam sold it in 1899.[89] He also borrowed money, using the house as collateral.[90] It appears that the house was considered to be in Sam's name (he did not use junior after his name), but with the understanding that Markie would continue to live in it. No record has been found to indicate that Markie was unhappy about the settlement of Admiral Carter's estate or the ownership of the house. A year after his death, she wrote to Blanche, "At present my affairs are not settled, but I think as to temporal things, I shall be comfortable probably."[91] No complaint. She did have other income: funds from her father's estate and a trust set up for her by Grandmother Martha Custis Peter[92] as well as a military pension of $30.00 a month. Six years later, on January 15, 1897, *The Washington Post* published an article about an increase in her pension:

> The House yesterday honored a great granddaughter of Martha Washington, Mrs. Martha Custis Carter, of this city. She is the widow of Rear Admiral S. P. Carter....The House voted to make the pension $50.00

a month. After the bill passed Mr. Loud, of California, said he had consistently opposed bills carrying so large an amount, and should have objected in this case had his attention not been distracted.

With the death of her husband, Markie's indomitable spirit was shattered. Her life had been intertwined with that of her husband. Now, under the heavy burden of grief, life had lost its purpose, its joy. She "longed to go, too." Although Sam and two servants lived in the residence, she felt so "alone with his vacant chair and all of its beloved associations." It reminded her that she no longer had a reason to watch from the parlor window to see her dear husband "step out of the streetcar with such elastic steps & with such a military air – a picture of perfect health and manly beauty – and how I ran to greet him [at] the door as was our wont when either of us returned & to exchange our fond kiss of welcome – and this for nearly fifteen years."[93]

Markie's friends and relatives encouraged her to visit them, but after a year, she still preferred to stay in her home where her "darling's spiritual presence" was around her. She received visitors who were family or close friends, and "Our servants are still here, faithful & good. My dear little niece & her darling boy come in every day or two...and dear Mr. U., Lum's husband, comes from B. (Baltimore) & stays a few days...and my dear Aunt B. (Britannia) comes occasionally to look after me." She left the house only to visit "some in sickness that I can help & I attend to my duties outside."[94]

In August 1893, Markie finally accepted the invitation of Sallie Williams, the widow of brother Laurence, to visit "Content Farm" in Cambridge, New York. "This 'Content' is a most charmingly comfortable luxurious home. Sallie drives twice a day in one of her elegant little equipages, but I really do not care to drive unless it is to accomplish something. I would like very well to have one of them in W. (Washington) when I want to take an invalid friend out or to facilitate my movements in any way." She was "happier in Washington doing my every day duties to the sick than anywhere else."[95]

Other than attending church, visiting the sick and taking flowers to her husband's gravesite, Markie could not motivate herself to lead an active social life.[96] As she had done throughout her life, she sought comfort at Tudor Place, her childhood home, where shared family memories were a source of consolation to her. She frequently spent the day and sometimes stayed for weeks. Armistead Peter, Jr., Britannia's grandson, often entered in his diary that Markie had "lunched and dined" or that "Markie dined *as usual* at Tudor," not adding that he, too, was a guest, as was his wife, Nannie, the daughter of Lolo and Sallie.[97] Nannie and Armistead were third cousins. They had married on April 25, 1894, in what *The New York World* described as "One of the prettiest and most elaborate weddings for a long time…at the Fifth Avenue Hotel…[in] Mrs. Williams' private drawing room….trimmed with a profusion of pink roses. An arch of these flowers formed a chancel…." The bride "was resplendent with jewels."[98]

In 1897 Markie moved to 2017 Q Street with a caretaker, cousin Maggie Peter,[99] perhaps because she was no longer able to care for her large house. When her health deteriorated further, she also hired a nurse.[100] Admiral Upshur, father of the children whom Markie cared for after their mother died, sent her a will to sign, giving "all property real & personal" to his four children. He may have learned that Markie had begun giving away items that she treasured, most of them to Nannie. She sent her a silver waiter with a note saying, "As it seems to be conceded by all, that the long discussed 'silver waiter' is mine to dispose of, I…give it to you…[it] was from the estate of our Parents…."[101] She also gave Nannie a silver vase which Armistead Peter, Jr. described as "a beauty with the Williams coat of arms engraved on one side and beneath it the letters 'A & W.' " (America and William, Markie's parents.)[102]

Armistead Peter, Jr., in his memoirs, wrote his version of events surrounding Markie's will. He reported that he learned from Cousin Markie that "her brother-in-law, Admiral John Henry Upshur, was trying to have her make a will leaving her entire property to his four children, thereby cutting out Nannie – her only other niece. Markie wept bitterly, saying that while she knew Nannie was amply provided for, that she had no wish to cut her off…as Harry wished her to do." Eventually, Admiral Upshur came from New York, and took Markie to her neighbors where the will was duly witnessed although, according to her neighbor, "Markie had wept bitterly, saying that she did not want to sign it." Upon hearing this, "Mrs. Williams (Sallie) was furious: That's Harry Upshur!....I had left money in my will to his children; I shall change my will, and not one of them shall have a penny; maybe in the end they will lose more than they have gained.' "[103]

"When Cousin Markie died, and her will was offered for probate, Admiral Upshur" asked Nannie to sign "certain papers." She replied that while she had "no wish for the money, there were certain family heirlooms that Aunt Markie had always told her she was to have. I suggested that if Cousin Markie's other will were placed on record, there could be no question as to the truth of Nannie's statement. Admiral Upshur was utterly dumbfounded to find that I knew of another will....That must have been one of the worst hours that the Admiral had ever passed through." This will was probated, and "Cousin Markie's original will, in her handwriting," was also recorded. "Apparently, Markie insisted on adding [to the will Admiral Upshur forced her to sign]: 'excepting such personal articles as I may devise later to other persons and mentioned in my codicil to be annexed.'" Nannie received the things that Markie had designated for her. Admiral Upshur's son, George, "told Nannie that she had been treated badly...that if there was anything that she wanted to tell him and she should have them." The next day Armistead picked up the two items: "a portrait of Captain Williams, her grandfather, painted by himself; also, the engraving of the Mt. Vernon Family." Armistead was delighted that Nannie got "the lion's" share of the trust that Grandmother Martha Peter left for Markie and her siblings. "The Admiral with all of his sharpness could not keep her out of this."[104]

Custis Upshur, the Admiral's oldest son, who lived in Washington, D.C., replied to letters from his sister, Gertrude, who resided in Montana: "As to dear Aunt M's personal effects. George (Upshur), Minnie (Upshur) and Nannie Williams had charge of the division....Kate's illness and consequent inability to act as administrator, I expect will cost the Estate a round sum." He complained because the personal effects had been divided equally among the four children, "No one got a full set of anything: a poor plan." The picture of their grandfather, painted by himself, "was desired by Nannie, and having in view the fact that she got nothing of value out of the Estate, and of her Mother's manifold kindnesses to you, Kate and George, the two latter thought...regardless of any feelings to let her have it, wh. was done – although unquestionably she will restore it to you, on demand." [105]

As to Gertrude's being displeased with the division, Custis wrote, "Kate has Aunt M's watch and likewise our Mother's miniature of Mrs. Washington, wh dear Aunt M had really no right to "leave" to anyone as it did not belong to her – and it was the only thing of my Mother's wh I can recall as having been promised me – so you see I too have a grievance!" (Custis turned twelve years old the day after his mother died.) Apparently, George tried to make everyone happy, but had not succeeded. Custis further complained, "George finding out that Aunt Lum had given me her old and damaged Washington lamp, took the one lately belonging to Aunt M., although I wanted it to mate mine and to use

209

it as a model in having mine restored, some day." As to Gertrude's other inquiries, each sibling received four each of cut glass tumblers, champagne glasses, wine glasses, and claret glasses. The Carter silver, including the silver forks that she wanted, and the Japanese and Chinese china, which belonged to Admiral Carter, were given to Sam, as requested by Markie.[106]

When Markie left two wills and a codicil, she must have anticipated, with sadness, that her estate would upset the dynamics of her rival families, both of whom she loved. As she had done during the Civil War, she found a way to lighten her worry. She had a strong faith and was a devout Episcopalian, but was comforted by reading Christian Science material. She always had been interested in medical matters, especially homeopathic medicine. Although both she and Admiral Carter had been treated by Navy doctors, they sometimes called upon homeopathic physicians. She treated herself as well as her family with homeopathic medicines. Now, she treated herself by reading Christian Science literature.

In 1894, Britannia wrote to Nannie Peter that "Your Aunt Martha is much interested in reading Christian Science every day for two hours to her friend Mrs. Derby. It occupies a portion of her time and she enjoys it.[107] Five years later, although Markie was under the care of a doctor and a nurse, Britannia wrote to Nannie, "It is very sad poor child to think of her condition, which I must ever believe was brought on by her C. S. taking such entire possession of her mind."[108]

During this last year of her life, Markie was an invalid. Niece Katie helped to take care of her during May and reported that the doctor said that she was no better, no worse.[109] But when Nannie and Britannia visited her on October 2, they found her in a troubled state of mind - "a very sad condition.[110] On October 19, Britannia wrote to Nannie, "I undertook the cars yesterday to go over to see poor Martha, who I found much changed, that I hardly think she can be with us much longer.... Life is really not to be desired under the circumstances."[111]

Martha Custis Williams Carter died of "Cerebral Softening" on Tuesday, October 31, 1899, at 8:30 AM.[112] The day of her funeral, November 2, was bright and beautiful; her long season of mourning was over. Her wish to join her husband had been granted. Services were held at 10:00 AM at Epiphany Church and "from there to Oak Hill [Cemetery], where the casket was placed in the same grave with Admiral Carter."[113]

The headline of the November 1st article of *The Washington Post,* announcing Markie's death, read: "Death of Mrs. Martha C. W. Carter, widow of Rear Admiral Carter and Great-granddaughter of Martha Washington." To be remembered with her dear husband and Grandmama Washington would please Markie.

It would please her, also, to know that she is remembered at two National Historic Landmarks: Arlington House and Tudor Place, two grand estates on hills overlooking the Potomac River, both dear to her heart. At Arlington House, where she was always welcome and lived for months at a time, hang the portrait of teenage Markie, painted by her father, and a sketch of Arlington which she drew for her young brother, William Orton Williams. Across the Potomac River, at Tudor Place in Georgetown, where she was born, grew up and married, there are many memories of her, but perhaps the remembrance that would please Markie most is a portrait of her with one of her "darling" beside her.

[1] Ltr., MCW to BB, September 18, 1877, Williams Family Collection, Eleanor S. Brockenbrough Library, The Museum of The Confederacy, Richmond, VA.

[2] Pressed Plants, TP Archives, MS-5 (5-2).

[3] Ltr., MCW to BB, September 18, 1877, Williams Family Collection, Eleanor S. Brockenbrough Library, The Museum of The Confederacy, Richmond, VA.

[4] Octavia Zollicopper Bond, *The Family Chronicle and Kingship Book of Maclin, Clack, Cocke, Carter, Taylor, Cross, Gordon and Other Related American Lineages.* Privately published, n. d.

[5] *Revolutionary War, Landon Carter of Early Tennessee*, C. Hammett for TNGenNet and Combs & Co. Research Group. (www.tngenweb.org/revwar/records/c/carter.html)

[6] Ltr., Beverly Lyall, Archives Technician, Dept. of The Navy, US Naval Academy, to Ms. Judy Carter, 13 January 1995; *"A Figure Unique In Annals of United States Army and Navy,"* The Princeton Alumni Weekly, October 11, 1929.

[7] *"A Figure Unique In Annals of United States Army and Navy,"* The Princeton Alumni Weekly, October 11, 1929.

[8] William Carrett Piston, *Carter's Raid: An Episode of the Civil War in East Tennessee*, Johnson City, TN, The Overmountain Press, 1989.

[9] Noel C. Fisher, *War At Every Door: Partisan Politics and Guerrilla Violence in East Tennessee, 1860-1869*, University of North Carolina Press, Chapel Hill, NC, 1997.

[10] *General Samuel Powhatan Carter, USA*, History Central, Union Generals, (www.mltied.com/Bio USGENS/USACarter.html)

[11] Ltr., Beverly Lyall, Archives Technician, Dept. of The Navy, US Naval Academy, Annapolis, Maryland, to Ms. Judy Carter, 13 January 1995; *"A Figure Unique In Annals of United States Army and Navy,"* The Princeton Alumni Weekly, October 11, 1929.

[12] *General Samuel Powhatan Carter, USA*, History Central, Union Generals, (www.mltied.com/Bio USGENS/USACarter.html)

[13] War Papers 19, prepared by Lt. Colonel G. C. Kniffin, for Military Order of the Loyal Legion of the U. S., Commandery of The District of Columbia, read at the meeting of March 7, 1894. LOC.

[14] *A Reminiscence of Burnside's Knoxville Campaign*, Paper read before the Ohio Commandery of the Loyal Legion, April 3rd. 1912, by Joseph W. Wilshire, Captain 45th O.V.I. (www.homestead.com/ohio45/wilshire~ns4.html)

[15] Ltr., Ella S. Pozell, The Oak Hill Cemetery Co., Washington, D. C., to Ms. Judy Carter, Sept. 18, 1987.

[16] Ltr., Beverly Lyall, Archives Technician, Dept. of Navy, Naval Academy, Annapolis, Maryland, to Ms. Judy Carter.

[17] *Notes on Oak Hill Cemetery, Lot No. 822*, TP Archives; Ltr., Beverly Lyall, Archives Technician, Dept. of The Navy, US Naval Academy, Annapolis, Maryland, to Ms. Judy Carter, 13 January 1995; "A Figure Unique In Annals of United States Army and Navy," *The Princeton Alumni Weekly*, October 11, 1929.

[18] Ltr., MCW to BB, September 18, 1877, Williams Family Collection, Eleanor S. Brockenbrough Library, The Museum of The Confederacy, Richmond, VA.

[19] *Family Papers Collected by Armistead Peter, Jr. (America P. & William G. Williams & Their Children).* TP Archives., MS-4 (69-21).

[20] Record of Marriage, page 118, Oct. 2, 1877, Clerk's Office of the Supreme Court, District of Columbia Archives.

[21] Deed of Settlement, Oct 2nd, 1877, 1:20 PM, District of Columbia Deed Book 865, pp 315-16. District of Columbia Archives.

[22] Ltr., MCW to BB, September 18, 1877, Williams Family Collection, Eleanor S. Brockenbrough Library, The Museum of The Confederacy, Richmond, VA..

²³ MCWC-SPC Wedding Announcement, October 3, 1877, Williams Family Collection, Eleanor Brockenbrough Library, The Museum of the Confederacy, Richmond, VA.
²⁴ Unless otherwise noted, diary information in this chapter came from MCW Diary F (1878) MS-6 (1- 6)
²⁵ Ltr., MCW to BB, September 18, 1877, Williams Family Collection, Eleanor S. Brockenbrough Library, The Museum of The Confederacy, Richmond, VA.
²⁶ Jacob, Kathryn Allamong, *Capital Elites: High Society in Washington, DC, p. 210,* Washington, DC: Smithsonian Institution Press, 1995.
²⁷ MCW Diary, 84 Cathedral St., Baltimore, MD., April 1, 1877, The Pierpont Morgan Library, New York. MA 1045(1).
²⁸ *Ibid.*
²⁹ Ltr., MCW to BB, May 25, 1879, Williams Family Collection, Eleanor S. Brockenbrough Library, The Museum of the Confederacy, Richmond, VA.
³⁰Papers of Laurence Williams, TP Archives, MS-12.
³¹ *Notes on Adolf Cluss, Adolf Cluss Biography* (www.goethe.de/ins /was/pro/vtour/dc1/clussbio.htm)
³² Washington, DC: A National Register of Historic Places, DuPont Circle Historic District. (www.cr.nps.gov/nr/travel/wash/dc50.htm)
³³ Allamong, *Capital Elites.*
³⁴ Building Permits-Plans, 1903-1904, RG 351, Box 107, Records of the Government of the District of Columbia. No. 4494, 1891, Estate of Samuel P. Carter, Inventory of the Personal Estate of Decedent, returned by American Security & Trust Co., No. 212 LPU, Inventories and Sales folio 319, District of Columbia, Register of Wills, District of Columbia Archives.
³⁵ Ltr., MCW to BB, March 29, 1892, Williams Family Collection, Eleanor S. Brockenbrough Library, The Museum of The Confederacy, Richmond, VA.
³⁶ Ltr., C. P. Upshur to Gertrude Hunt, December 22, 1899, TP Archives.
³⁷ Ltr., MCWC to Nina, August 1, 1883, TP Archives
³⁸ Constance McLaughlin Green, *Washington Capital City, 1879-1950,* Princeton University Press, New Jersey: 1963.
³⁹ MCWC Photographs, Photograph Collection, TP Archives.
⁴⁰ Avery Craven, ed., *To Markie, The Letters of Robert E. Lee to Martha Custis Williams,* Cambridge, MA: Harvard Univ. Press, 1933.
⁴¹ Ltr., MCW to BB, May 25, 1879, Williams Family Collection, Eleanor S. Brockenbrough Library, The Museum of the Confederacy, Richmond, VA.
⁴² Ltr., Ellen C. Bonaparte to MCWC, April 10, 1879, The Pierpont Morgan Library, NY, MA 1045 (1).
⁴³ Papers of Laurence Williams, TP Archives, MS-12.
⁴⁴ Ibid..
⁴⁵Ltr., Congressional Research Service, Knowledge Services Group, to Senator George Allen, September 8, 2006.
⁴⁶ Ltr., MCW to BB, May 25, 1879, Williams Family Collection, Eleanor S. Brockenbrough Library, The Museum of The Confederacy, Richmond, VA.
⁴⁷ Madeline Vinton Papers, Georgetown University. (http://www.library); Georgetown.edu/dept/speccoli/cl122.htm); Allamong, *Capital Elites.*
⁴⁸ *Introduction to 19ᵗʰ Century Etiquette.* (www.centerforhistory.org/pdfdoc); (www.literacy-liaison-com/article026.html.)
⁴⁹ Ltr., MCP to MCW, March 25, 1847, TP Archives, MS-6 (1- 5).
⁵⁰ MCW Diary, 1856, Arlington House Archives, MCWC Papers, folder 8.
⁵¹ MCW Diary, 1858-1859, Arlington House Archives, MCWC Papers, folder 14.
⁵² BPK Account Book, 1892, TP Archives, MS-7 (Folder 12).
⁵³ Ltr., MCWC to BB, January 5, 1881, Williams Family Collection, Eleanor S. Brockenbrough Library, The Museum of The Confederacy, Richmond, VA.

[54] Ltr., MCW to BB, September 18, 1877, Williams Family Collection, Eleanor S. Brockenbrough Library, The Museum of The Confederacy, Richmond, VA.

[55] The New York Avenue Presbyterian Church, Washington, DC, History. (www.nyapc.org/history)

[56] Trip Jones, Parish Archivist, *Taking Our Place in Washington History,* The Church of the Epiphany, May 2005. (http://www.epiphanydc.org/history.html)

[57] Ernest B. Furguson, *Freedom Rising – Washington in the Civil War,* NY: Alfred A. Knopf, 2005.

[58] Jones, *Taking Our Place in Washington History.*

[59] *The Evening Star, Wednesday, February 20, 1889,* p. 6. *National Presbyterian Church History.* (http://www.nationalpres.or/hisport.php).

[60] *The Evening Star,* Wednesday, February 20, 1889, p. 6.

[61] *The Washington Post,* June 21, 1887, p. 1

[62] National Presbyterian Church History. (http://www.nationalpres.or/hisport.php).

[63] Ltr., J. Theodore Anderson to F. M. Scott, August 31, 2005, The Library and Archives, The National Presbyterian Church, Washington, DC.

[64] *The New York Times,* June 2, 1881, p. 2.

[65] *The Washington Post,* March 4, 1885, p 1.

[66] *The Washington Post,* May 29, 1891, p. 2..

[67] *History of Military Order o f the Loyal Legion of the United States.* (www.suvew.org/mollus)

[68] *The Washington Post,* December 14, 1884, p. 5.

[69] The *Washington Post,* July 24, 1884, p.1.

[70] The *Washington Post, February 26, 1885,* p. 2.

[71] *Woman's National Indian Association* (http://en.wikipedia.org/wiki/Woman's_National_Indian-Association.)

[72] *The Washington Post,* August 10, 1880, p. 3.

[73] *Cloudland Hotel.* (http://toto.lib,unca.edu/.WAC_hotels_ABE/cloudland_hotel.htm)

[74] Ltr., MCWC to BB, January 5, 1881 , Williams Family Collection, Eleanor S. Brockenbrough Library, The Museum of The Confederacy, Richmond, VA

[75] Ltr., MCWC to Gertrude Upshur, August 17, 1882, TP Archives.

[76] *The New York Times,* February 7, 1883, p. 5.

[77] Robert Irving Upshur & Thomas Teackle Upshur IV, *Upshur Family in Virginia.* Second Edition, Lynchburg, VA: Warwick House Publishing, 1993.

[78] Williams-Upshur Genealogy, TP Archives.

[79] Ltr., MCWC to Hon. William H. Hunt, March 24, 1884, TP Archives.

[80] Ltr., Samuel P. Carter to General Henry M. Cist, September 10, 1889, TP Archives.

[81] Holice and Debbie, *The History of Otsego, NY – Richfield Springs,* September, 2001. (http://www.usgennet.org/usa/ny/county/otsego/book/richfield/richfieldsprings.html)

[82] Certificate of Death No. 77844, Permit 77900, May 26, 1891, Health Officer, Washington, DC, District of Columbia Archives.

[83] Ltr., MCWC to BB, June 14, 1891, Williams Family Collection, Eleanor S. Brockenbrough Library, The Museum of The Confederacy, Richmond, VA

[84] *The Washington Post,* May 29, 1891, p.5.

[85] Ltr., Ella S. Pozell, The Oak Hill Cemetery Co., to Judy Carter, September 18, 1997; James M. Goode, *The Outdoor Sculptures of Washington, DC: A Comprehensive Historical Guide,* 1974.

[86] *Tennessee Historical Markers,* The Tennessee Historical Commission, Nashville, Tennessee, 1996.

[87] Case No. 4494, In the matter of the estate of Samuel Powhatan Carter, deceased. Supreme Court of The District of Columbia, Special Term for Orphans Court Business, 1891, District of Columbia Archives.

[88] *The Washington Post*, June 13, 1891, p. 4; S. Morgan Friedman, *The Inflation Calculator* (http://www.westegg.com/inflation)

[89] Real Estate Records, 1889-1900, Washingtoniana Division, Martin Luther King, Jr., Memorial Library, Washington, DC; Deed, Samuel P. Carter to Andrew R. Fillebrown, 6 August 1899, Liber 2430, folio 401-403, Office of the Recorder of Deeds, District of Columbia Archives.

[90] Deed of Trust, Samuel P. Carter, Lambertville, NJ, & Fitch & Brown, 12 March 1896, Lib. 2101, pp. 363-68, recorded 19 March 1896; Deed of Trust, Samuel P. Carter, Lambertville, NJ, & Fitch & Brown, 7 Aug. 1897, Lib. 2223, pp. 461-65, recorded 19 Aug. 1897, Office of the Recorder of Deeds, District of Columbia Archives.

[91] Ltr., MCWC to BB, March 29, 1892. Williams Family Collection, Eleanor S. Brockenbrough Library, The Museum of The Confederacy, Richmond, VA.

[92] AP, Jr. Diary, November 11, 1899, TP Archives, MS-14.

[93] Ltr., MCWC to BB, March 29, 1892. Williams Family Collection, Eleanor S. Brockenbrough Library, The Museum of The Confederacy, Richmond, VA

[94] Ibid.

[95] Ltr., MCWC to BB, August 8, 1893,. Williams Family Collection, Eleanor S. Brockenbrough Library, The Museum of The Confederacy, Richmond, VA

[96] Ltr., MCWC to SWP, November 1, 1892. TP Archives, MS-11 (1-5).

[97] Armistead Peter, Jr., Diaries 1891-1898, TP Archives, MS-14.

[98] *The New York World*, April 26, 1894.

[99] *Family Papers Collected by Armistead Peter, Jr. (America P. & William G. Williams & Their Children).* TP Archives, MS-14 (69-21).

[100] Ltr., Maggie G. Peter to Armistead Peter, Jr., June 27, 1899. TP Archives, MS-14 (2-7).

[101] Ltr., MCWC to SWP, June 4, 1894, TP Archives MS-12 (1-2)

[102] Ltr., AP, Jr. to AWP, March 21, 1899, TP Archives, MS-14 (2-10).

[103] *Family Papers Collected by Armistead Peter, Jr and his diaries,* TP Archives, MS-14 (69-23).

[104] Ibid.

[105] Ltrs., C. P. Upshur to Gertrude Hunt, December 9, 1899 and December 22, 1899, MS-6.

[106] Ibid.

[107] Ltr., BPK to AWP, August 28, 1894, TP Archives, MS-18 (5-4)).

[108] Ltr., BPK to AWP, May 29, 1899, TP Archives, MS-18 (5-5.

[109] Ibid.

[110] AP, Jr. Diary, October 2, 1899, TP Archives, MS-14.

[111] Ltr., BPK to AWP, October 19, 1899, TP Archives, MS-18, Box 5.

[112] Certificate of Death Record No. 127707, Permit No. 127840, Martha Custis Williams Carter, November 1, 1899, Health Officer, Washington, D.C., District of Columbia Archives; AP, Jr. diary, October 31, 1899, TP Archives, MS-14.

[113] AP, Jr. Diary, November 2, 1899, TP Archives, MS-14.

THUMBNAIL BIOGRAPHIES

ADOPTED BROTHER. See Austin Flint, Sr., M. D.

JOHN JAMES ABERT (1788-1863). Chief, U. S. Corps of Topographical Engineers, superior officer of Markie's father. Lolo (Laurence Abert) was named for him. Markie was a schoolmate and friend of Louisa Abert, and maintained a friendship with the Abert family for many years.

BLANCHE BERARD (1824-1901). Markie's friend and confidante with whom she corresponded most of her life. Christened Augusta Blanche Berard; as an author used "A. B. Berard."

ELIZABETH PATTERSON BONAPARTE – "Betsy" (1785-1879). She and Markie met at a boarding house; remained friends until death intervened. Wife of Jerome Bonaparte (a brother of Napoleon). Son: Jerome Bonaparte, Jr.; Grandchildren: Jerome Bonaparte II and Charles Joseph Bonaparte.

BRIT or AUNT BRIT. See Britannia Wellington Peter Kennon.

BUNNY or BUN. See William Orton Williams.

SAM CARTER. Admiral Samuel Powhatan Carter's son.

ADOLF CLUSS (1825-1905). Architect of house built for Markie and Admiral Carter on Connecticut Avenue in Washington, DC. Designed public buildings in Washington, including several schools and the Arts and Industries building of Smithsonian Institution.

COUSIN M or COUSIN MARY. See Mary Anna Randolph Custis Lee.

GEORGE WASHINGTON PARKE CUSTIS (1781-1857). Markie's "Uncle Custis." Grandson of Martha Washington; husband of Mary Lee Fitzhugh; father of Mary Anna Randolph who married Robert E. Lee. Custis built Arlington House on land inherited from his natural father and planned as a memorial to his adoptive father, George Washington.

JOHN PARKE CUSTIS - "Jacky" (1754-1781). Martha Washington's son. Married Eleanor Calvert. Children: Elizabeth Law -"Eliza" of Mount Washington (1776-1832); Martha Custis Peter of Tudor Place (1877-

1854); Eleanor Lewis - "Nelly" of Woodlawn (1779-1852); and George Washington Parke Custis of Arlington House (1781-1857.)

MARY LEE FITZHUGH CUSTIS – **"Molly"** (1788-1853)."Aunt Custis" shared her love of flowers and books with Markie. See George Washington Parke Custis.

AUSTIN FLINT, SR., M.D. (1812-1886). Markie referred to him as "one of the dearest friends I have on earth" and "my adopted brother." He was a pioneer of heart research and had great influence on the early course of medicine in the United States.

GIP. See Walter Gibson Peter.

BRITANNIA WELLINGTON PETER KENNON – **"Aunt Brit"** (1815-1911). Younger sister of Markie's mother (America); 12 years older than Markie. Married Commodore Beverley Kennon. Daughter: Martha Kennon.

SARAH LAW (WILLIAMS) – **"Sallie."** See Laurence Abert Williams.

MARY ANNA RANDOLPH CUSTIS LEE (1808-1873). Daughter of George Washington Parke Custis and Mary Lee Fitzhugh. Married Robert E. Lee, a distant cousin. In letters to Markie, Robert E. Lee often referred to his wife as "Cousin M"; Markie referred to her as "Cousin Mary." The Lees had the following seven children:

1. **GEORGE WASHINGTON CUSTIS LEE** - "Custis" (1832-1913). Major general in the Confederate Army. After the war, taught at the Virginia Military Institute and reluctantly became president of Washington and Lee College.

2. **MARY CUSTIS LEE** - "Daughter" (1835-1918). Shared a bedroom with Markie. She was away most of the time on extended visits to friends and relatives, leaving Markie with a large bedroom on the front of the house and a great view of the Potomac River and Washington, DC.

3. **WILLIAM HENRY FITZHUGH LEE** – "Rooney" (1837- 1891). Youngest man in the Confederacy to hold the rank of major general. After the war returned to White House Plantation and later moved to Ravensworth Estate, married, farmed and became involved in politics. He served in the U. S. House of representatives from 1887 until his death in 1891.

4. **ANNE CARTER LEE** – "Annie" (1839-1862). She was self-conscious of her appearance because of a birthmark on her face and the loss of an eye. She died during the war.

5. **ELEANOR AGNES LEE** – "Agnes" (1841-1873). She was said to be the most beautiful of the Lee girls. She and Orton Williams were friends from the time they played in the nursery, but she refused his marriage proposal.

6. **ROBERT E. LEE, JR.** – "Rob" (1843-1914). Captain in the Confederate army. After the war, lived at Romancoke Plantation, married, farmed, became a business man and author of *Recollections and Letters of General Rboert E. Lee.*

7. **MILDRED CHILDE LEE** – "Precious Life" (1846-1905). Baby of family, spoiled and willful. Close to her father who called her Precious Life because he said that she brought light into a room.

ELEANOR CUSTIS LEWIS - "Nellie" (1779-1852). Markie's "Aunt Lewis." See John Parke Custis – "Jacky."

LO or LOLO. See Laurence Abert Williams.

MARGARET WILLIAMS ORTON. Markie's "Aunt Margaret." Only sister of Markie's father; married Thomas Orton. Children: John and Philadelphia (Mrs. John Edmond) - "Phillie." Markie visited "Aunt Margaret" in Paris, Washington, DC and Philadelphia.

ARMISTEAD PETER, JR. (1870-1961). Son of Martha Kennon and Dr. Armistead Peter. Married Anna "Nannie" Wright Williams, daughter of Sallie Law and Laurence Williams.

MARTHA CUSTIS PETER (1777-1854). Markie's maternal grandmother with whom she and her siblings lived at Tudor Place. Mrs. Peter was the second child of John Parke "Jacky" Custis and Eleanor Calvert and was the only one of Martha Washington's grandchildren to be born at Mount Vernon. Married Thomas Peter, son of Robert Peter, first mayor of Georgetown. Siblings Elizabeth -"Eliza;" Eleanor - "Nelly;" and George Washington Parke Custis. Children: John Parke Custis, George Washington, Columbia Washington, America Pinckney Williams (Markie's mother), and Britannia Wellington Kennon.

MARTHA KENNON PETER (1843-1886).Markie's cousin. Daughter of Britannia Wellington Peter and Commodore Beverley Kennon. Married Dr. Armistead Peter. Children: Walter Gibson; Beverley Kennon; George Freeland; Agnes; Armistead, Jr.

WALTER GIBSON PETER – "Gip" (c. 1841-1863). Served with Orton Williams in Confederate Army. Brother of Dr. Armistead Peter who married Martha Kennon, Britannia's daughter.

PHILLIE (Philadelphia). Markie's cousin. See Margaret Williams Orton.

BENJAMIN PERLEY POORE (1820-1887). Popular newspaper correspondent, editor and author. Markie met him when he visited "Uncle Custis" while she was living at Arlington.

LOUIS A. SAYRE, M.D. Physician who treated Lolo for typhoid fever and related illnesses.

ANNA MARIA THORNTON (1775-1865). Wife of Dr.William Thornton and close friend of Martha Custis Peter. Markie is often mentioned in her diaries.

WILLIAM THORNTON, M.D. (1759-1828). Physician and architect. President George Washington chose him to design the Capitol; Martha Custis and Thomas Peter chose him to design Tudor Place.

EDWARD DAVIS TOWNSEND (1817-1893). Markie met him when he was a second lieutenant. They remained life-long friends and she often called on him for help with family military problems. He became the Adjutant General of the Army with the rank of Major General.

COLUMBIA WINGFIELD WILLIAMS UPSHUR - "Lum" (1828-1886). Markie's sister, a year younger than Markie. Married Abel Brown Upshur (1821-1895), cousin of sister Kate's husband, John Henry Upshur.

JOHN HENRY "Harry/Harri" UPSHUR (NOTTINGHAM) (1823-1917). Kate Williams' husband. He chose his mother's maiden name as his surname. He was a West Point graduate and attained the rank of Lt. Admiral.

KATHARINE ALICIA WILLIAMS UPSHUR - "Kate" (1834-1864).

Markie's sister, seven years younger than Markie. When she died in 1864, Markie cared for her four children until their father (John Henry Upshur) remarried. Children: Custis Parke (1852-1920), George Littleton (1856-1938), Katherine – "Katie" (1861- ?), Gertrude – "Gertie" (1862-1944).

AMERICA PINCKNEY PETER WILLIAMS (1803-1842). Markie's mother. She met Captain William G. Williams at a party given for General Lafayette in 1824 by her parents, Martha Custis and Thomas Peter.

ANNA WRIGHT WILLIAMS (PETER) – "Nannie" (1872-1961). Markie's niece. See Armistead Peter, Jr.

LAURENCE ABERT WILLIAMS – "Lolo" (1833-1879). Markie's brother, six years younger than Markie. Graduate of West Point. Major in the Union Army; became seriously ill with typhoid fever from which he never fully recovered. Married Sarah "Sallie" Law, daughter of George Law, one of the wealthiest men in New York City. Children: George Law Custis – "Georgie" (1868-1891); Anna Wright – "Nannie" (1872- 1961), who married her cousin, Armistead Peter, Jr.

WILLIAM GEORGE WILLIAMS (1801-1846). Markie's "Papa." A captain and engineer with Army Corps of Topographical Engineers; amateur artist. Killed in Battle of Monterey in the Mexican War. See America Pinckney Peter Williams.

WILLIAM ORTON WILLIAMS (1839-1863). Markie's brother, 12 years younger than Markie. When a child, was called Bunny or Bun; as an adult, called Orton. Was a first lieutenant in the Union Army, but resigned and enrolled in the Confederate Army; became a colonel. Hanged as a spy.

FAMILY TREE

Daniel Parke Custis (1) m. Martha Dandridge m. George Washington (2)
(1711-1757)   (1731-1802)   (1732-1799)

John Parke Custis (1) m. Eleanor Calvert m.David Stuart (2)
(1754-1781)   (1758-1811)

Martha Parke Custis m. Thomas Peter   Eleanor Custis m.Lawrence Lewis
(1777-1854)   (1769-1834)   (1779-185)   (1767-1839)

William Fitzhugh m. Ann Randolph
(1741-1809)   (1747-1805)|

Mary Lee Fitzhugh m. George Washington Parke Custis
(1786-1853)   (1781-1857)

America P. m. Wm. G. Williams   Britannia W. m. Beverly Kennon
(1803-1842)   (1801-1846)   (1815-1911)   (1793-1844)

Katherine m. J.H. Upshur   William Orton Williams
          (1823-1917)   (1839-1863)

Mary Anna Randolph m. Robert E. Lee
(1808-1873)   (1807-1870)

Martha Custis m. Samuel P. Carter   Columbia m. Abel Peter   Laurence m. Sarah Law   Katherine Williams
Williams   (1819-1891)   (1828-86) (1826-95)   Upshur Williams (1837-1912) (1834-64)
(1827-1899)   (1833-79)

Anna Williams m. Armistead Peter, Jr.
(1872-1961)   (1870-1960)

Lee children:
G.W. Custis (1832-1913)
Mary Custis (1835-1918)
Wm. H. Fitzhugh (1837-91)
Ann Carter (1839-62)
Eleanor Agnes (1841-73)
R.E. Lee Jr. (1843-1914)
Mildred Childe (1846-1905)

Upshur children:
Custis Parke (1852-1920)
George Lyttleton (1856-1938)
Katherine (1861- ?)
Gertrude (1862-1944)

BIBLIOGRAPHY
MARTHA CUSTIS WILLIAMS CARTER

Primary Sources

"Arlington and Mount Vernon 1856," letter of Augusta Blanche Berard, published in *Virginia Magazine of History and Biography*, v. 57, no. 2 (April 1949), pp. 140-175.

Arlington House Manuscript Collections: Papers of Martha Custis Williams.

Custis, George Washington Parke. *Recollections and Private Memoirs of Washington*. Washington, DC: Printed by W.H. Moore, 1859.

District of Columbia. Records Office.

George Washington's Beautiful Nelly.   Edited by Patricia Brady. Columbia: Univ. of South Carolina Press, 1991.

Growing Up in the 1850s: The Journal of Agnes Lee. Edited and with a foreword by Mary Custis Lee deButts. Chapel Hill: Univ. of North Carolina Press, 1984.

Historical Society of Washington, DC: Photograph Collections, Vertical Files.

Library of Congress:
    MMC-3710 -- De Butts-Ely Collection
    Diary of Anna Maria Thornton

Eleanor S. Brockenbrough Library, The Museum of the Confederacy: Blanche Berard Papers

Library of Virginia:
    Custis-Lee-Mason Collection
    D.S. Freeman Collection

The Pierpont Morgan Library:
    Literary and Historical Manuscripts – Continental –
    Martha Custis Williams Carter

The Southern Churchman. Friday, May 15, 1857, v. 23, no. 19, p. 76.

To Markie, letters of Robert E. Lee to Martha Custis Williams, ed. by Avery Craven, from manuscripts in the Huntington Library. Cambridge, MA: Harvard Univ. Press, 1933.

Tudor Place Manuscript Collections:
        MS-2 – Thomas and Martha Peter Papers
        MS-5 – Custis-Lee Papers
        MS-6 – Papers of Martha Custis Williams Carter
        MS-7 – Papers of Britannia Wellington Peter Kennon
        MS-10 – Lee Family Papers
        MS-11 – Papers of Sarah Law Williams
        MS-12 – Papers of Laurence Williams
        MS-13 – Papers of Dr. Armistead Peter
        MS-14 – Papers of Armistead Peter, Jr.
        MS-18 – Papers of Anna Williams Peter
        MS-25 -- Knox Family Papers

The Upshur-Brown papers, a family collection in Richmond, VA.

U.S. Census Records.

U.S. Department of the Navy. Naval Academy. Letter, 13 January 1995.

Virginia Historical Society, Lee Family Papers, MSS2.

Washington & Lee University Special Collections:
        064 – Lennig Collection, Robert Edward Lee Papers
        170 – Lee-Jackson Papers

Washington, DC Public Library, Washingtoniana Division
        City Directories

Secondary Sources

Berard, A.B. *School History of the United States*. Philadelphia, PA: H. Cowperthwait & Co., 1860.

Beauchamp, Tanya Edwards. "Adolph Cluss: An Architect in Washington during Civil War and Reconstruction." *Records of the Columbia Historical Society*, v. 48 (1971-1972), pp. 338-358.

Bond, Octavia Zollicoffer. *The Family Chronicle and Kinship Book of Maclin, Clack, Cocke, Carter, Taylor, Cross, Gordon and Other Related American Lineages.*

Bourguignon-Frasseto, Claude. *Betsy Bonaparte – The Belle of Baltimore.* Baltimore, MD: Maryland Historical Society, 1988.

Carter, David Wendal. *Notable Southern Families – Carter of Tennessee Including the Taylors – Descendants of Colonel John Carter of Tennessee.* Chattanooga, TN: The Lookout Publishing Co.

Carter, W.H. *From Yorktown to Santiago with the 6th U.S. Cavalry.* Austin, TX: State House Press, 1989.

Coulling, Mary P. *The Lee Girls.* Winston-Salem, NC: John F. Blair, 1987.

Doughtry, Mary Bandy. *Gray Cavalier – The Life and Wars of General W.H.F. "Rooney" Lee.* Cambridge, MA: Da Capo Press, 2002.

Eisenhower, John S. *So Far from God: The U.S. War with Mexico, 1846-1848.* NY: Random House, 1989.

"The Execution of Williams and Peter." *Harper's Weekly: A Journal Of Civilization.* New York, July 4, 1863.

"A Figure Unique in Annals of United States Army and Navy." *Princeton Alumni Weekly.* October 11, 1929.

Fisher, Noel C. *War at Every Door: Partisan Politics and Guerrilla Violence in East Tennessee, 1860-1869.* Chapel Hill: The University of North Carolina Press, 1997.

Freeman, Douglas Southall. *R.E. Lee – A Biography.* NY: Charles Scribner's Sons, 1942.

Furgurson, Ernest B. *Freedom Rising: Washington in the Civil War.* NY: Alfred A. Knopf, 2004.

Green, Constance McLaughlin. *Washington: Capital City, 1879-1950.* Princeton, NJ: Princeton University Press, 1963.

Jacob, Kathryn Allamong. *Capital Elites: High Society in Washington, DC after the Civil War.* Washington, DC: Smithsonian Institution Press, 1995.

Kail, Wendy. "George Washington's Great-Granddaughter and the Topographical Engineer: The Life and Times of William G. Williams, Class of 1824." West Point *Assembly*, v. 58, no. 6 (July/Aug. 2000), pp. 35-39, 47.

Kail, Wendy. "Surveying Roads, Canals, and the Trail of Tears: The Life and Times of Williams G. Williams, Class of 1824." West Point *Assembly* (Nov./Dec. 2002), pp. 52-57.

Kail, Wendy. "Captain William G. Williams {Class of 1824} Goes To War: 1842-1846." West Point *Assembly* (Nov./Dec. 2005), pp. 24-26.

Kundahl, George G. *Alexandria Goes to War: Beyond Robert E. Lee.* Knoxville: University of Tennessee Press, 2004.

Lee, Capt. Robert E. *Recollections and Letters of Robert E. Lee.* NY: Garden City Publishing Co., 1924.

Leech, Margaret. *Reveille in Washington: 1860-1865.* New York: Harper & Bros., 1941.

Lessoff, Alan and Christof Mauch, eds. *Adolf Cluss, Architect: From Germany to America.* NY: Berghahn Books, 2005.

Lumbard, Frances Barbour. *The Changing Face of St. John's: 200 Years in Georgetown.* Washington, DC: St. John's Church, 1998.

McPherson, James M. *Battle Cry of Freedom – The Civil War Era.* NY: Ballantine Books, 1988.

Meade, William. *Old Churches, Ministers, and Families of Virginia.* 2 vols. Philadelphia: Lippincott & Co., 1857 (reprinted by Heritage Books, Inc., 1992).

Mitchell, S. *A Family Lawsuit: The Story of Elisabeth Patterson and Jerome Bonaparte.* NY: Farrar, Straus and Cudahy, 1958.

Navarro, Irene Guggenheim. "Hairwork of the Nineteenth Century," *Antiques Magazine*, March 11, 2001.

Nelligan, Murray H. *Arlington House: The Story of the Robert E. Lee Memorial*. Burke, VA: Chatelaine Press, 2001.

New York Times.

Perry, John. *Lady of Arlington: The Life of Mrs. Robert E. Lee*. Sisters, OR: Multnomah Press, 2001.

Sanborn, Margaret. "The Ordeal of Orton Williams, U.S.A., C.S.A." West Point *Assembly*, v. 28, no. 4 (Winter, 1970).

Tennessee Historical Commission. *Tennessee Historical Markers*. Ed. by Cathy Tudor Forester. Eighth ed., 1996.

Thomas, Emory M. *Robert E. Lee – A Biography*. NY: W.W. Norton & Co., 1995.

Upshur, George Lyttleton. *As I Recall Them: Memories of Crowded Years*. NY: Wilson-Erickson, Inc., 1936.

Upshur, John Andrews. *The Upshur Family in Virginia*. Second Edition by Robert Irving Upshur & Thomas Teackle Upshur IV. Lynchburg, VA: Warwick House Publishing, 1993.

Washington Post.

Washington Star.

White, John. *Chronicles of the Episcopal High School in Virginia*. Dublin, NH: William L. Bauhan, 1989.

Wiley, Bell Irvin. *The Life of Billy Yank: The Common Soldier of the Union*. Baton Rouge: Louisiana State University Press, 1971.

INDEX

INDEX

INDEX

230

INDEX

Quincy, Josiah, 1

Richfield Springs, NY,205
Riggs Bank,187
Rives, Judith Walker,76,78
Roan Mountains, NC,204
Rockbridge Baths,171
Roosevelt, Theodore,55

St. Catherine's Well,131
St. John's Episcopal Church, Georgetown,14
Sanborn, Margaret,156-157
Saratoga Springs, NY,204-205
Sayre, Mr. & Mrs. Lewis W., 143,149-150,178
Scott, Winfield,130,132,179
Scribner's Magazine,57
Seven Days' Battles,142
Shepherd, Alexander,189
Shiloh,137
Shiras, Alexander,14,185
Slavery, 82-83,101-104
Slaves at Arlington,100-123, 134-135
Slaves at Tudor Place,197-198
Smithsonian Institution,108-109
Society of the Cincinnati,203
Southern Churchman,46,106
Stacia,197-198
Stanton, Edwin M.,200
Stone, Lucy,170
Stowe, Harriet Beecher,82,89
Stratford,167
Stuart, J.E.B.,141,183
Sumner, Charles,111

Taylor, Zachary,68
Thornton, Anna Maria,69,108, 135
Thornton, William, 1
Topographical Engineers, Corps of, 1,11,27,32,120

Townsend, Edward D.,42-43, 134,139,151,177-179,199
Traveller,43,169-170
Treasury Dept.,187
Tudor Place,1-4,10,12,13,27,29, 33,43-44,65-67,70,97,107,123, 134,141,168,171,185,197-198, 207,211
Tyler, John,21
Tyler, Mrs.,82
Typhlitis,205

Uncle Tom's Cabin,74-75,89
U.S. Naval Academy,182-183, 202
Upshur, Abel Brown,51,102, 183,192,207
Upshur, Abel Parker,24
Upshur, Columbia Williams, see Williams, Columbia
Upshur, Custis,167,209
Upshur, George Lyttleton,167, 209
Upshur, Mrs. George L.,49
Upshur, Gertrude,173,197,204, 209
Upshur, Katherine C.,173,193, 197,199,204,209-210
Upshur, John Henry,68,97,135, 158-159,169,208-209
Upshur, Katherine Williams, see Williams, Katherine Alicia

Van Buren, Martin,5
Virginia Magazine of History and Biography,49
Virginia Military Institute,167
Visitation, Convent of,12,80

Warm Springs, VA,172
Washington and Georgetown Railroad Co.,144
Washington College,167

INDEX

Washington, DC,46,141,145, 160,207,209
Washington, George,22,54,57, 86,97,108-109,129,138,158, 195,197
Washington Infirmary,145
Washington & Lee Univ.,167
Washington, Martha, 1,41,54, 138,197,206,209,211
The Washington Post,50,195-196,202-206,211
Webster, Daniel,55
Weigel, Mr.,88-94
West, Benjamin,129
West Point, NY,11,14,26,42,50-51,55,62,65,68-70,119-120
White House on the Pamunkey, 138-139,172
White House (Washington, DC),21,117
White Sulfur Springs,171
Williams, America P.,1-8,64, 208
Williams, Anna "Nannie",174-176,208-210
Williams, Columbia W.,3,1119, 20,34-35,51,57,68,114,143,179, 184,192,195,209
Williams, Katherine A.,3,11,19, 20,32,34,45,68-69,137,143,158-159
Williams, Laurence Abert,3, 7,11,13,16,27-28,30,32,35,45, 55,57,64-69,84,114-115,128, 135-136,139-141,143,149-150, 159,175-179,186,194-195,207-208

*Williams, Martha Custis (see also Carter, Martha Custis Williams)
   clothing,191-193
   diaries,19-25,45-47,51-59, 73-94,95-124,128-129,136-147, 165,185-201
   early life, 3-8,10-38
   education,10,12,14,19,25
   love of flowers,96,122
   and Madame Bonaparte,51-59
   in Paris,73-94
   religion,14,15,19,30,62,96, 98-99,199-201,210
   views on slavery,82-83,101-104
   will,208-210
   and women's suffrage,170
Williams, Sarah Law,155,174-177,194,207-208
Williams, William G.,1-8,12-38,42,45,64,174,208-209
Williams, William Orton,3,4,11, 14,20,22,25,34,45,63-64,68,97, 118-120,128,130,132-34,147-159,173,197,200
Williamsburg, VA,138
Women's National Indian Association,203-204
Women's National Relief Association,203

Yellow Sulphur Springs,204
Yorktown, VA,137

---

* Only selected topics have been listed here, since Markie appears on almost every page.

Made in the USA
Columbia, SC
15 April 2018